THE CHARGING BUFFALO

THE
CHARGING BUFFALO

A HISTORY OF THE
KENYA REGIMENT

GUY CAMPBELL

**LEO COOPER
IN ASSOCIATION WITH
SECKER & WARBURG**

First published in Great Britain 1986 by
Leo Cooper in association with
Secker & Warburg Limited,
54 Poland Street, London W1V 3DF
Copyright © 1986 Guy Campbell

ISBN: 0-436-08290-X

To all former members of
the Kenya Regiment

Typeset in 10/12pt Ehrhardt by
Hewer Text Composition Services, Edinburgh
Printed and bound in Great Britain by
The Bath Press, Bath

CONTENTS

LIST OF ILLUSTRATIONS

ACKNOWLEDGMENTS

I am deeply grateful to my wife for her assistance, advice and forbearance over the last six years; also to Mrs Harfujah Bell who typed and edited my script and to all those members of the Regiment who sent me their memories and their photographs.

G.C.
1986

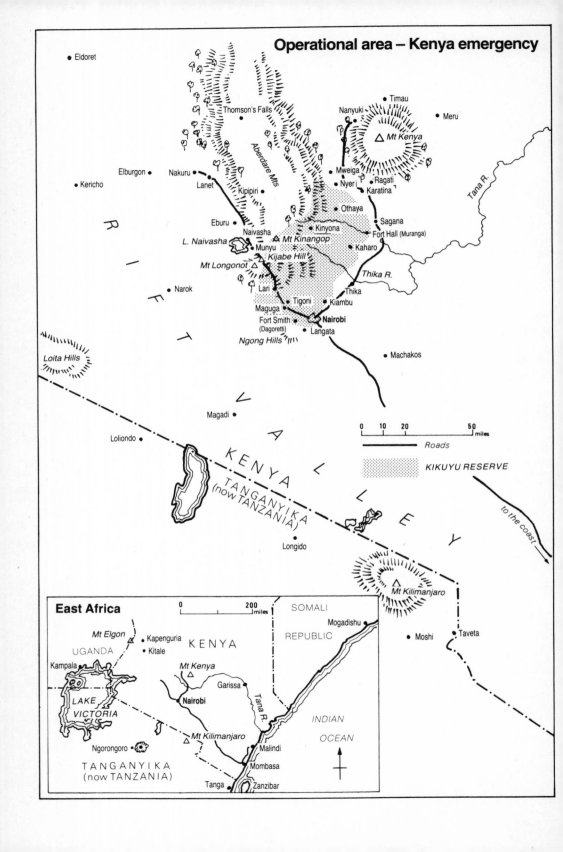

INTRODUCTION

THE KENYA REGIMENT now only exists in the memories of those who served in it. Its short life covered two periods: the first, 1936–45, when the Regiment was active in the Second World War in Africa, Madagascar and Burma; the second, 1950–63,when it helped to cope with the Mau Mau Emergency in Kenya and continued to train soldiers until the Declaration of Independence in 1963. It was the most junior of the regiments on the Army List and it was the shortest-lived.

It was a Territorial Force, as the regimental badge shows, having the letters TF beneath the charging buffalo. From its ranks were produced leaders for the battalions of the King's African Rifles between 1935 and 1945, over 3500 men in all. Of these more than 1500 were commissioned as officers.

It was different from all other regiments in the British Services in that only for a brief period during the Mau Mau Emergency of 1952–6 did it operate as a regiment. All too soon much of its operational value was lost owing to its obligation to provide officers and NCOs for the numerous forces of the Crown after the Emergency was declared. It also provided others who were to prove the bulwark of the multiple posts vital to the administration in crushing the terrorists.

In the chapters which follow, its actions will be recorded, always against the background of Kenya, the country and its peoples, African, Asian and European.

For a long time it has been felt that its history should be told before it was too late. Suggestions as to an author were mooted. I have found two in the files, dated 1961 and 1963, but no action was taken. Late in 1980 I took on the task myself. To me it was a labour of love, full of interest and a journey back into my memory. As it is now just over twenty-nine years since I left after four years in command of the Regiment it has proved a mammoth task. Much has happened in the intervening years. Kenya has been independent since 1963 – twenty-three years which have seen many changes. European settlement still survives, though many whites have left.

In the following pages I shall attempt to tell the story of the Regiment, the major part of the book dealing with the years between 1951 and 1956 which covers the period of the Mau Mau Rebellion.

I started to write in the third person but soon realized that it impeded and stultified my thoughts because it inhibited my writing. Any errors or innaccuracies will be my own but I have made every effort to pick the brains of those who served with me and who know so much more about Kenya and its peoples than I do. Life was full, though fraught with problems, and to start with I had to learn how to think like a Kenya settler and adjust my judgments to come more in line with those who had carved out of raw Africa a prosperous land after years of failure and disappointment. It must not be forgotten that the early pioneers faced untold tragedies and frustrations. It made them a hardy community with a passionate love of their land but not necessarily the ideal material for military service. Even after training and initiation into the customs of the British Army there was always a difference, possibly of outlook or priorities, and in their more direct approach to life in Africa. This, I learned, was the key to their character. To get the best results with your wireless you tune in. In time I hope I learned the right touch and for this I have to thank the eleven years I had already served in Africa.

The various incidents in this history are, whenever possible, recorded in the words of those who took part. This, I hope, will give individual views of the actions as they occurred and not just bare facts as is common in 'situation reports'. It does, too, give a more genuine flavour to the narrative.

To relate the story of the Regiment, its formation and short life, it is necessary to go back to the turn of this century when Kenya gained its name and Europeans first decided that it was a country fit for settlement. In one way or another the descendants of the early settlers from Great Britain, South Africa, Asia, Australia, New Zealand, Persia, the Seychelles, Armenia, Israel, Greece and Italy have all helped to build this new country.

CHAPTER 1

THE EARLY HISTORY
OF KENYA

BEFORE THE latter part of the nineteenth century little was known in Britain about Kenya. When the first British explorers arrived they found no history, no written records, no buildings of architectural significance, no roads or bridges, no tracks or crops, machinery or irrigation, few graves or tombs. Yet the area is considered to have been the birthplace of the earliest man! In 1937, near Lake Nakuru, at Hyrax Hill, some stone habitations were discovered, together with neolithic tools from 1000 BC, while recent finds by the Leakeys' archaeological team have unearthed remains of human beings of a type earlier than any previously discovered.

Central Africa has its natural defences which keep their secrets: dense forests, swamps, rivers and mountains, and monsoon rains that can obliterate any signs of habitation in a matter of days. One has only to fly over the vast interior to realize how nature can cover its past. Soil erosion has added to the problem and the spread of the desert still hides many treasures. The coast of North Africa has only recently disclosed cities, viaducts and the remains of forgotten civilizations. What is now Cyrenaica and Tripolitania was once the granary of Rome.

Alexander the Great visited the Kufra Oasis and the Fezzan, and the Romans are known to have reached Sennar on the Blue Nile. In that area in January, 1941, my company of the Sudan Defence Force came across the unmistakable outline and ramparts of a Roman fort near the junction of the Sara and Kossa Rivers, tributaries of the Blue Nile. The square outline still had entrances at the cardinal points. The Romans wanted gold and possibly ivory. The Blue Nile had gold deposits and it was very rich at the Sara junction: gold dust came to the surface when crossing the stream. Further south in the Bani Shangul we drove off the Italians who worked a gold mine of 14-carat gold, faced in inch veins.

What historical records there are of East Africa may be found in the writings of the Greeks and the Arabs. Herodotus wrote about the source of the Nile being in the 'Mountains of the Moon', while an account written in AD 80, *Periplus of the Erythraean Sea* (Indian Ocean), by a Greek merchant seaman of Berenike, a port on the Red Sea, describes in a matter-of-fact way how the coast of Africa was 'under the authority of the people of Muza [Mocha] who send thither many large ships, many Arab captains and agents who are familiar with the natives and intermarry with them and who know the whole coast and understand the language'. He also mentions ships from India coming to the coast. Among the settlements he described were Mogadishu, Malindi, Mombasa, Zanzibar, Kilwa and Mozambique.

In the fourteenth century the Arab traveller Ibn Battuta described Kilwa as 'one of the most beautiful, well-built towns', Mombasa as a 'large' and Mogadishu as an 'exceedingly large' city. In 1498 Vasco da Gama found the Sheikh of Mozambique and his retinue dressed in 'robes of velvet and silk and gold thread, with turbans of silk and gold, swords and daggers mounted in silver' and at Mogadishu he saw a large town with houses of many storeys with big palaces at the centre.

Ten years later Duarte Barbosa described Kilwa as 'a Moorish town with many fair houses of stone and mortar, with many windows after our fashion. . . . The doors are of wood, well carved with excellent joinery.'

The Arabs' chief interest in East Africa was in ivory, the other most profitable trade being slaves. In search of these 'commodities', they penetrated deep into the interior as witnessed by Charles New in 1871, who asked for information from a Swahili caravan at Taveta, and from this made a map of the principal caravan routes, with comments about the terrain and the peoples: some 'peaceably disposed, though very rude and barbarous,' some agriculturalists, growing such crops as 'Turkish maize', and others 'very wild and furious'. The map proved to be surprisingly accurate and showed that great areas of East Africa were well known to the Arab traders long before the British arrived.

The earliest Europeans to establish themselves in Africa were the Portuguese in the city of Gondar in the sixteenth century. They set up trading posts in Mozambique, while the British and Dutch occupied parts of Cape Province and Natal. During the scramble for Africa, more Portuguese, German, French, Belgian and Italian colonists came, but none reached Kenya. Some missionaries and explorers, like Sir Richard Burton (who reached Harar from the Red Sea) and Dr David Livingstone, ventured into nearby countries, but, although by the mid-nineteenth century exploration was a matter of prestige among European powers, Central Africa was still virtually unknown to them and only the much-coveted prize of discovering the source of the Nile could attract brave men, like Speke, into these wastes.

Distances were vast, there were no maps, no information about what lay ahead and there were the dangers of tropical diseases and rinderpest, as well as stories of savage warriors who inhabited the interior. Few dared to travel there and no porters could be bribed or persuaded to make such a journey. The Anti-Slavery Society did much to encourage exploration of these areas as they were known to be the source of supply for the slave trade.

Among the earliest Europeans to visit Kenya was the missionary Krapf, who was based at Mombasa in the late 1840s and who was interested in exploration, chiefly in the search for the source of the Nile. It was while on one of his journeys, in 1849, when he was visiting the leader of the Wakamba tribe at Kitui (whose name was Kivoi) that he first saw Mount Kenya. The Kamba pronunciation of the name 'Kay -ee- nya' was the basis of that which was adopted by the Europeans. Until 1920 Kenya was called the East African Protectorate and after that the Administration changed the name to Kenya Colony. Kenya Province was one of the original eight provinces of the Protectorate.

In 1890 the British East Africa Company arrived to trade and in 1892 Fort Smith (Dagoretti) and Fort Hall (Muranga) were built. In 1895 the name East African Protectorate was given to the area. In 1896 a railway was started at Mombasa to go as far as the shores of Lake Victoria. It was intended to open up the country, help the missionaries and to complete the suppression of the slave trade. Livingstone had urged that tribal wars could be ended by planting permanent settlements of Europeans and establishing the 'Pax Britannica'. Crops were planted and Europeans took over 'unoccupied' and uncultivated land, believed to belong to no one and not used by the Kikuyu tribesmen. No Europeans were allowed to settle in the tribal/native reserves. The settlers were allotted blocks of land on long leases from the Protectorate Government. There were no written laws before the Government took over the country. Fertile land was lying idle and it was not used by the native population, nor at the time did any Kikuyu claim ownership. The first British settlers arrived in 1902, followed by the Dutch in 1904, coming from South Africa. After the military operations in German East Africa (1914–17) an East African Women's League was formed 'for the welfare of all races, including votes for women and the happiness of all'. From 1920 the Soldier Settler Schemes encouraged old soldiers to settle in East Africa, the last of these schemes being the one for retired members of the Indian Army in 1947. Hotels, like the New Stanley Hotel, began to open, run by early European settlers.

Most of these settlers were independent in their outlook and no lovers of petty government restrictions. They were capable of challenging the authority of government from Whitehall and the Governor was on one occasion besieged in Government House. Much of this attitude stemmed from the differences that divided the officials from the settlers. This was reflected by the annual sporting fixture when cricket teams from the officials took on the settlers on the Gymkhana Ground in Nairobi.

The two best-known clubs in Nairobi observed the same rules: the Muthaiga Country Club has never admitted government officials, its members being drawn from the up-country farming community. An older club, the Nairobi Club, caters for the business and official fraternity. Both clubs have always opened their doors to British officers serving with battalions of The King's African Rifles and to the Royal Navy.

From the earliest days of land settlement the settlers who lived in a particular area chose one small settlement which later became a town with post office, shops and a club which all could join. This did not apply to Asians or Africans, and the same rule forbade non-Europeans to enter the major hotels and restaurants. This sounds nonsensical and indeed it was! Even in 1951 the Aga Khan could not book in at the New Stanley Hotel, although he could stay with the King at Buckingham Palace! It is not difficiult to see why there was a rift, certainly in outlook, between the officials – i.e. government servants, bankers, businessmen and traders – and the settlers, or, to stretch it more widely in some instances, the landed gentry who lived up-country and made their own rules of conduct and conditions. In the twenties and thirties when a young man in England kicked over the traces or got into financial difficulties the answer was often a passage to the 'Colonies' with the warning not to return. But to say that this set the standard for settlement is ludicrous and an insult to the many fine people who chose to make Kenya their home, often with limited resources. Rich or poor, they faced a future which was largely unknown and with no guidelines to follow. No insurance company in the world would safeguard losses from drought, pestilence, disease, floods or famine. Few policies included protection from wild animals, tsetse fly, rinderpest or the safari ant.

The early settler was facing a struggle for existence beset with unknown dangers. For the pioneers were journeying into unknown land, on foot or by ox wagon. They were armed, since the tribes who occupied the land through which they travelled might resent their presence. This was in the days before there were established posts of police or soldiers. These pioneers had at most sporting guns with which to shoot game and this was their only protection. The labour they had recruited might desert when danger approached, and trade goods such as coloured beads are no protection against the spears of warlike tribesmen. There are many tales of how the first settlers survived and the perils they faced. These experiences influenced the outlook not only of those who faced them but successive generations to whom the knowledge was passed on. Few can deny the courage of these men and women and it should be no surprise that their descendants have inherited their spirit and daring.

To the average Kenyan the problems of daily life are expected; they do not lose any sleep if the rains are late or a crop fails; it has all happened before and you just have to be enterprising and resilient. This attitude has sustained the European settlers for eighty years and it shows no sign of changing. Do not forget that these early settlers brought up their children in the starkest of conditions: doctors could only be reached with difficulty; there were no recognized roads; trekkers carried all their goods, supplies, seeds, tools, tentage; they had language problems; there was no law and order, no hospitals, no trains, hotels or shops.

Not all had money behind them. One Mr Block, father of Jack and Tubby, trekked from South Africa with all his goods and possessions on one donkey. There were many like him. Others came without any experience of farming or business. Some jumped ship and made their way northwards. The Mayers, who originated from near Andover, emigrated to New Zealand, then moved to Australia. The head of the family made a fortune in sugar, became Mayor of Cairns and moved to East Africa later. Some families had capital and land was available at a low price; after that it was only their ingenuity which brought success to their venture. The Cole family, Earls of Enniskillen, was one such.

A large number of Voertrekkers came with their wagons from South Africa. The bitter feelings caused by the Boer War (1899–1902) might have proved a serious handicap when Roienek and Boer met in the new land of Kenya, but this seldom occurred as the South African pioneers tended to strike deeper into the interior. No horizon was too far for them to conquer. Racial differences did exist though: the Afrikaner tended to take what he wanted from the land and move on and was generally more heavy-handed with the local African. No Afrikaner chose to hold any position in the government administration.

By 1930 Kenya had a government with administrative posts throughout the country. Police maintained the law and, for both internal security and protection against external aggression, the King's African Rifles occupied stations in the Three Territories of East Africa: Kenya Colony, the Uganda Protectorate and Tanganyika Territory. The early trading posts were protected by military posts like Fort Hall. For recreation there was the racecourse at Nairobi and many sporting clubs for polo and all manner of other sports, including rifle shooting. Leave to the UK took time by ship from Mombasa, until Imperial Airways introduced a new dimension in travel. The danger of disease remained and precautions were necessary. At first these were primitive, but in time quinine, M & B and penicillin knocked out many of the killing infections. For many years the sun was thought to be the greatest danger to the human body: pith helmets, safari hats, flannel shirts, spine pads, kamar-bands, veils, and heavy boots and clothing were considered essential. It was not until the Second World War that the British soldier himself punctured most of the accepted theories on health: hats, dark glasses and trousers went out; berets, shorts and sandals were the only clothes in normal use even under the hottest sun, except in places where thorn bushes or heskenit grass were painful. However, it is to the early, pith-helmeted soldiers of the First World War and before that our story now turns.

FORMATION OF THE KING'S AFRICAN RIFLES

The last two decades of the nineteenth century were years of great change in Africa. East Africa in particular was under the greatest pressure in the scramble by the European nations to bring light to the Dark Continent. Commerce followed the Cross and Church missions and trading posts were set up. These events led to the gradual introduction of a simple administrative system which in turn required the raising of police and military units to maintain the peace. Small numbers of Sikhs were recruited from India to form the nucleus of a force. Guards were recruited, armed and trained to look after the administrative and trading posts, and armed porters escorted the caravans. These elementary forces were used with tribal allies to deal with malcontents. As military officers arrived in increasing numbers so the military became more organized and formal. Rates of pay were defined, terms of service established and equipment standardized. Nevertheless each territory went its own way and it was not until Whitehall began to take full responsibility for government that any steps towards uniformity were taken.

Contingents of Sikhs made up the first military units in Nyasaland. They were formally recruited through the India Office and had recognized terms of service. Many ad hoc units were recruited from local tribesmen as required and, inevitably, some acquired a degree of permanence. As time went by it was obvious that the various rifle companies must be reorganized, so in 1896 the Central African Regiment came into being. It saw foreign service in Mauritius, Somaliland, Ashanti and The Gambia. In 1898 it was split into two battalions, the 1st and 2nd Central African Regiment, and in 1900 its name was changed once more and the battalions became the 1st and 2nd Central African Rifles.

Lugard arrived in Uganda in 1890 and was soon raising and organizing armed units for the Imperial British East Africa Company, which governed the country by royal charter. An Indian contingent again formed the backbone of the newly raised rifle company. Selim Bey, an intelligent and tough Sudanese officer, had brought his troops south with Emin Pasha and was waiting in Uganda for the opportunity to return to his master, the Khedive of Egypt. Selim Bey, loyal to the Egyptian ruler, refused to join Lugard but agreed to form an alliance. Terms were drawn up and he continued under the Egyptian flag. Lugard, with Selim Bey's troops and a motley collection of locally raised rifle companies, supported by hordes of tribal allies, set to work to stop slave raiders, curb tribal wars and, most important, stop the Catholics and Protestants slaughtering each other. All this required constant campaigning. Once more it became obvious that these loosely grouped units must be tightly organized for efficient control, and so on 1 September, 1895, the Uganda Rifles was formed.

In 1891 the Imperial British East Africa Company started to administer the Coast, supported by a contingent of Indian police. Caravans were escorted by untrained armed porters. By 1894 it was necessary for Ainsworth, the Administrator at Machakos, to raise a local militia to protect and garrison the company's station. Permission was granted provided he did not intervene in any tribal fighting. On 1 July, 1895, Whitehall stepped in and a British Protectorate was declared. On 11 September of that year all miscellaneous troops were amalgamated to form the East African Rifles with its headquarters at Fort Jesus (Mombasa). As with the regiments in the other Territories the East African Rifles fought many hard campaigns.

By the turn of the century it was clear to all concerned that a closer relationship between the regiments was necessary. This would increase military efficiency, and standard equipment would save money. Proposals were called for and the problem studied. The plan put up by Colonel W. H. Manning was accepted and on 1 January, 1902, the regiments became the King's African Rifles. Manning (later GCMG, KBE, CB) was promoted Brigadier-General and appointed the first Inspector-General of the King's African Rifles. The battalions were organized as follows:

1st Bn KAR	formerly 1st Bn CAR
2nd Bn	2nd Bn
3rd Bn	EAR
4th Bn	African companies ⎫ of Uganda Rifles
5th Bn	Indian companies ⎭
6th Bn	to be formed later from three infantry companies, camel corps, militia and mounted infantry of local forces in British Somaliland

When the Great War started the King's African Rifles were greatly expanded and in 1919 the force strength was 1297 officers, 1916 British NCOs and 29,137 Africans. Casualties were 1311 killed, 3806 wounded, 3103 died of disease.

Between the wars the Regiment was consolidated and conditions of service improved. Reserves were established and equipment improved. In the Second World War the Regiment fought with distinction in Somalia, Abyssinia, Madagascar and Burma. Forty-four battalions plus garrison companies saw service, supported by East African engineers, artillery, transport, supply, medical and other ancillary units. Many won gallantry awards and many gave their lives.

Today, after Independence, we have the Tanzania Rifles, the Uganda Rifles and the Kenya Rifles with their own supporting units standing ready to protect their countries in the tradition of their fathers.

THE EAST AFRICAN MOUNTED RIFLES

When war was declared on 4 August, 1914, a mounted regiment was formed from the European settlers the following day. It was initially envisaged as a strike force to attack and defeat the forces defending the German colony of Tanganyika, which were a threat to Kenya. Its life was to be short, however, as demands were made on it for leaders by the King's African Rifles. At its peak it

9

was intended to have six squadrons, a Maxim gun section and signallers. Any man was eligible who could ride a horse and carry a rifle. By the end of August its strength had reached about 400 volunteers but within months many were transferred to other units. One reason for this was that the newly formed divisions also required officers and NCOs.

The type of man who rallied to the colours in 1914 was no different from his counterpart in 1952. It meant leaving his farm or job in the hands of his wife and family and riding off to join up. Very few had any military service, except those who might have served in the South African war or in India. What they lacked in knowledge they made up for in enthusiasm and individualism. For example, all members of Bowker's Horse who joined the EAMR retained the BH on their helmets, with EAMR on their shoulder-straps. Many were glad to escape the drudgery of a succession of bad crops or losses of stock. They set forth on a great adventure, many armed with pig-spears which they intended to use as lances, but a few near-fatal accidents to horse or rider eliminated this ancient weapon and a rifle was to prove the only friend of the mounted soldier. At one stage they even camouflaged their mounts as zebra.

The Regiment did have experienced men as Commanding Officer, Second-in-Command, Adjutant and Regimental Sergeant-Major. They were all former regular soldiers, as were the Quartermaster, the Regimental Quartermaster-Sergeant and Squadron Quartermaster-Sergeant. A special force of scouts was raised by Captain F. O'B. Wilson (later Sir Frank, CMG DSO). Originally they were known as the Magadi Defence Force. Many were famous big-game hunters of British or Dutch ancestry. They were mounted on mules and armed with every conceivable kind of rifle except the service .303. They did good work reconnoitring Longido, Kilimanjaro and Meru and the slopes of Ngorongoro. They travelled by night and lay up by day, often 30-40 miles behind the German lines. Water was always a problem. Their wide-ranging scouting was to prove invaluable in the advance of 1916.

It is not my intention here to describe this bush war in detail. It was one of long marches through extremes of heat by day and bitter cold by night, through rough country of thorn, full of game. Fires had to be lit at night to prevent lions eating the mules or horses. The tsetse fly was another major problem. Defence against these natural dangers was more important at times than defence against German attack: elephant, rhino, buffalo or lion can stampede any camp. Contacts with game were frequent. One man, diving fast for cover from a German machine-gun, landed on a leopard who was more surprised than he was and bolted! Giraffes damaged communications by bringing down telegraph lines. One of the greatest anxieties for a commander was how to evacuate the wounded through such territory with very limited means of transport.

Meanwhile, in November, 1914, at Tanga, on the coast, a landing by British forces proved disastrous and it was soon apparent that the calibre of some of our forces was not equal to the task. The British commander was inept and most of his troops were not fully trained and after a long sea journey had to make a beach landing against well-defended German positions. Heavy casualties were suffered in the swampy ground. A swarm of bees added to the discomfiture and on more than one occasion Indian sepoys and their leaders turned tail. Admittedly the Germans held the stronger position, but well-trained troops with good leaders would not have been routed.

Afterwards the fighting became a game of hide-and-seek with the German force, brilliantly led by von Lettow-Vörbeck, always one jump ahead of our very mixed troops of many different nationalities, under the command of officers past their best and generally lacking imagination. In due course Jan Smuts was appointed supremo and younger and more daring brigade commanders were selected. One of these was later to become Governor of Kenya; Major-General Sir Edward Northey, a 60th Rifleman.

The German commander, Colonel Paul von Lettow-Vörbeck, although greatly outnumbered, succeeded in disconcerting his opponents for three years. The British forces were laid low with disease and must have been the most demoralized British Force ever to be raised. Some of the British officers seconded to command the African askaris could not speak Swahili. Those who were Kenya settlers were much better equipped mentally and proved capable officers and NCOs.

Throughout the campaign great courtesy was shown by both sides. Von Lettow-Vörbeck was a magnificent leader of men who fought with old-fashioned chivalry. Strange though it may sound these days, the British, Indian and African troops admired him more than they did their own commanders. But eventually weight of numbers told and he and his gallant troops were forced to surrender to Lieutenant-Colonel E. G. B. Hawkins of the 1st/4th KAR and were granted all the respect due to a much-admired enemy. Thirty-seven years later when Her Majesty the Queen presented new colours to the 4th Battalion KAR at Jinja in Uganda, a telegram was received which read as follows: 'Greetings to the old enemy.' It was signed 'von Lettow-Vörbeck'.

The last date of importance in the East African campaign was 12 November, 1918, when a brisk engagement was fought on the River Melina. It was the final action of the campaign and, as it was fought after the Armistice, it was also the last of the First World War. Von Lettow signed the surrender document on 14 November, 1918.

With the surrender of the German forces, Tanganyika had to be administered by the victors and any pockets of resistance rounded up. With the eventual total defeat of Germany, Tanganyika became part of the British Empire and was taken over by the Colonial Office. Local troops were raised who became the 6th Battalion of the King's African Rifles on the same basis as the Kenya, Uganda and Nyasaland battalions. British officers and NCOs were on the same terms of service. It is more than likely that former German askaris who had served under von Lettow-Vörbeck were glad to change their coats. After years of warfare, a good job with pay, a firm base and married quarters must have appealed to any man. The German askari had proved that he was a good soldier and was soon to prove he was a good citizen too. Under British administration German settlers were permitted to retain their land, provided they kept the peace and accepted that they were under British sovereignty.

CHAPTER 2

BETWEEN
THE WARS

AFTER THE First World War life in Kenya settled down to the concerns of normal life: farming, business and generally making a living. To illustrate this, here are a few stories of men who were connected in one way or another with the Regiment and who have described what they did between the wars.

Colonel A. Dunstan-Adams OBE MC TD, having served during the First World War in West Africa and Egypt, the Somme, Ypres, etc, found himself in 1918 temporarily in command of his battalion and was awarded the Military Cross and Bar for gallantry in action. Unfortunately, however, his lungs had been affected by mustard gas which prevented him studying medicine in England and he was advised to move to a warm climate.

After a year in North Africa he returned to England where he married Eileen Thornton in 1925, the year they decided to settle in Kenya. He tried farming for a short time before joining W.C. Hunter and Co. and McIvor Motors. Then he started his own practice as a chartered accountant. Associated with him were Angus Lawrie, Denis May, John Story, David White and others.

In the following years the rise of Nazism under Hitler troubled many of the settlers who realized the weakness of Kenya's defences, and Dunstan-Adams was one of the foremost supporters of the formation of a European regiment to support the KAR. He was appointed commanding officer of the Kenya Regiment in 1937.

Lieutenant-Colonel Cecil J. Valentine OBE ED* was another of the original officers of the Kenya Regiment in 1937. Born in India, educated in England, he arrived in Kenya in 1925 and worked for a number of firms connected with trading and export of produce. He married Sheena, one of the five McLachlan daughters, another of whom married Philip Morcombe CO of 5th KAR in

---

* Efficiency Decoration

Madagascar and Burma, who later did so much to form the Kikuyu Guard. He was commissioned and appointed to command A Company of the Kenya Regiment in Nairobi, and in 1939 was an instructor at Eldoret.

During peacetime Kenya maintained a defence force on a territorial basis, much on the same lines as a Territorial battalion of the British Army. It was formed in 1928 and was known as the Kenya Defence Force (or 'Kenya Damned Fools' by some!). Its members served part-time and were men who could be spared from civilian occupations to attend regular training sessions during the year and various weekend camps, as well as the compulsory annual camp. Many of the first volunteers had fought in the First World War and were experienced men. They and the younger recruits had one thing in common: Kenya was their country and they recognized the need to have a European force, particularly in view of the rise of Nazi Germany.

KDF camps were held in the Eldoret District at the Soy Hotel, a few miles out of Eldoret. The manager of the hotel, an ex-lieutenant-colonel from the First World War, was very helpful in letting the Force use barns and empty stores on the hotel grounds for training and accommodation for the five-day camps. The training sessions were commanded by Colonel Swinton-Home, and actual training was conducted by Permanent Staff Instructors (PSIs) from the Brigade of Guards, such as Sergeants-Major Bobbitt and Broomfield. Many of those attending the camps were Afrikaners from the Uasin Gishu plateau area around Eldoret. The Afrikaners in general terms disliked the military discipline, but as attendance at the camps was compulsory they had no option. There were occasional amusing verbal outburst between the PSIs and those being instructed.

They were 'quite a tough bunch', according to this account by Charlie Broomfield. He writes:

I attended the 1939 Kenya Regiment camp and, true enough, we were giving instruction and drilling in English, being watched with great interest by the local Africans of the hotel staff and a few of their friends. After a while the Dutch chaps said that they couldn't understand English, so the PSIs got together, conferred and said: 'O.K., we'll teach them in Swahili,' so off we started, much to the amusement of the watching Africans! This, of course, really got up the Dutch chaps' backs up and it wasn't long before they said; 'O.K., Bwana, we understand English'. After that it was plain sailing.

Charlie Broomfield and RSM Jimmy Cummins had another brush with the Afrikaners on the Kenya Regiment's Uganda platoon's first parade at Kampala. This time, when they complained they did not understand English, the RSM dismissed the parade and conferred with CSM Broomfield. They managed to find a recruit who spoke both English and Afrikaans, and he spent the next two hours teaching the RSM all the necessary words of command in Afrikaans.

When the bugler again blew the 'Fall In', the platoon, looking forward to foiling their instructors again, fell in expectantly with barely disguised mirth on their faces. They were soon disillusioned as their RSM, with a roar in fluent Afrikaans, proceeded to double them around the parade ground with fixed bayonets. Most of them collapsed after fifteen minutes or so, only a few of the tougher individuals keeping it up a little longer, but after that they ate out of his hand.

THE KENYA REGIMENT (TF)

By the end of 1936 Italy was firmly established in Abyssinia. In Europe signs were manifest to those with open eyes that the God of War was getting tired of mere sideshows. In Kenya the military resources were pathetically inadequate and it had become evident that the situation in the Colony was fraught with unjustifiable risks. The Commander of the Northern Brigade KAR, Colonel J. A. Campbell DSO (later Major-General) was doing his utmost to improve matters within the regular battalions of the KAR, the Coast Battery and the KAR Reserve. He had no power over the irregular local Defence Force and this force, through misunderstandings, lack of encouragement and funds had reached the lowest ebb of its efficiency.

Something had to be done, so Sir Joseph Byrne, Governor of the Colony, appointed a committee under the chairmanship of Colonel Campbell to examine the position with regard to the local Defence Forces of the Colony and to make recommendations for their reorganization. He was helped in this task by Lord Stratheden, a captain in the Coldstream Guards, who went out to Kenya in 1936, with the dual job of raising a TA-style officer-and-NCO-producing battalion of white settlers and to reorganize the Kenya Defence Force, which he describes as 'an internal security scheme'. He continues:

Nearly all of my time was used in drafting with the Attorney-General the Bill which we hoped would be the Act to allow a regiment to be formed, and trying to see it go through LegCo [the Legislative Council] – a major task, as no one had heard of such an idea before, and every detail seemed to have to go back to the Colonial Office in London. During this time I could not do any actual work on the battalion, but did rough out the areas which I thought should be covered by the various sub-units.

I was never actually Adjutant, as with my dual job I was Staff Officer Local Forces. When the battalion took shape I appointed a chap called Redhead as Adjutant; he was a schoolmaster and rather good. Dunstan-Adams always called me Adjutant because he wanted to keep me 100 per cent Kenya Regiment. He got very impatient and furious at the delay, but eventually the

Bill did get through LegCo and I could start proper work on organizing the future battalion.

I had to be jolly careful that I did not cause anybody any sort of affront. I therefore avoided seeing or even being thought to hear any odd 'goings on'. I got very unpopular because I ordained that the uniform should be trousers and not shorts. I was put up to this by the new Governor, Brooke-Popham, who was even more fair-skinned than I was. I was more or less forgiven when some of the stubborn ones on their own exercises wore shorts and found that after lying in the sun on their tummies for an hour or two the backs of their knees were raw.

Before I left I got as far as organizing an annual camp. It was not far out of Nairobi on the way out to Magadi. A boob I made there was to forget that every member came in a car, and I hadn't got nearly a large enough car park. During the conference at the end of one exercise a small herd of giraffes came through, which caused considerable amusement. There were various reports from night patrols during the camp that buffaloes, or some other dangerous animal had been past them.

Before I left there was a scheme that I should raise a 4th Company in Uganda. I got as far as writing a paper for the Chief Secretary and Governor of Uganda and then I left for home.

The Campbell committee published its report early in 1937. Its main recommendation was that a voluntary territorial force of all arms be established in addition to the compulsory existing Defence Force. The Territorial Force was to be called the Kenya Regiment TF and it was to be raised from the age group 18-35 years. The Kenya Defence Force applied actively to men between the ages of 18 and 30 only and involved the extremely limited period of training of a hundred hours per annum. This training was to be carried out in short annual camps and included nights and times off-duty. In point of fact the actual training never occupied more than fifty hours. This training was compulsory and unpaid.

The training of the new Kenya Regiment, however, involved a minimum of sixty hours of actual training during the year, plus such additional instructions as might be ordered, plus an annual camp of twelve clear days. In actual fact the minimum periods were more than doubled in many instances. Time spent in camp was paid.

Service in the Regiment was for four years, followed by a minimum of four years with the Reserve. Service with the Reserve involved ten hours of actual training annually. The general standard and type of members of the Regiment was to be based upon the requirements governing the primary purpose for which the establishment of the unit was recommended. This was the provision of a reservoir of trained junior leaders, both commissioned and non-commissioned, to cope with an inevitable expansion of the King's African Rifles and ancillary forces in the event of war.

16

Regulations were suggested to ensure that only men having potential leadership qualities should be enlisted into the Regiment.

The formation of Cadet Units and of a Special Reserve were also recommended. The Special Reserve was to include such men as might have served in the Regular Army, the Territorial Army or any other Volunteer Force and those having other special qualifications, or any suitable men for whom no vacancy in the Regiment was available.

It was also proposed that a permanent staff of instructors be sought from the Brigade of Guards and that these be on a minimum basis of one PSI per company, in addition to a serving officer as Staff Officer or Adjutant and a Quartermaster.

These were the main recommendations of the committee and they were implemented by the Kenya Government in the Kenya Regiment Ordinance and Regulations of 1937 assented to in His Majesty's name on 29 March, 1937. Under this ordinance the Kenya Regiment (TF) was established by notice in the Gazette on 1 June, 1937.

The role of the Regiment in peacetime was threefold:

1. to train its members for its wartime function of providing junior leaders for the KAR
2. to provide instructors for KDF training camps
3. to be prepared to assist the regular forces – army and police – to maintain order within the Colony and to repel aggression from outside until such time as reinforcements could be made available.

Unfortunately at first the establishment of only two companies was authorized. This was due to two things: first, a doubt that sufficient young men would respond and, second, the general niggardly financial attitude to any military proposals obtaining, not only in Kenya, but throughout the Empire at that time.

Fortunately, however, the proposals regarding permanent staff were complied with wholeheartedly. The appointment of Captain (later Brigadier) Lord Stratheden of the Coldstream Guards as Staff Officer was a happy one in every sense of the word. To his efficiency, keenness and kindly tact and guidance is owed a great deal of the progress subsequently made by the Regiment. He was supported by Lieutenant Cummins (Irish Guards) the QM, whose knowledge of the country and its population gained in nearly ten years' service with the KDF was invaluable, and by CSM Bobbitt (Welsh Guards) and CSM Carter (Grenadier Guards). The Regiment was extremely fortunate in its permanent staff.

Five officers were gazetted on the formation of the Regiment. These were: Lieutenant-Colonel A. Dunstan-Adams MC (late CO of the 1st Nairobi Battalion KDF) as Commanding Officer with the rank of major, Major O. Lennox-Brown (late Machine Gun Corps) as Captain Commanding the country company, Captain C.J. Valentine (late 1st Nairobi Battalion KDF) as Adjutant and Captain J. Forrest (late 1st Nairobi Battalion KDF) as OC Prince of Wales' School OTC.

At the same time Brigadier-General A. C. Lewin CB CMG DSO ADC was appointed Honorary Colonel of the Regiment. His personal interest and practical encouragement during the two years before the war were an inspiration to all ranks of the Regiment.

Recruiting was inaugurated in a letter to the Press signed by the Governor calling on young men to join the Regiment. The response was immediate and enthusiastic. It confounded the pessimists who had doubted the spirit of the young men of the Colony. Out of an estimated number of about 2000 eligible men, over 500 of the type required had enrolled before the end of June. The Commanding Officer was in England representing the embryo of the Regiment at the Coronation of His Majesty King George VI and it was during these ceremonies that the uniform and badge of the Regiment first appeared on parade. Captain Lennox-Brown therefore commanded the Regiment during the initial recruiting period. With Lord Stratheden and other officers, he was responsible for interviewing and enlisting the first 500 men.

As a result of the astounding response, government approved the addition of a third company and Captain W. W. Mackinlay (RARO RA) of Njoro was gazetted to the Regiment and appointed a company commander. The third PSI, CSM Broomfield (Grenadier Guards) joined shortly after.

The battalion was organized with its headquarters and that of No. 1 Company in Nairobi, No. 2 Company in Nakuru and No. 3 Company in Eldoret. Training began in August, all the members having been uniformed and equipped. The uniform was as follows:

No. 1 Dress: pith helmet with pugri and Kenya Regiment flash (brown/red/ green; *brown* to represent the African soldiers, led by *green* – the young Europeans of Kenya – trained and supported by *red* – the Permanent Staff Instructors of the Regular Army. Popularly but inaccurately the colours were thought to mean 'Through mud and blood to the green fields and beyond' – the motto of the Royal Tank Regiment.) regimental badge (charging buffalo), KD jacket with long sleeves, lay-back lapels, KD trousers or KD shorts; long hose stockings with no foot, short hose top with regimental colours; khaki puttees, with regimental boots; hose tops; khaki shirt with collar; khaki tie.

No. 2 Dress: as above except that for KD jacket red bush shirt with four pockets, and delete khaki shirt and tie.

In towns, parades were held in the evenings and at weekends and in quarterly five-day camps. Progress was rapid and the first combined exercise with the KAR took place in Machakos in February, 1938, when No. 1 Company fought an encounter battle with the 3rd KAR. The Inspector-General, Major General George Giffard (later General Commanding the Army Group in South East

Asia), and the Brigade Commander were present and both congratulated the company on its state of training and conduct during the exercise.

In February, 1938, twelve members of the Regiment were granted commissions, thus providing a commander for each platoon. Two other members, both schoolmasters at the Prince of Wales' School, were commissioned and posted to assist Captain Forrest in the OTC. This was trained by the Kenya Regiment Permanent Staff Instructor based in Nairobi, in conjunction with its own officers, and training usually took place on one evening per week and every Saturday morning, with an annual camp at the Ngong Hills. Several of the OTC joined the Kenya Regiment when they finished their training.

The names of these first fourteen officers of the Kenya Regiment were: Branston, Berkeley, Bompas, Buxton, Crawford, Dorrington, Gledhill, Goldhawk, Hart, Lean, Luckham, Manning, Sweatman and Redhead.

The first annual camp was held in March, 1938, on the slopes of the Ngong Hills. A platoon of the KAR under Lieutenant R. Marsh was attached as a demonstration platoon and assisted very materially in training. Brigadier Campbell, who remained in the camp throughout the period, expressed himself astonished at the progress made when he addressed the battalion on the final parade of the camp.

The general principle adopted for training was that arms drill, weapon training, section leading and minor platoon tactics were carried out during the year and the annual camp was given over to platoon, company and battalion tactical training with one afternoon for sports. The programme in camp was as strenuous as it could be made and included evening lectures by regular officers of the KAR and RAF. In tactical exercises it was sought to test every man's interest and progress by giving each private the opportunity of acting as section leader and – as far as possible – as platoon commander; by giving all senior NCOs a chance of commanding the platoon and when possible the company; and by giving all junior officers command of the company in at least one of the operations. In the light of experience it is now realized that not enough time was given to general administrative training which, except for a few lectures, was neglected. In spite of this, the first camp was undoubtedly a success and increased the enthusiasm by a healthy inter-company rivalry.

Visitors included HE Sir Robert Brooke-Popham, Major-General George Giffard who spent a day with the battalion, and Brigadier General Lewin who spent two days in camp. Throughout the camp the medical care of the battalion was in the hands of the MO, Surgeon-Captain J. A. Carman, whose talks on hygiene and health were among the most popular of the daily lectures.

Throughout 1938 efforts were made to obtain authority for the completion of the battalion by the addition of a fourth company. This authority was granted in February, 1939. Captain Redhead was given command. Lieutenant Buxton became a company commander in place of Captain Lennox-Buxton who was promoted and appointed second-in-command of the battalion, the Commanding

19

Officer being promoted to Lieutenant Colonel. In view of the formation of the fourth company five new subalterns were commissioned. They were: Second Lieutenants Furse, Garvey, Grant, Hopcraft and Simpson. The fourth PSI, CSM Allen (Scots Guards), also joined for duty.

Captains Boyd and Oates, both engineers, had by this time been commissioned as the first officers in the Special Reserve.

With the growing political uncertainty in Europe in the first half of 1939 came renewed concern for the poor state of military preparedness in Kenya and Uganda. In May HE Sir Philip Mitchell, Governor of Uganda, invited the Brigade Commander to send the Commanding Officer to Uganda with a view to recruiting a platoon to be part of the Kenya Regiment. In June the Commanding Officer, accompanied by Lieutenant Cummins, visited Uganda and from the extremely small numbers available enlisted over thirty young men to form the Uganda platoon of the Regiment. Command of this platoon was given to Second Lieutenant Crittenden who was commissioned into the Regiment.

In the same month the Brigade Commander obtained authority to form a reconnaissance platoon as part of the Regiment. Recruiting immediately started and by the end of the month twenty-six men with special qualifications had been added to the strength. These were men with a greater than average knowledge of the country; most of them were white hunters. The age limit for this platoon was increased to forty-five.

In August, 1939, the second annual camp was held – again on the Ngong Hills. The camp ended on 23 August for all except the Reconnaissance platoon, which had started a week later. Its members had been hard at map-reading, field sketching and report writing and compass work and, on the day the camp broke up, had set out for Nanyuki where they were to be attached to the 5th KAR for field work in the NFD (Northern Frontier District). They went in box body cars owned by the men themselves.

At the conclusion of this camp Brigadier Campbell said goodbye to the Regiment as his tour of duty in East Africa was coming to an end and he did not expect to see the battalion on parade again. He thanked the men for their response to the efforts of the staff to train them. He said they had a long way to go but that he could ask for nothing better, in the event of war, than to find himself in command of a body of men as fit and keen as those of the Kenya Regiment. Should war come soon, he added, they would be of the utmost value to the KAR.

No regular soldier ever gave more help and encouragement to a territorial unit than did Brigadier Campbell.

On the breaking-up parade the Commanding Officer warned the men of the possibility of an early mobilization and told them that he thought the situation in Europe indicated that they should make immediate arrangements to put their civilian affairs in order.

The camp had been even more successful than that of 1938. 480 men took part in the march past out of the 534 who attended. Of the remainder a number were in England on leave and these were sent back to rejoin the Regiment about four months later.

The training had progressed more rapidly than had been hoped for by the most sanguine. This did not mean that the men were fully trained soldiers but it did mean that they had come a long way from being raw recruits. At least 75 per cent were capable of instructing in the use of rifle and Bren gun and more than that number had acted with greater or lesser success as junior leaders in the main tactical exercises and taken part in many TEWTs. They still lacked administrative training and had little idea of the ordinary duties of NCOs in an African battalion, but the majority were holding positions of moderate responsibility and nearly all could speak Swahili and had had some experience of African labour. Best of all, they were keen and anxious to learn.

On 26 August, 1939, the Commanding Officer was ordered to report for duty at Nothern Brigade HQ, with instructions to bring the mobilization posting lists up to date. On 28 August the first calling-up telegrams were sent to country members and the town members ordered by telephone or orderly to report for duty.

The boys' boarding block at the European Primary School, Nairobi, was put at the Regiment's disposal as a mobilization barracks. As fast as men came in they were mustered into parties and sent off to various battalions of the KAR as junior officers and senior NCOs. By 3 September over 240 officers and men were actually with the KAR. The men of the Reconnaissance Platoon at Nanyuki had been assisting the 5th KAR in mobilizing for several days before war was declared. At this time there were thirteen members of the Regiment on leave in the British Isles; among them was Captain B.M.R. Gale, who tried to enlist in units in England but was prevented from doing so by the Colonial Office. Instead he received orders from the Colonial Office, in two envelopes, the inner one of which was suitably stamped 'Secret', to stand by ready to join the Regiment at 24 hours' notice.

The thirteen 'duly met on board the *Empress of Australia*' at Southampton. They had to haul their own luggage from the van and the usual lights of course were not in use. The only illumination was two Dietz lamps. Their cabins were 'far down and the port holes were only just above water level. These never could be opened because the ship zig-zagged continuously, so the atmosphere was thick to say the least of it. The ship was blacked out at night, but gin was around 4d a tot which was some slight consolation.'

Basil Gale recalls:

At first we had to feed far aft, far down and over the propellors. We did not much like those conditions and so, being true Kenyans, said as much in no uncertain terms. We were moved up one deck and found ourselves not quite so far aft. Although the food was still dished out in pails and so on, conditions were a little better after that.

21

Back in Kenya new recruits were being enlisted daily and training was in full swing. By the end of September over 400 had been sent to active units as well as a few to Supply and Transport. In the middle of September the battalion moved to the Nairobi Show Ground (now occupied by No. 1 General Hospital) and on 6 October it moved to Kampala. During this period the formation of the 1st East African Light Battery was authorized and, with the exception of one officer, it was drawn entirely from the Regiment. It was commanded by Major Mackinlay. The Reconnaissance Platoon had returned to Nairobi and, after re-equipping, was divided into two sections. One section returned to Nanyuki where it was attached to 5th KAR and the other went to Garissa where it was attached to 4th KAR. Later this platoon was again withdrawn and increased in strength largely from the Regiment to become the East African Reconnaissance Squadron, popularly known as the 'Recces', who so constantly harassed the enemy when, in June, 1940, the Italians crossed the northern border of Kenya. It was from this unit that the first Kenya Regiment casualties were reported.

It was at about this time that Captain Michael Biggs of KAR Northern Brigade was instructed to give a lecture to the Kenya Regiment Intelligence Platoon, camped at Langata. He was somewhat taken aback by his pupils:

The subject of my lecture was, I think, 'Fieldcraft' but when I stood in front of the Kenya Regiment's Intelligence Platoon I faced such chaps as the Cunningham brothers, Temple-Boreham, Ker and Downey and other such white hunters who knew far more about my subject than I did, so mostly I talked about military intelligence, getting identifications etc. in the field.

The Regiment remained at Kampala until the end of the year – a difficult time, during which it was almost impossible to obtain any training stores, clothing or equipment. Recruits were still pouring in and often had to work in their civilian clothes for weeks. At the beginning of January, 1940, it moved into camp on the racecourse at Eldoret. By this time over 500 members were serving with the KAR, NRR (Northern Rhodesia Regiment), Light Battery, Recces, the S & T and the EAE, and a small number who had gone to the RAF and 100 to the Royal Navy (including John Laing). About 120 were completing their training at the newly-formed OCTU at Nakuru where one of the officers, Captain Redhead, was an instructor, and about 150 were training at Eldoret.

One of the Regular Army PSIs at Eldoret was CSM Davo Davidson (Worcestershire Regiment). Davo had served part of his army service in Palestine, where apparently he used to ride on the front of railway engines to give warning of any mines on the lines. Also at one time he was supposed to have been in America fighting against gangsters, taking part in several shoot-outs. Fellow PSI Charlie Broomfield recalls:

1. Early days in Kenya.

2. Men of the Kenya Regiment leaving Nairobi for action stations in East
Africa, Madagascar and Burma, 1939.

3. Colonel A. Dunstan-Adams,
OBE MC TD.

4. General Sir William Platt, the victor of
Keren, formerly Kaid El A'am of the Sudan
Defence Force.

5. Kenya Regiment Camp in the Ngong Hills, 1939.

6. General Sir George Erskine, GOC-in-C
Kenya, 1953–55.

7. The Reverend James Gillett, Regimental
Padre, 1936–53.

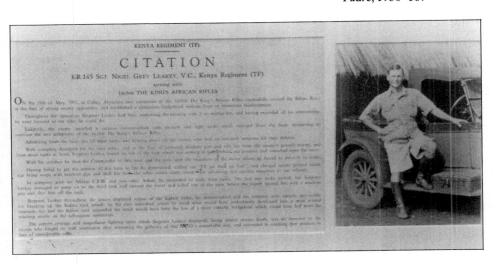

8. Sergeant Nigel Grey Leakey, VC.

9. Waiting to take over the range. A cheerful crowd of Kenya National Servicemen, 1952.

10. Passing Out Parade, Kenya National Servicemen, Salisbury, Southern Rhodesia, 1952.

I had given him instructions to take some members of the Kenya Regiment to the 30-yard range and give them pistol instruction. After a while I went to the range to see how the pistol training was progressing and what should I find but Davo giving demonstrations on how to use a pistol against gangsters in doorways, windows, etc.

One contingent of recruits arrived at Eldoret from Mombasa. Reg Collins, who was among them, writes:

I suppose the composition of the Mombasa contingent could have been regarded as typically Kenyan, even down to one member joining us at Mombasa station under a prison warder escort, for he had been prematurely released from Fort Jesus in order to serve King and Country (he was later commissioned and served – admittedly not in a very distinguished Corps! – in a fairly senior rank).

The altitude of the camp at Eldoret after Mombasa proved to be a problem:

Early morning PT comprised a run around the full circuit of the racecourse. The first couple of mornings for the Mombasa contingent were pretty horrendous, with several of us keeling over and the rest (including me) feeling distinctly weak and unwell. We were as a consequence excused PT for our first week, by which time we were well adjusted to the altitude.

Another trial was the food:

I cannot remember a morning when the porridge was *not* burned. Whether as a result of practical work study, I do not know, but the tea was made in the same cauldrons (or was it one giant cauldron?) in which the porridge had been made. Time or inclination to clean the cauldron(s) properly after the porridge-making was evidently lacking. This meant that the tea carried a certain 'body' by the presence of a multitude of flecks of burned porridge. More than forty years on I can remember the taste. Many of us had been to boarding schools and were less than faddy about our food but the Kenya Regiment, we agreed, provided a nadir of cuisine then and in terms of later experience.

Conditions at OCTU were fairly primitive as well. D.W. Skerratt

was peacefully perambulating the Square at Eldoret when the RSM descended on the Platoon and roared at me to fall out and get over to the Orderly Room at the double. In fear and trepidation I, a young private, barely 19 years of age, reported to the Adjutant who informed me that I must leave for Nakuru immediately. I left about 2 pm that day by car with a certain Private Bewes. I was to teach the KR RAF Squad the morse code and to ensure they qualified, sending and receiving at 12 wpm. Bewes was to teach them map-reading and we were given twelve weeks to complete the task.

On arrival at Nakuru I was whipped up in front of the great man himself, Brigadier General Lewin, who welcomed me and said: 'Glad to have you; get on with the job.' (Being a flier himself he was very keen on the RAF.) I was given a basic hessian-walled banda as a classroom and when I enquired about equipment I was told, 'You're the qualified telegraphist, it's up to you, chum.' All I had was a rifle and bayonet. I made a hurried visit to Nakuru Post Office, borrowed a couple of morse keys, purchased a very old 1914–18 DIII buzzer from the local sale room and had a Sikh *fundi* (mechanic) make more morse keys for practice. So was born an unsophisticated morse-operating class and I think most of those chaps qualified before leaving for their RAF training proper.

In February a small company under command of Lieutenant Branston was attached to 6th KAR for inter-brigade manoeuvres in the NFD. Its conduct, bearing and stamina during the fairly strenuous exercises earned praise from all senior officers and was an excellent example to the Askaris. Among those who praised most generously were some who had previously criticized the Regiment through ignorance of its role, its spirit and its pre-war training. The officers not on duty with this company acted as umpires throughout the exercises.

Months before, it had become evident that the young men from other East African territories could best be trained by means of the organization already existing in the Regiment and so gradually the purely Kenyan and Ugandan character of the Regiment was modified by the inclusion of recruits from Tanganyika, Nyasaland and Northern Rhodesia. Some men anxious to be in at the beginning had come up from South Africa and Southern Rhodesia at their own expense and enlisted in the Regiment. The selective rules for membership had been given up at the beginning of hostilities, fitness being about the only qualification left.

By the middle of 1940 the number enlisted was over 1500 of which most were serving in the various units already referred to, besides a steadily increasing number who had gone to the RAF.

In September Lieutenant-Colonel Dunstan-Adams was posted as Sub-Area Commander in the NFD and Lieutenant-Colonel ('Sweetie') Barkas (East Yorks) late of the 5th KAR took over command. At that time the numbers had risen to over 2300 due to the spur to recruiting given by the entry of Italy into the war.

At about the same time facilities were extended to include Southern Rhodesians and a batch of recruits who arrived from South America. The resultant change in the purely East African character of the Regiment was accompanied by a further breaking away from the pre-war traditions by the posting of all the remaining officers of the Regiment to other units. They had done a good job and it was time they were given better opportunities for promotion by going to other units. In some cases pre-war officers on joining their new battalions found themselves junior to men who had enlisted after war was declared and whom they had put through their recruit's training little more than a year before.

The places of the Kenya Regiment officers were mostly taken by officers from home. Naturally these officers knew nothing of the short history of the Regiment nor of the *esprit de corps* of which it was so proud, and so it lost much of its unit consciousness and became merely a training depot. Command changed again from Lieutenant-Colonel Barkas to Lieutenant-Colonel Stitt DSO MC who, though not an officer of the Regiment, had been Second-in-Command for nearly a year.

By the middle of 1941 the supply of recruits had been very nearly exhausted and the maintenance of the organization was no longer economic. From that time onwards recruits were enlisted into the Regiment only. Their training was carried out at various depots from Gwelo in Southern Rhodesia to Nakuru in Kenya. The last recruits to be trained in Southern Rhodesia were a small number of British subjects set free to enlist on the occupation of Madagascar by British forces. Those trained at the Nakuru Battle School were drawn largely from young men who had left the Prince of Wales' school at the end of 1943 and had therefore done a sound course of training in the school OTC.

Before the Regiment was discontinued in service, it acted as a depot and training centre for potential leaders and, with the exception of the Chaplain's Branch, there was no branch, arm or service which was not provided with officers, NCOs or men from the Regiment. Officers and men of the Regiment took part in many actions during the war. The following quotations from *The King's African Rifles* illustrate a few of their actions:

On 15 November Captain N. M. C. Cooper with a patrol of D Company surprised and put to flight a party of thirty-five Japanese, killing four and capturing a machine-gun, equipment and maps.

The Japanese air raids caused some casualties, particularly in 11th KAR, who lost Captain I. S. Adler (RAMC) the regimental MO killed, and Captain H. R. C. Curtis (Royal Sussex Regiment) and Second Lieutenant H. Maclean wounded. While sheltering the last-named, Sergeant Mwanza (an M'Kamba) of B Company was mortally wounded.

Lieutenant P. G. W. Anderson (Kenya Regiment) of 2nd KAR, who was acting as mortar FOO to D Company (4th KAR), then volunteered assistance and worked his way along the edge of the ridge to deal with a sniper who had knocked out three successive Bren gunners of No. 16 Platoon in as many minutes. With Sergeant Sparkes and the mortar askaris, Anderson rushed the fox-hole and killed the sniper.

Lieutenant Norbury, commanding No. 16 Platoon, was wounded while crossing the wire, but with great courage continued to lead his men to the top,

25

where he was wounded again. He was awarded the first MC of the campaign, and two African other ranks were awarded the MM.

Both Captain Cooper and Lieutenant Anderson were awarded Military Crosses. Others were Colin Campbell, Gregor Grant, Tubby Block and Donald Powrie, while John Garvey was awarded the MBE and Cecil Valentine the OBE. In Abyssinia, at the Battle of Colito:

Sergeant N. G. Leakey of the mortar platoon, having used all his bombs, had joined the infantry for the last phase of the attack. As the leading tank approached he leapt upon it, shot one of the crew by firing his revolver through the crack of a badly fastened lid, climbed inside and forced the tank to stop. Failing to bring the gun into action against the other tanks, he went after them on foot, and as they withdrew was last seen attempting to force open the top of another tank as it bore him away into the bush. Leakey's subsequent fate was never ascertained, but his courageous example had done its work. He had killed the commander of the tanks at his first assault and this action, coupled with concentrated fire from the artillery, rallied the askaris and prevented the enemy tanks from exploiting a situation initially in their favour.

Sergeant Leakey was awarded a posthumous VC. The citation ended with the words: 'There is no doubt that by his self-sacrifice and devotion to duty Sergeant Leakey, single-handed, halted a most dangerous counter-attack which threatened to destroy all our infantry who had crossed the river.'
In memory of Sergeant Leakey, 6th KAR celebrate Colito Day each year.
A letter from a Second-Lieutenant who served with the 1st/6th KAR describes the conditions in which some of the troops had to serve, and a highlight of their campaign:

3 June 1941

Well Ma Darling,

We are still battling along forcing the Italians back, the artillery is in action and at the moment our planes are bombing and machine-gunning their gun positions. I really have hopes that things may be over up here by mid or late June, but who can really say? Rain is our most delaying event and yet we are still pushing forward.
We have had a few more nights out of bed but I have managed to keep dry. An Italian groundsheet – 6'×6' – pitched as a tent has kept off light and medium rain and we have been fortunate not to have had heavy rain the last couple of nights. Last night was annoying. Although our transport could not get up to us the boys were sent off on foot with our beds etc. and I was looking forward to a comfortable night. The guns were firing, though we were not

26

being shelled and there was some rain; the boys *lost* the way and returned so we had to sleep again in our clothes under our little tents while they slept in comfort by the lorries. Was I annoyed!

When we are away from our first line there is usually trouble of some sort. Once three bottles of whisky and five of brandy were stolen from our limited stocks while we were living in discomfort forward. We generally have a night or two like this before a battle and then one or two after it while a bridge is being built; we are therefore quite often 3-4 days without bed and bedding or washing kit. Food is brought up but of course it is cold when it reaches us; we have, however, a large thermos pot which is most useful for tea. Although often wet we don't always fare badly for the nights after the battle we can get groundsheets and blankets from the battlefield; the night before any action is not so good for whatever we have for the night we generally have to take into battle with us the next morning.

I had a wonderful experience the other day. News came in from some tanks on patrol that a party of the enemy, about 500, wanted to surrender, so my Company Commander took me and my platoon out to collect them. We got the remains of a Division – a General, two Brigadiers and their staffs, about 1000 Italians, 2000 natives and hundreds of pack animals. It *was* a job collecting all their arms, binoculars etc., searching their kit, getting them into some sort of order and sending them in to a place five miles away. I had only my British sergeant, 20 Askaris, and a few tank people to help me. It took about five hours and I had not a minute's rest. The big bugs went in with my Company Commander in a lorry; the officers then went off on foot and without an escort. I had to keep my askaris to look after their askaris and mule teams – and later the other Italians unescorted. What a procession! Several of the natives had wives and there were a fair sprinkling of children. If only there had been a few more of us we could have had lots of loot. I managed to get a few things, including some rope which came in useful as a truncheon when dealing with the natives.

My next letter *might* contain news of another successful battle, which battle *might* be the last of this campaign; let us hope it will.

Love to Bunny and her bairns and to YOU darling Ma,

John

In all over 3500 members of the Regiment joined the East African Forces. Of these more than 1500 were commissioned as officers in the battalions of the King's African Rifles from Kenya, Uganda, Tanganyika and Nyasaland, and in the Northern Rhodesia Regiment.

They served in General Cunningham's campaign which, with General Platt's force, defeated the Italian Armies on two fronts. After the Italians surrendered, some officers were specially selected to serve as administrative officers in the former Italian colonies of Ethiopia and Somalia. Others remained with their

KAR battalions and took part in the campaign in Madagascar before proceeding to Burma where they helped to defeat the Japanese.

Throughout the years of war, while their husbands and sons were on active service, mothers and wives looked after the farms. A few experienced the disasters which had confronted their predecessors at the beginning of the century but the spirit of comradeship still existed and neighbours rallied to assist those who had lost their stock or crops.

At the time there was no organization to rehabilitate the African askaris who had been overseas for many months. Nor had anyone seriously envisaged what effect service abroad would have on 'Private Majji Baridi'. They had met soldiers from other Commonwealth countries, the West African contingent of Nigeria, Gold Coast, Sierra Leone and Gambia, not to mention those from Somalia, the Sudan Defence Force, the South African Forces and others from the Belgian Congo and India. They also may have been surprised when they met British battalions and realized, perhaps for the first time, that the white soldiers did the same sort of fatigue work as they did. This point had been laboured needlessly in my opinion as for centuries British officers have always joined in with their men on any task without losing face. 'Majji Baridi' would have had much to tell his *bibi* (wife) when he returned home.

Very few Kikuyu joined the forces as front-line combatants. Mostly they acted as back-up services, like the 'boys' mentioned in the letter above. The African contingent consisted mainly of Wakamba, Somalis and others, who were never allowed to rise above the rank of senior NCO. One or two Kikuyu did, however, serve in combat, notably Dedan Kimathi and Stanley Mathenge, the last of the Mau Mau 'Generals' who were later to trouble the East African Security Forces.

CHAPTER 3

THE REGIMENT
RE-FORMED

STEPS WERE taken immediately after the war to re-form the Regiment and final approval was given in 1950 when it was re-formed into four companies: A and HQ Companies at Nairobi, B Company at Nakuru and C Company at Kitale/Eldoret. One soldier who joined up at this time tells of his experience:

I joined the Kenya Regiment TF in 1950 when recruiting started after the War. I remember queueing up with all my Nairobi friends of about the same age, twenty or so, outside Bruce Ltd. First in the queue was Clifford Connell who was determined to be first and achieve some glory! I think having achieved this he took little interest in the Regiment thereafter.

After a brief medical examination I was accepted and became KR 3609 Private F. J. McCartney. The Nairobi area recruits were all in A Company or HQ and it was our lot to train on the occasional Tuesday evening and on one Sunday a month at our HQ which occupied a number of long wooden shacks opposite the Aero Club at Wilson Airport. CSM Croft lived there. I think we will all remember him!

I believe I was the first to be put on a charge. We had just been issued with our khaki No.1s from the QM's store when we were called on parade. Hurriedly I put my uniform into Private Campbell-Gillies' unlocked car – and that was the last I ever saw of it (no reflection on Private Campbell-Gillies)! I was charged before Colonel Valentine and fined 100 Shs which I thought was a bit excessive in the circumstances.

Annual Camp at the foot of the Ngong Hills was great fun – in retrospect. Having to do night sentry duty for interminable hours, or so it seemed, has always made me feel rather sympathetic towards night watchmen who fall asleep.

29

On one big exercise we did I was the Company Commander's runner. Initially it appeared to be a cushy number, riding around in his jeep. The Company was deployed along a track in the foothills of the Ngongs. Suddenly down below a reedbuck broke cover and instantly a dozen rifles took a bead on it, including those of Nigel Bulley and Mickey Shaw. Francis Erskine was the only one to pull the trigger. The resultant bang of course gave the whole show away. Erskine was put on a charge by our irate Company Major and I was despatched on foot with a message to another company. That was the last I saw of the jeep, and I spent the rest of the day trailing my major and never quite catching up, and all the time with an appalling attack of hay fever. Needless to say I avoided that 'cushy number' on future operations.

Lieutenant-Colonel C. J. Valentine OBE ED, who during the latter part of the war had held the appointment of AA and QMG to the East African Division in Burma, was appointed to command, with the Permanent Staff coming for the first time from the King's Royal Rifle Corps and the Rifle Brigade (The Green Jackets). The first RHQ was in temporary buildings at Nairobi West.

In March, 1950, the foundation stone of the present RHQ was laid by HRH The Duke of Gloucester, the guard of honour being provided by Old Comrades of the Regiment, and the building was formally opened by Her Majesty The Queen, then HRH The Princess Elizabeth, at a parade on 2 February, 1952.

The Regiment is possibly the only one in the Empire whose Colours bear no battle honours in spite of the fact that its members saw action in most of the campaigns of the last war. The Colours were subscribed for by the women of Kenya through the East African Women's League, and by officers of the Regiment. Their presentation to the Regiment was authorized by His Majesty King George VI. On 4 November, 1950, the Colours were presented to the Regiment by His Excellency the Governor, Sir Philip Mitchell GCMG MC at a ceremony at Nairobi West. The Colours were consecrated by the Right Rev. Percy Crabbe, Lord Bishop of Mombasa.

On 20 November, 1950, the Regiment was honoured with the Freedom of the City of Nairobi and, in accordance with its privilege, marched through the city with 'bayonets fixed, drums beating, band playing and colours flying'. Fergus McCartney remembers the occasion:

We marched along never-ending streets until I thought my left elbow and arm would be permanently deformed from carrying my .303 service rifle at the slope for such a considerable distance – it was absolute agony. In spite of this I remember we all felt proud and honoured and after the parade many citizens made a point of being particularly nice to us.

Two very useful and enjoyable camps which were held before the declaration of the State of Emergency in 1952 showed that the original *esprit de corps* existed unchanged. In January, 1952, the first call-up under the Compulsory Military Training Ordinance of 100 young men was flown to Southern Rhodesia for six months' training. This was done in Salisbury pending the completion of the Kenya Regiment Training Centre at Nakuru. When the recruits passed out they joined the Regiment as territorials and attended the annual camp in 1952, finding no difficulty in identifying themselves immediately with the territorial tradition.

Much excitement surrounded the official opening of the new Regimental Headquarters on 2 February, 1952, by Princess Elizabeth. Fergus McCartney remembers 'an awful lot of rehearsal for the Parade and if I remember rightly at the last full rehearsal at 4th KAR HQ, Nanyuki, there were a lot of hitches'. One of these was when the lady representing the Princess tried out the lavatory and looked up to see a smiling African face, politely asking: 'Do you want some more water, Memsahib?' However,

> when the actual day came such was the occasion that the Regimental Guard of Honour excelled itself. The Princess, wearing a pink and white polka-dot dress, looked absolutely radiant as she came along the lines. She stopped to talk to the man next to me, so my view of her was more than just a fleeting one. The whole parade by the CCF, the Old Comrades and the Regiment was an outstanding success.

The Princess was to have gone on to present the Colours to 4th KAR but within a few days of the Parade while staying at Treetops Hotel, Mweiga, she heard of her father's death from Major Eric Sherbrooke Walker and had to return home. She did eventually return to present the Colours in 1954 at Jinja in Uganda.

TRAINING

The Kenya Regiment Training Centre was commanded by Major A. D. (Tony) Lewis DSO of the Dorset Regiment, with Major A. C. K. ('Rogue') Barkas (Durham Light Infantry), Major Harry Bell (York and Lancaster Regiment) and Major Kenneth Coutts (Royal Army Education Corps). The Company Sergeant-Major was CSM Cameron of the Scots Guards.

The Rhodesian Government allotted the King George V Barracks to the Kenya Regiment National Servicemen and the use of the Southern Rhodesian Forces' training facilities. The Royal Rhodesian Regiment was already affiliated to The King's Royal Rifle Corps so another bond was forged. During both World Wars Royal Rhodesians served with the 60th Rifles. Their Honorary Colonel was Colonel Ferris, whose son Bob had been attached to 2/60th in BAOR in 1951.

The first courses went to Salisbury but in 1954 the KR Training Centre was moved to Lanet near Nakuru. The move was probably inevitable but something was lost which was important – those who trained away from home benefited from the experience as they served in another country and with people both black and white who had different backgrounds. One added advantage – they could not get home for weekends. Those who were trained at Salisbury realize the great influence it had on their development.

Throughout the life of the Training Centre, Officers, WOs and NCOs changed, but the standard of instructor never dropped and the youth of white Kenya had much to be grateful for. For some, military discipline may have been a rude shock but I never heard of one man who did not value his introduction to Military Service. The Training Centre was active from January, 1952 to 1963 when the Regiment, by then multi-racial, was finally disbanded.

Major 'Rogue' Barkas writes:

I was a soldier for twenty years but I think the best posting I ever had was when I was told that I was going to Salisbury in Southern Rhodesia to train young Kenya National Servicemen. The chap who commanded the project was Tony Lewis of the Dorsets, who was the same sort of age as we were. He'd been a very distinguished soldier in the war – he got a DSO at 24 and was the ideal chap to come out and command this small unit. There was also a fellow called Harry Bell in the York and Lancaster Regiment – he was to command one group of these fellows – and myself, who had been out in Africa for quite a long time during the war. I was selected to command the other half. Kenneth Coutts of the RA Educational Corps was expected to imprint the three Rs on Kenya skulls.

The soldiers themselves were an extraordinary sort of muddle-up: there were blokes from farms, from the game department, from Nairobi and the government service. They were all personally excellent Kenya blokes. As it worked out, Harry Bell commanded the farmer chaps and I had the town types.

In one platoon one ended up with about fifty, all highly educated fellows – and it was a unique situation when all your private soldiers had passed Cert A – like commanding a platoon of potential major-generals, and coming to Rhodesia for them was like sending them to university: it rounded them off, broadened their outlook – they all say to this day that it turned them into men.

When all the training was over they came back up to Kenya and joined the Regiment. In the Emergency these chaps did a terrific job, entirely because of that basic training. I remember when the first lot arrived in Salisbury though. They got off the plane with short shorts, open-necked shirts, scruff order, to be greeted by the most terrible fellow – CSM Cameron of the Scots Guards. They all said, 'Huh, who's this bloody fool who thinks he's going to hammer us? Nobody is going to defeat us.' They were in a bolshy frame of mind, thinking: 'We come from Kenya: none of these bloody pommies are going to tell us', but within a couple of weeks he had them doubling round the square carrying rifles above their heads. If they didn't behave themselves they were sweeping the square with toothbrushes. CSM Cameron – they called him 'Rumbleguts' – gave them absolute hell from morn till night. After a month or two they were eating out of his hand. He'd call them 'bloody hairy-backs' and shout on parade 'Get hold of your rifle, boy – you're 'olding your rifle like a tart holding a navvy's prick.' Things like that used to come out automatically on parade in the morning. Nobody took offence – they all jumped and got a move on. The competitive spirit produced was second to none – they turned into the most excellent unit I've ever served with.

When King George VI died, CSM Cameron walked into the barrack rooms during a rest period after lunch and ordered all the cadets out onto parade. When they had fallen in he addressed them as follows: 'Have you heard the news, very sad news, His Gracious Majesty King George VI has died?' A pause and then: 'I don't blame him – he probably heard he had got you horrible lot in his army. Parade dismiss – back to your Egyptian PT. Move!'

When all this Kenya Regiment training business was over in Rhodesia I came back and served another eighteen months in the same set-up in Nakuru in Kenya. It wasn't quite the same as going down to Rhodesia. The blokes were at home: they could ring Mum, they could skive off for weekends. They had a different feel from the blokes that actually went away.

Life at the training centre was never allowed to get too serious. 'Rogue' Barkas tells of another incident which 'reflects the whole attitude of the Kenya Regiment – the way we all got on and enjoyed life to the full' – a visit of the CO to the passing-out parade at Salisbury:

The CO Colonel Guy Campbell came down from Nairobi to visit us and watch the passing-out parade. This happened at the end of each six-months' course and was a great thing for us – the preparation was terrific and on this occasion the chap taking the parade was the Governor of Rhodesia, Sir John Kennedy. The soldiers were so smart, the weather was beautiful: it was the real day of the Kenya National Servicemen's Training Centre. I was commanding the first half of the company and we were proceeding down the front rank, the Governor in front, me going along on his right-hand side, holding my sword, thinking I was so smart. Following me up was Guy, the CO, plus the normal retinue of ADCs and hangers-on who always accompanied Governors and people on this type of occasion. When we got to the end of the front rank we were doing a left turn when I suddenly felt two fingers up my backside and Guy whispered in my ear hole:

'How's that for centre?' How I managed not to laugh I don't know! During the whole of this time we were walking down the front rank, up the rear rank and a slow march was being played and I remember as a boy the words of that song used to be:

'Somebody shat on our doorstep and Mother swore blind it was I'. This is how the whole day went on.

I was serving in the British Army of the Rhine in the summer of 1951 when I was informed that I was to be posted to Kenya. We were in the 33rd Armoured Brigade in the 11th Armoured Division, and I was Second-in-Command of my regiment, the 1st Battalion 60th Rifles. Most soldiers became used to changes of environment but, after only five months in BAOR, with many years abroad (eleven of them having been in Africa), I was a little surprised and my heart beat a little quicker when my Colonel informed me of the posting. Ken Collen and I were old friends from Eton days and he had served with the King's African Rifles. Between 1927 and the present date we had met rarely and the most recent occasion was when we both took part in the victory parade near Gondar at the final surrender of the Italian Army in Ethiopia in November, 1941. He warned me that the Kenya Regiment were a very tough lot of chaps and that some of their senior officers were probably older than I was and that they had a reputation of independence and straight talk. As usual it took the War Office some time to organize my passage. When the posting order finally arrived, my departure was more hurried than I would have liked and my leave in UK was only brief.

In the last week of November, I reached London and migrated to my favourite haunt, the Cavendish Hotel in Jermyn Street which was still run by the famous Mrs Rosa Lewis, whom I had known since I was seventeen. Staying at Rosa's were two people, Major Tony Lewis (posted to command the KR Training Centre) and a charming American girl, Tania, who was married to Frank Waldron, late Scots Guards. In the next four years I was to see much of Tony Lewis, and Frank and Tania were to serve on the staff of my Tactical Headquarters. The final advice I had from Rosa was to 'keep my wick trim'.

Just before I left England I heard from the Public Relations Officer, East African Command in Nairobi – an old companion who had served with me in the British Military Mission to Ethiopia – Séan Galwey. He and I had had amusing times together in the beautiful city of Harar and wonderful trekking in the Ogaden province of Somalia. He told me that he had ensured my posting by informing the GOC East Africa, Lieutenant General Sir Arthur Dowlar, that I could certainly outswear and outdrink most Kenyans and hold my own in other respects!

I landed at Nairobi West Airport on 9 December, 1951, where I was met by the Adjutant Teddy Phillips, and embarked on four years of a very full and interesting life in one of the most beautiful countries in Africa. It proved to be a great contrast to the places in which I had served: the Sudan, Eritrea, Ethiopia, Somalia, Libya, Palestine and Egypt. It was not only the way of life but the difference in attitude, customs, language and administration.

I had no briefing before I left so I decided to play it off the cuff. I spent the first four months as Second-in-Command, which can be no sinecure, as the very last thing you must ever do is to look as if you were waiting for your boss to retire.

As is customary, my heavy baggage took months to arrive and I lodged in various dwellings before eventually being given a rented house. The Regiment was still being shaped and forged into a battalion but the companies were widely

34

dispersed and each company commander, officer, NCO and man knew how *he* intended to do things. I was quite prepared for this. As I was the first regular soldier to be posted in command I was watched very closely. So as not to be accused of favouring one section or another I decided not to align myself in any particular sport, although I could watch them all.

I sensed early on that one or two persons regarded me with suspicion, as, for example, the time when, at a regimental dance, the then Mayor of Nairobi rather scathingly told me that I was the 'first Imperial ever to command our Regiment'. I looked at my partner enquiringly. 'Don't worry about him,' she said, 'he's only a silly old basket,' and we continued round the room. As she was an old friend and a Kenya girl I put it out of my mind. Thinking about it later, I realized that I might have to prepare myself to meet some resistance as I was a Regular Soldier and the Kenya Regiment was a newly formed Territorial Unit.

Among the people I met at this time were the Nairobi members of the Regiment, Colonel Dunstan-Adams, the CO, Cecil Valentine and members of the HQ and A Company. In addition there were of course our Regular permanent staff: Adjutant, Quartermaster, Regimental Sergeant-Major, Regimental Quarter-master-Sergeant. With senior sergeants at Headquarters and the three Rifle Companies in Nairobi, Nakuru and Kitale, there were quite a number of people to get to know.

The main emphasis of the work at that time was preparing for the visit of HRH Princess Elizabeth. I noticed that the permanent staff were expected to provide all the answers and to take action without reference to the higher echelons of the army machine. When it came to approval from the Secretariat for expenditure of a large sum of money for some item vital to our needs we often short-circuited them and bought it ourselves. Loud noises were heard later but by then it was too late.

I also noticed and was determined to break the idea that we PSIs were expected to do all the work. Once we got it across that we were not stooges we had a much better understanding. Fortunately, all the Company Commanders left the PSIs with a free hand: they even taught us a few tricks of evasion, or masterly cover-ups. I had thought that I knew them all, but I was mistaken. I am the first to salute master operators! Nevertheless I think we all agreed that we must train company officers to realize that organization and administration were just as important as shooting straight.

One only had to attend a company or platoon parade to realize their keenness and enthusiasm. Some revelled in responsibility, others reckoned it a waste of good drinking time. One thing was common to all of them: a spirit of adventure. As the weeks passed I met more and more members of the Regiment either on duty or in the clubs of Kenya which played a big part in their lives, but also watching games in which our chaps were taking part. All weekend parades were well attended. They were bursting with health and did their best to take the mickey out of their PSIs – who were more than a match for such antics. One of the major problems was to prevent some of our up-country members from reducing

35

the length of their shorts and rolling their sleeves up to their armpits. They did not have to try to look tougher; they were already tough!

Each company had a spirit of its own, imbued with the outlook of their environment and also of their birth as we had some of British or European origin and others of Afrikaans descent. There was a distinct difference of outlook between these two groups but it was never serious. All were proud to have a Kenya Regiment number.

Within a week I was on my way to meet B Company of the Regiment whose HQ was in Nakuru, ninety miles to the north through the Rift Valley. The road of murram twisted down the escarpment after Dagoretti, originally called Fort Smith, and for some of the journey the railway track ran close by. Mount Longonot was to the left over Lake Naivasha and the Kinangop with the rich farms of what was called the White Highlands was under the shadows of the Aberdare Mountains which rose to over 13,000 feet. Nakuru was one of the principal towns between Nairobi and the Uganda border. It had a hotel, a European club, hospital, bank, post office and shops mostly run by Asians and Africans. There were, of course, sports grounds for those who played rugby, cricket, tennis, golf or polo. European farms were all around, some extending to many thousands of acres. Every variety of crop was grown from wheat to sisal or sunflowers, and thousands of acres were solely for cattle. Further north in the Highlands of Molo settlers had imported merino sheep from Australia. Elsewhere coffee, tea and tobacco were grown.

The roads were not metalled and punctures were frequent – jacks, wooden boards and tow ropes were carried by all travellers. Most cars required a high wheelbase as stones could cause damage to axles or sumps. I was to stay with an old friend who had formerly served in 5th KAR. He lived at Sabukia, seventeen miles north-east of Nakuru with a wonderful view overlooking Lake Nakuru with its flocks of flamingo and the high hills of Mau Summit behind. The air was bracing and the nights could be chilly.

Naturally we discussed the task ahead of me and he gave me some sound advice. He described the true Kenyan as an extrovert who had never fully grown up, with a very simple outlook on life, who was quick to take offence and who would fight for a principle. There was no in-between: it was red or white, never pink. This meant they could be uncompromising; spades might be spades, but to a Kenyan they were 'bloody shovels'. Over the years I was to find this assessment accurate, but of course there were exceptions. I was also warned not to be critical as there were always two ways of tackling any problem. Here I could thank my years in the remote Sudan and the Ogaden Province of Somalia and the Abyssinian Highlands for teaching me tact. As well as tact I had to rely on a sense of sympathy, justice, absolute fairness and a cheerful outlook. If I had a maxim it was very simple: I sincerely believed that a smile, a greeting and a handshake could bring the sun from behind any cloud. No commander is expected to be either Godlike or a genius, but he should be approachable. He must also be recognized as one who will stand up for his men, right or wrong, and be able to joke and drink with them and yet put his foot down firmly when necessary.

The next day we attended a dance given by the company in Nakuru, where I met other leading settlers, the local mayor and prominent citizens. This was my first view of the up-country settlers and they certainly looked a healthy collection of people. Practically all the Kenya Regiment members present had war ribbons and their handshakes were crunchingly hard. They also looked you straight in the eye and smiled easily. During the course of the evening we were entertained by the Company Second-in-Command, Captain Ray Mayers, an Australian by birth and already a legend. He had run a large area of Somalia for the Civil Administration of the Ogaden. He was one of the few men I have met who could turn a bigoted gathering of saints into a hilarious rave-up. For the first of many times I watched him 'dance with the muffin man' and do his egg trick.

It was also at this dance that I learnt that the owner of a 50,000-acre farm with a university degree was a private in the Regiment, while another of limited means and often broke was his platoon commander. This was the first time I fully understood the Regiment's saying: 'An officer in the Regiment is only one favoured amongst equals.' Never in my life had I seen so many healthy and uninhibited males take over a party. The girls were well looked after, but I sensed that when the noise reached its crescendo they might well look at each other and edge towards the door! It was as if Moira said to Helen – this is where we girls peel off – David and Ray and the rest will return with the dawn.

Samweli, my African driver, took me back to Nairobi and I was able to reflect upon my first meeting with the farming element in the Regiment. It was an impact which one rarely meets as it was a startling introduction into the character of the men I was going to serve with. One of them had explained how their system of promotion worked, which was certainly novel. They chose their own nominees. A stripe or a pip was an important acquisition but it had to be earned in the most democratic way. The up-country men were even more forthright than those I had met in Nairobi, but it was only a question of environment; the responsibilites of running a farm were obviously more testing than a safe job in a commercial firm or a sedentary office job.

I had much to mull over.

I was told by a Kenya settler after I arrived that the Government felt more secure with a Regular CO who would not be politically motivated. As a stranger to the situation I played my cards close to my chest. However, in retrospect I can say this: I hold the view, which is open to argument, that the citizens of every country should have the right to gain advancement in conditions of work, pay and education, and the opportunity to take part in the administration.

When compared with the Foreign Office, the Colonial Office was far behind in its policy of developing the educational standards in medicine, law, veterinary science, agriculture and technical development. In 1952 there were no Kenyan African doctors, surveyors, judges, lawyers, solicitors, army officers, dentists, business executives, agriculturalists, tenant farmers nor skilled tradesmen, biologists, ships' captains or senior policemen. The schooling was low-standard and few, if any, had even been to Makerere College, let alone to a European school (Jomo Kenyatta was an exception to this, and was educated in Russia for seven years as well as living in England with an English wife for some time). There were no recognized African football, rugby, tennis or hockey teams, and athletics were not organized. It was not until 1961 that two Kenya sprinters ran in an AAA meeting at White City. Derek Erskine had brought them over and he told me that one day they would be world beaters. All the middle-distance Kenya runners who are record-holders now come from a small area north of Eldoret.

In 1952 there were no Kenya, Uganda, Tanganyika or Nyasaland officers in the KAR. Idi Amin Dada (nicknamed 'VD and scars'), was one of the first two NCOs chosen as officers in the 4th (Uganda) Battalion of the KAR in 1962. In 1954 he was a lance-corporal.

This lack of development was prevalent in African colonies and elsewhere in our Empire, apart from India (administered by the India Office). By contrast, in the Anglo – Egyptian Sudan, administered by the Foreign Office, development had been far advanced. From the days of the Egyptian Service the Sudan had trained Sudanese doctors, lawyers, army officers, etc. In 1925 Gordon College at Khartoum rated as a school of high standards. Sudanese held posts in the Political Service and other branches of the administration. They also played some of the games played by the British and held senior posts in banks, commercial firms, customs, prisons, etc.

I am not suggesting that the Colonial Office had a deliberate policy of not developing the chances of the Kenya Africans. It may have been lack of financial resources, and one must remember Central Africa was unknown until the late 1870s and '80s.

One Sudanese *shaib* (old man), when asked what British rule had meant to him, stated quite simply: 'For the first thirty years of my life I never knew if I would return home safely; the last thirty years I have known peace and security' – testimony to what the British achieved there.

One can always be wise after the event and criticize our shortcomings but, notwithstanding these, the scholar who looks back upon the history of our Empire can also see that we put down slavery, planted the crops and developed the land, ministered to the sick, organized efficient police and armed forces, and introduced missionary societies while recognizing all religions. In Kenya in the space of a few years, schools and hospitals were established and other amenities provided in all the main townships, with a railway that reached the shores of Lake Victoria.

Kenya already had a council of tribal chiefs, who as representatives of their tribes could debate and put forward suggestions. The Kikuyu were not only the largest tribe in Kenya, they were also the closest to the Europeans in that the first Europeans encountered them as the railway from the coast to Lake Victoria passed through their lands. This the Kikuyu turned to their own advantage as they made good money working for the settlers. There was no resistance shown to the Europeans except in certain remote areas nearer the coast. The new type of European had not come for slaves.

However, there had been for some years a belief among the Kikuyu that the Europeans had stolen a large area of their tribal lands. L. S. B. Leakey, who was brought up from childhood among the Kikuyu and knew and understood them so well that he was made a blood-brother of the tribe, explained in his book *Mau Mau and the Kikuyu*, published in 1952, how they arrived at this belief.

The Kikuyu were an agricultural tribe, whose nearest neighbours had been the Wa-Nderobo, a hunting/gathering people. As the Kikuyu prospered and grew in numbers their land became 'one vast garden' but even this became too small to feed them and they started to seek new land to farm. Leakey writes: 'Undoubtedly, by virtue of their greater numerical strength, they could have driven out the Wa-Nderobo by force, but to them such action . . . would have been futile, for the land so obtained would have been valueless to them for settled occupation and for crop-growing, since God and the spirits would not bless activities carried out under such conditions.' They therefore evolved, in cooperation with the Wa-Nderobo, a system of land transfer by agreement and adoption into the Kikuyu tribe of the Wa-Nderobo party, with payment being made in the form of goats and sheep and other things in exchange for the land. The transfer involved marking of boundaries and agreements involving all members of the families concerned, so that there was no bad feeling. Land thus acquired belonged to the Kikuyu family in perpetuity, to be passed on to, and divided up between, all its members. A Kikuyu landowner could also have tenants or *ahoi* who used the land temporarily but who had to make way for the family when the land was needed.

However, in 1902, when the first Europeans arrived, the land appeared to be vacant because the tribe had been decimated by four major disasters: the great smallpox epidemic, the great rinderpest outbreak, an intense drought and consequent famine and a devastating locust invasion.

Each of these disasters is commemorated in the names given to Kikuyu initiation age-groups over this period [writes Leakey]. Land that had been under cultivation generally returned, as it does in Africa in a year or two, to bush. This sudden and unprecedented reduction in the population and the alteration from 'one vast garden' to virtually uninhabited bushland was . . . accentuated by the fact that thousands of Kikuyu moved away – temporarily – from the stricken land and went back to live with relations and friends in the Nyeri and Fort Hall districts of Kikuyu country where the drought had been less severe and the smallpox epidemic . . . less widespread.

The Europeans 'in practically every case' made payments to the Kikuyu when alienating land for farming, and 'attempts were made to explain that these were for purchase', but the British were 'wholly unaware that from the point of view of Kikuyu law (oral law) these payments did not and could not ever rank as purchase of the land; at best they could only rank as payments for the right to cultivate, subject always to the real owner being allowed, at some future date, to evict the occupier.' According to Kikuyu law:

a) no transaction for the transfer of the *ownership* of land to a person or another tribe could take place unless first of all the two parties had been linked by a ceremony of mutual adoption.
b) no final transfer of ownership could be completed unless the boundaries of the land so sold were marked out in the presence of witnesses and to the accompaniment of a religious ceremony.
c) no sale of land was valid unless other members of the landowning family had been given first refusal; neither was it valid without the sanction of all the members of the landowning family.

With the increase in population aided no doubt by better medical care from Europeans, and better education in the ways of the Europeans, some of the Kikuyu began to be aware

that European farmers claimed the complete ownership of the lands they occupied by virtue of title deeds, and they began to demand that 'Tidlydee', as title deeds were called, should be granted to such Kikuyu as still actually owned land. This demand came from a genuine fear – if one without foundation – that, as the European population increased, still more land would be alienated for European farms. Nor was it allayed by the fact that they were refused such title deeds, on the ground that all Kikuyu land ranked as 'Crown land' under the Crown Lands Ordinance, and that the Kikuyu were, in effect, only tenants at the will of the Crown.

The majority of government officials were still wholly unaware (and when informed usually sceptical) of the fact that the Kikuyu system of land tenure, in the Kiambu area, was on the basis of ownership of estates with well-marked boundaries. It was still believed that the land was held communally by all members of the tribe, and that any person could build huts and cultivate any piece of land, wherever he chose, provided it was not already being used by someone else. This belief was probably not dispelled until 1929, after the report of the Kikuyu Land Enquiry Committee, of which I [Leakey] was a member. Since this report was not as widely read as it might have been, the old idea continued in the minds of many Europeans.

In 1932 the Morris Carter Land Commission was appointed by the Crown to look into the question of native lands, as by then the government had realized that there were genuine grievances and cases of hardship throughout the Colony, especially among the Kikuyu.

Unfortunately the Kikuyu, ill-advised by the leaders of the Kikuyu Central Association, put such outrageous claims before the Commission that many just claims were set aside and the whole matter was obscured. Had this not occurred, it is likely that the recommendations of the Commission would have taken a more generous form. As it was, the Commission recognized that the Kikuyu, especially of the Kiambu Division, had lost a considerable amount of land, and compensation was recommended, as well as the provision of certain new land for Kikuyu settlement. These recommendations, moreover, were implemented. Unfortunately, some of the land thus made available – although it was not part of the Kikuyu reserve as then demarcated – was land which the Kikuyu claimed to have been theirs originally. . . .

The recommendations of the Carter Land Commission were accepted by the government as a final settlement of all Kikuyu land claims [but] . . . the Kikuyu were far from satisfied.

Leakey described the land in the Kikuyu reserves in 1952 as 'very overcrowded' 'even for subsistence' and says the Kikuyu then were in any case 'not content merely to grow enough for subsistence. They wanted to improve their conditions of living, wear better clothes, educate their children and do many other things that [were] manifestly impossible for the majority to achieve since . . . most people only [had] a very small acreage at their disposal.'

According to Leakey, tens of thousands of Kikuyu were then living as squatters on European farms where, like the *ahoi*, they had no security of tenure and there was nowhere for them to go if they were evicted. Some tried to find places, for instance in the forestry schemes, in the lands of other tribes, or in the cities, but there wages were so low that it was necessary to retain a piece of land to provide for old age in the absence of a pension.

In 1955, before I left Kenya, I wrote in a report the following:

The most important aim for the future is that a sound Kenya African Administrative service is instituted in the form of a career and promotion structure as applies in others of our colonies and dependencies. The same aim should be equally applicable in Uganda, Tanganyika and Nyasaland. What is needed is more education, more opportunities and more posts to be filled over the whole spectrum of the administration, in all civil branches, the armed forces, medicine, law, agriculture, finance, trade and education.

In the future it should be possible for Africans, male and female, to achieve high rank in all departments of government. One day these members of the service could become the leaders of Kenya.

At the time of writing these observations, I do not imagine that a single

41

member of the Kenya Government could envisage an administration with Africans acting as senior grade officials as existed in the Sudan or India. I believe that the Colonial Office must accept that there is a great need to start a broader African participation in appointments throughout the service.

As an example, East and West Africa, both administered by the Colonial Office, lagged far behind the Anglo-Egyptian Sudan Service which was more advanced since the Sudan occupation at the beginning of this century. This means quite simply that they are fifty years behind! The start must come soon. Why not begin the re-think now, as within ten years much might be achieved?

The arrival of airlines has made the world much smaller and the cry for education, a career and opportunity will become of increasing importance and demand. It might also conceivably lessen the hunger for more land!

Even then such ideas were not well received, but in 1952 there was little or no general awareness among Kenya settlers of the frustration felt by the Africans. The rise of the Mau Mau happened in secret, probably instigated by former members of the banned Kenya Central Association, some of them taking part in a replacement organization, the Kenya African Union. Leakey writes:

There is reason to believe that it was in the latter part of 1948 or early in 1949 that [it] really got under way and that this was linked with the news that the Duke of Gloucester was coming out to Kenya, as His Majesty's Representative, to confer city status on Nairobi. It is certain that as soon as the news of this decision . . . was released, a number of Kikuyu agitators, most of them former members of the banned KCA, started spreading the fantastic story that the raising of Nairobi to city status was to be accompanied by 'further thefts of land' from the Kikuyu by the British authorities. Since 'save the land' is the battle cry that can stir a Kikuyu more than anything else, it was not surprising that a number of people, more particularly those who already felt a strong grievance about land matters, rallied to the call. Many meetings were held and people were called upon to boycott the city celebrations and everything to do with them.

It seems that the boycott made little impression on the European community at the time, if indeed they noticed it at all. Leakey adds:

It seems most unlikely that the leaders of this movement to boycott the city celebrations seriously believed that there was to be any further alienation of native land for European settlement, for they must have been fully aware that under the Natives' Land Trust Ordinance the lands that had formally been called 'Native Reserves' and which had once ranked as Crown Lands were now fully safeguarded.

However, the leaders of this movement were for some reason anxious to stir

42

up further anti-British feeling, and they were fully aware that by saying the land was in danger they were sure to get a following.

Though some of their causes may have been based on justice, it is the methods by which they tried to achieve their aims that I would criticize.

The following chapters which take up so much of the story of the Regiment concern the Mau Mau rebellion. Not all of it may be palatable to those who are ignorant of the details of what occurred or of who motivated the rise against the Government. A rising did occur which took over four years to quell. The whole Kikuyu tribe was caught up in the maelstrom which tore them apart, loyalist against insurgent, family against family, brother against brother.

CHAPTER 4

THE MAU MAU
EMERGENCY

AT MIDDAY on 24 August, 1947, the village green at Kahuro, in the heart of the Fort Hall reserve, was packed with thousands of Kikuyu men and women, colourful in their Sunday best. They listened eagerly to the cunning words of the orators who had driven up from Nairobi. Time and again they would burst forward with menacing shouts. It took brave men to approach a meeting of this sort, but Ignatio Murai calmly walked into the crowd and, assisted by his two Tribal Police Constables, arrested the two leading speakers. The crowd took a little time to react. Then they picked up sticks and stones and set off in pursuit. When Chief Ignatio and his two Constables saw the mob was out of control and closing in, they opened fire. One rioter fell dead, another was wounded. The rest disappeared.

A District Officer, Tommy Thompson, who served in the Fort hall district during the five-year build-up of Mau Mau strength, culminating in the Emergency, comments:

If one looks back one can see the set pattern of Mau Mau agitation from that incident in 1947. After it everything went quiet, very quiet indeed, and it was quite obvious that Jomo Kenyatta, with his friends James Beauttah and Petro Kigondo of Fort Hall, decided to look around again and re-plan. Their plan took the form of arousing people against the Government at the frequent meetings of the Kenya African Union in Fort Hall. . . .

[Later] Kenya African Union meetings were banned in the Fort Hall district itself, but they continued to be held in neighbouring towns like Nairobi and Thika and were attended by hundreds if not thousands of Fort Hall Kikuyu. Kenyatta, Beauttah and Kigondo were usually on the platform. The propaganda followed the set pattern of 'more land, more money, more opportunity and self-determination' . . .

Things became really grim in the months of August and September, 1952. If an officer went on safari, young men would turn their backs on him and spit on the ground. They were beginning to wear Kenyatta beards and long hair. In particular, schoolmasters in the Kikuyu independent schools were turning out propaganda . . . I visited Chui School with the Health Inspector and as we entered the headmaster said: 'What do you Europeans want here? I am busy educating Kikuyu children. Go away.'

Tommy Thompson was by no means the only District Officer to report unrest. There were also, during this period, instances of rifles, shotguns, pistols, sporting rifles and ammunition being stolen from Europeans all over Kenya. Burglaries were particularly prevalent in Nairobi, Karen and Muthaiga. The old method of using a fishing line on the end of a stick thrown through a downstairs window (ninety per cent of Europeans' houses were single-storey buildings) was a favourite with the thieves. Any attempt to grab the line would have been dangerous as razor blades were attached, but in any case such robberies were conducted with so much skill that the sleeping occupants were rarely awakened.

Incidents of cattle being hamstrung and dogs and cats killed on settlers' farms were recorded. Many Kikuyu and *shamba* (farm) boys left the service of Europeans; some had been with the same families for years. This spread to the Luo tribe; the Meru and Embu, blood-brothers to the Kikuyu, were also sympathetic, if not actively hostile.

Police warnings had been issued to all householders to take extra precautions in safeguarding weapons but thefts continued, many of them unreported, especially since later the authorities imposed fines for lost weapons. At the time, and even after the Emergency had been declared and European and African Kenyans had been murdered by terrorists, many Europeans refused to believe that their own staff could be influenced by the Mau Mau oath. Although Mau Mau meetings and oathings had taken place openly in the Fort Hall area since 1947, the evidence was never recorded or, if it was, it never came to light until too late.

The initial aim of Mau Mau was secretly to unite, discipline and foster political consciousness among the Kikuyu. The origin of the name 'Mau Mau' is obscure and various theories have been put forward. Kitch Morson (ex-Kenya Regiment 1937–45), who knew the Kikuyu as well as any man, believed it referred to the mother spirit of the tribe, 'Mumbi'. Séan Galwey who served in the KAR during the war and at that time was Public Relations Officer, East African Command, concluded from his enquiries that: 'The name Mau Mau is obscure in meaning and the most likely translation is that it is a *kinubi* (backslang) corruption of the Kikuyu expression *Uma! Uma!* meaning "Get out".' Another explanation is that it is a corruption of the KiSwahili word for the female genitalia, *kuma*. This

45

gained credence from the obscene nature of the Mau Mau oaths of initiation. A Kikuyu elder, Harry Thuku, said: 'The true name of the society should be *Gikuyu na Mumbi* or the "Adam and Eve People", the real owners of the land – in fact Mau Mau means "The Adam and Eve People".'

L. S. B. Leakey's full account of the development or rather degeneration of the Mau Mau oathing ceremonies, in *Defeating Mau Mau* (1954), shows how the need for secrecy changed what was originally a voluntary and reasonably moderate oath according to Kikuyu laws and customs of both the Kikuyu and the European communities. In order to preserve secrecy, unwilling people, even women and children, had to be forced to take the oath and the ceremonies had to take place in private places after dark, whereas Kikuyu law stated that an oath had to be voluntary and witnessed by the community. The rites began to involve elements usually associated by the Kikuyu with black magic, such as the piercing of sodom apples and sheep's eyes with thorns, which was also against their laws.

> Those who resisted Mau Mau did not necessarily do so out of loyalty to the Government but because they just could not tolerate degradation and depravity and they also foresaw that the Mau Mau would bring nothing but sorrow and ruin to the tribe. The elders of the Kikuyu tribe, personified in and led by Senior Chief Njiri, resisted because they saw that Mau Mau violated all their traditions and background. Those who had embraced Christianity resisted because they saw that there could be no compromise between their faith and the teachings of Mau Mau. (extract from *The Kikuyu Guard*)

Those who did follow Mau Mau were the ones caught in between the two religions, dissatisfied with the British forms of Christianity and yet also unclear as to the merits of their old religion and customs. Breakaway churches and schools were set up and many of the oathing ceremonies took place in such churches.

The terms of the original oath were as follows:

1. If I ever reveal the secrets of this organization, may this oath kill me.
2. If I ever sell or dispose of any Kikuyu land to a foreigner, may this oath kill me.
3. If I ever fail to follow our great leader, Kenyatta, may this oath kill me.
4. If I ever inform against any member of this organization or against any member who steals from the Europeans, may this oath kill me.
5. If I ever fail to pay the fees of this organization, may this oath kill me.

As the Mau Mau gained strength, the terms of the oath were amended to include the following clauses:

1. If I am sent to bring in the head of my enemy and I fail to do so, may this oath kill me.

2. If I fail to steal anything I can from the European, may this oath kill me.
3. If I know of an enemy to our organization and I fail to report him to my leader, may this oath kill me.
4. If I ever receive any money from a European as a bribe for information, may this oath kill me.
5. If I am ever sent by a leader to do something big for the house of Kikuyu, and I refuse, may this oath kill me.
6. If I refuse to help in driving the Europeans from this country, may this oath kill me.
7. If I worship any leader but Jomo, may this oath kill me.

What the Mau Mau capitalized on was the significance of tribal oaths in the life of the Kikuyu. Even though Kikuyu custom prohibited the administering of oaths by night, by force, or to women (so that Mau Mau oaths were a transgression of accepted custom), the rituals attached to the taking of these oaths had a powerful effect on the superstitious nature of even the less politically motivated Kikuyu. And where superstition failed, the oather and/or his family were under threat of death by Mau Mau loyalists should they not conform. One Kikuyu confessed to the South Kinangop Screening Team to having taken the following oaths:

1. If I do the platoon wrong, they will kill me.
2. If either my wife or my child does the platoon wrong, they will either take their heads or mine.
3. If I am told to kill a European, I will do so or be killed.
4. If I am told to go and burn a farmer's wheat or his maize, I will do so or die.
5. If I am told to kill or maim a farmer's sheep or cattle, I will do so or lose my head.
6. If I am told to help to release prisoners from jail, I will do so or this oath will kill me.
7. If the platoon want my wife for any reason, I will give her to them or they will take my head.

The administration ceremonies described in confessions varied, and appeared to have assumed more gruesome forms as the campaign progressed. The following is a translation from the Kikuyu of an original document captured from a Mau Mau hideout:

1. The first oath is taken by having cuts made. The blood is mixed with millet and the mixture swallowed. There are five stages in taking this oath.
2. To be pricked on the thumb (eight stages).
3. To place a piece of meat in the anus of an old woman and consume it while taking the oath.

4. *Captain's Oath* – the administrator waves his hand over the head of the initiate seven times, and the fingers of the right hand of a dead man are bent seven times.
5. *Major's or Treasurer's Oath*– the brain of a dead African is bitten seven times and then eaten.
6. *Colonel's Oath* – to drink the blood of a menstrual discharge seven times.
7. *Brigadier's Oath* – the brain of a dead European is bitten seven times and then eaten.
8. *Njeru* – to drink the urine of a woman during menstruation seven times.
9. *The taking of the oath in the forest* – the group taking the oath have to kill a man and a boy. The head of the man is used, the blood being mixed with that of the oath takers. Then the brain of the boy and the man and some of the magere tree are mixed together and eaten seven times. The oath takers swear never to disclose the whereabouts of the arms and ammunition. The heart of the child is then cut from the body and pricked seven times with a sharp nail.
10. *General's Oath* – the wrist bones of the left hand of a boy are broken and mixed with excreta, earth and blood and the mixture eaten seven times.
11. This oath is taken by a woman. The tail of a dog is cut off and placed in the woman's vagina.
12. To approach a Mau Mau hideout the signal is to touch the jaw with one hand, look downwards and, at the same time, snap the fingers of the other hand. Those in hiding retire to another hideout nearby and, when they are in hiding, a single shot is fired. The visitors then approach the hideout – where one man has been left – and having been recognized, those in hiding are warned that all is well by a cry repeated three times. The cry is the noise of a chicken when laying an egg. The hiders reply with the same cry once.

Oathing ceremonies could be administered to mass numbers. Tommy Thompson, the District Officer, had been on safari ten days before the declaration of the Emergency, when, in his own words:

A Church Elder of the African Inland Mission, who has since been murdered by Mau Mau, came along to me and said that he could show me a Mau Mau oathing ceremony in session. I had one Tribal Police escort, Mwaura Gakomo, who later became a corporal, and the only weapon we had between us was a walking stick. We sat on the side of a hill and watched about 900 people oathing. There was nothing we could do. The people laughed and spat at us.

Looking back, one is tempted to ask: 'Why was nothing done sooner?' – but it is always easy to be wise after the event. In fairness it must be stated that, except in areas where Mau Mau was active, life continued as normal. American film

48

companies enjoyed the Kenya sunshine, holidays were taken on the coast and bars were full. Business went on as usual, and clubs, hotels and cinemas flourished. The preludes to terrorism were being played out, for the most part unheard, on isolated farms in the Kikuyu reserve, in the Aberdares and on Mount Kenya. As the Mau Mau attacks became more violent, with victims being tortured and mutilated, they were still mostly restricted to isolated villages and farms, schools, mission stations, police and Home Guard posts. Protective measures to defend European farmers and those Kikuyu who had not accepted the Mau Mau call to rid Kenya of the whites were to become of paramount importance.

But there were no attempts to damage roads or railways, to blow up telephone lines or municipal buildings. It was known that throughout the Emergency the Mau Mau used the railway like commuters. No stops or searches were ever made as far as I know, although the trains passed through several battalion areas and police posts. For many life went on as usual: race meetings and sporting events were unaffected and as yet nobody walked abroad armed with a pistol – though later both sexes were moving arsenals. A few areas were completely unaffected even then and a visit to these spots brought a sense of unreality. The sheer size of Kenya, and the type of terrain utilized by the Mau Mau, must indeed have dissipated the urgency that was there. Many Kenya settlers felt that Nairobi was out of touch and that not enough was being done. It was hard to bridge the gap and to explain what it was like in the Aberdares or Mount Kenya. People whose farms had been burned and their livelihoods lost, or whose friends and neighbours had been killed, were frustrated by what appeared to be the sluggish reactions of the Government. Close proximity to the ever-prevalent danger brought stronger resolution and a determination not to be driven from their land. It is not surprising that weak reaction to a raid on a friend's house brought instant condemnation. It was possible that District Headquarters did not do enough to inform those living in their area just what was being done – there was always a risk of breaking security, which might enable a gang to escape by giving away the follow-up action. Club and hotel bars as well as the farms themselves were generally staffed by Kikuyu or Luo and any of them might have had Mau Mau sympathies.

In addition, Kenya had been left rather in limbo as the Governor, Sir Philip Mitchell, had retired, and the country was left in the hands of a locum tenens. I had assumed command of the Kenya Regiment in April, 1952, when Colonel Valentine relinquished command, and one evening I was dining with the Chief of Staff, Brigadier Geoffrey Rimbault, the stand-in Governor, and an old friend of mine, Major-General Douglas Packard. At the end of dinner Douglas stated that he could not understand why the new Governor, Sir Evelyn Baring, had not arrived. He began to labour the point and, although I did my best to kick his ankle under the table, he finally said: 'It's always the same, they leave some clot in charge who hasn't a clue about what he is supposed to do and of course there's a balls-up.' I had to use all my self-control to prevent myself falling off my chair –

49

the 'clot' was sitting next to him! However, it is not the intention of this history to apportion blame, and no doubt the acting Governor could do little but follow the policy of Sir Philip Mitchell.

Sir Evelyn Baring, who had been Governor of Southern Rhodesia and High Commissioner South Africa, arrived in Nairobi on 29 September. He immediately made a tour of the Kikuyu areas and it was during this time that Senior Chief Waruhui, a loyal Kikuyu, was murdered by the Mau Mau. On his return Sir Evelyn sent a telegram to the Secretary of State at the Colonial Office. Five days later, on 21 October, 1952, a State of Emergency was declared. Jomo Kenyatta and around a hundred other Mau Mau leaders were arrested at dawn on that day.

The three companies of the Kenya Regiment were immediately embodied, and I became overall commander of civil and military forces in the Nairobi area, where activity was now stirring. Staffs with typists swelled the police headquarters in River Road. Girls appeared as assistant staff officers and often gummed up the telephone exchange with frivolous calls, but they made the place more cheerful. The traffic thickened. Members of the widely dispersed and suddenly embodied Kenya Regiment, many of them veterans of the Second World War, were busy getting the necessary release from their employers, or finding somebody who would keep an eye on their farms. This was not always easy, but when the Emergency code words 'John Peel' went out, B Company acted quickly. Actually, the word 'John' had been the warning and 'Peel' the word for action. When dozens of private cars loaded with sleeping bags, cases of beer, servants and dogs and drivers in various orders of dress arrived on HQ Square, it was obvious that 'Peel' had preceded 'John'! By midnight the percentage of this company present was 99 and the bars and messes in Nairobi were doing a roaring trade. Some needed accommodation – we could provide blankets but not beds – others headed for the Muthaiga, Nairobi or Railway Clubs or dossed down with friends.

Events always speed up after the balloon has become airborne, and destinations were marked on the map in the CO's office and preparations for a rushed move were initiated. Inevitably there were snags and shortages: whatever one ordered from the Ordnance Depot – from latrine screens, picks and tents to Fort Issue Bromo – they never seemed to have it. Most weapons were shotguns or sporting rifles – the men's own – and there were hardly any uniforms. Except for the few heavier vehicles that could be hired for carrying stores, tentage, etc, moving the company meant that private cars had to be used. It was decided to mark all our various vehicles with distinguishing white circles of paper; front, rear, sides, roof and bonnet were marked to enable us to pick out Kenreg personnel anywhere. Later, company signs in red were added for easier recognition. Searches of locations were initiated in and around towns, villages and farms, and large sweeps in Kikuyu areas, intended to pick out suspects for interrogation. Weapons were occasionally discovered in the rafters of a hut, or a man might break cover to be chased and caught for questioning. Operations rooms were set up in the various areas and interrogation centres were established.

The Lancashire Fusiliers were dispatched from Egypt and three more battalions of the KAR arrived in support of those already in Kenya. The military cooperated with the civil administration, PCs (Provincial Commisioners), DOs and police. Much of one's time was spent in conference and discussion. Despite the urgent appeals of the Regiment that a war was on our doorstep and that it should be treated as such, we were still only acting in support of the civil power.

Members of HQ and A companies were posted to the KAR battalions; B Company moved as a body over to Nanyuki, one of the areas worst affected, and one platoon of C Company was sent to act as a guard to Jomo Kenyatta and the other Mau Mau leaders at Kapenguria near Mount Elgon. It is rare for a revolution to succeed once the leaders have been arrested and few Kenyans suspected that this was the start of a war which would last for the next four years. The revolt, after all, was not organized by a modern army; there were no skilled armourers or technicians, and their only modern weapons were those acquired by robbery. They constructed some makeshift guns using doorbolts. They had no transport and no intelligence service other than by word of mouth. What the Mau Mau did have, however, was the secret cooperation, whether voluntary or forced, of countless household servants, *shamba* (farm) staff and herdsmen of the Kikuyu and of tribes friendly to them. This was to prove the strength of the Mau Mau: themselves remaining under cover, they could always get advance warning of the Security Forces in the area and of course they used their knowledge and experience of the terrain to full advantage. In the Aberdares where the forest clings to the ridges and gorges and is broken by scarcely a clearing or track, the Mau Mau could move silently and unseen. They would lie up in bamboo shelters until night, then descend to the reserve to be given or to steal food, or to attack some loyalist target, only to disappear again without trace.

Against them were pitted up to six British infantry battalions, as well as the other Security Forces, and they suffered from the disadvantage of operating in conditions very different from those they had been accustomed to, although many had served since 1945 in Malaya, Korea and Aden, and those from Malaya had the advantage of experience in jungle conditions, much of which was applicable to the forests of Kenya. Even so it was found that new techniques were still necessary and all had to accustom themselves to high altitudes. British battalions did not have the same dedication to killing the enemy as the Kenya boys: wherever the enemy was, however long it took to find him, the Kenyan's incentive was that he was fighting for his home, way of life and the country he loved. However, each British battalion had Kenya Regiment Officers and NCOs attached to them. The Officer generally joined the battalion's special fighting patrol and helped out with language problems and interrogation of prisoners; their experience of Africa was of great value.

51

CHAPTER 5

RAY FORCE, I FORCE AND THE KPR AIR WING

THE REGIMENT was based at Mweiga on Marrian's Farm from early 1953; it was to be our Tactical Headquarters for over a year. The site was chosen because it possessed an airfield, a plentiful supply of water and in particular because it bordered the Aberdare Forest. Peter Marrian (farms were known by their owners' names) was a coffee planter but also, like many of the local settlers, an active member of the Kenya Police Reserve, and a close liaison was soon forged. All farms were visited frequently or used as bases for operations and the farmers accepted the regimental patrols as guests and often provided valuable information about movement of Mau Mau gangs.

Within weeks of our arrival our companies, now seven in number, were based on spurs at over 8000 feet up in the Aberdares. Each fort, defended by stockades, wire, moats and *panjis* (sharpened stakes of bamboo driven into the ground) was manned by only 15–30 Europeans. To aid their fighting capability we had recruited trackers from the other tribes used to forest conditions. To start with we had Masai – they were lifelong enemies of the Kikuyu – but they were not in their true element in the forest. The best forest and bush fighters proved to be the El Geyo, Turkhana, Nderebo, Wakamba, Nandi, Samburu and loyal Kikuyu.

Kenya Regiment posts were installed throughout the Nyeri, Fort Hall and Kiambu reserves, the three groups being under the command of Captain (later Major) Ray Mayers of the Regiment. The name 'Ray Force' soon achieved much distinction and became a household label in Kenya. Each of the three platoons, commanded by a temporary captain, had fifteen posts with two young members of the Regiment in charge of a varying number of Kikuyu Home Guard.

The Home Guard, or Kikuyu Guard, had been built up slowly and carefully over a period of months by the administration in the Central Province, from loyal members of the Kikuyu, Embu and Meru tribes. A very large percentage of the

52

Kikuyu had taken the first oath and in so doing they swore not to give away Mau Mau secrets; if they did they were told they would die and this the vast majority believed implicitly. One or two came into a chief or an officer and confessed what they had done or been made to do. Gradually people realized that those who confessed did not come to harm from supernatural causes as they had expected. Others who wished to resist the Mau Mau came forward to confess. The Kikuyu called it *Kahungwa muhori* or 'to have the lungs cleaned'. Before any Kikuyu could be a member of the Guard he had to confess fully in this manner; only then was he eligible to be taken on probation into the Guard as a junior recruit.

Initially the movement was based on volunteer effort and self-help. There was no pay for them; activity and interest were maintained by the Guards' own desire to fight against the forces of Mau Mau. Special funds were available, however, to cover incidental expenses and for the payment of occasional reward money for such special items as arms and ammunition recovered. Officers in charge of Kikuyu Guard units were encouraged to learn Kikuyu and gain the trust of the men.

Later, the Guards were not only recruited on a volunteer basis, but by 'direct encouragement', if necessary with armed support from the King's African Rifles. Mau Mau prisoners, once made to implicate themselves thoroughly on the government side, became some of the best fighters in the Home Guard. They were, unlike many loyalists, men who had no families living in the Reserve and little to lose, but who, because of their previous connections with Mau Mau, would certainly be killed by them were they to desert the security of their newly-formed loyalist cause.

On 20 April, 1953, Major-General Hinde formally issued a directive establishing the Home Guard as the Kikuyu Guard and defining its tasks in the fight against Mau Mau as:

1. in cooperation with the other forces of law and order, so to deny to Mau Mau the Kikuyu reserves that they become in due course a secure base from which our regular forces can be withdrawn to hunt down Mau Mau in the forests and mountains.
2. to provide information of Mau Mau activities and plans.

Under the direction of General Hinde, Colonel Philip Morcombe formed the Kikuyu Guard with help from young men from the Kenya Regiment as District Officers. The Guard was based on the *Athengeni*, the traditional warriors and scouts of the Kikuyu. In their guard posts they often operated with patrols of the Regiment, especially after the Mile-Strip Policy was introduced. (Anybody spotted inside this strip could be shot on sight. All huts, buildings, etc, were burned down and the ground was cleared for better spotting.)

The Kikuyu Guards were ideally suited for work in the Aberdares; they knew

53

the country as intimately as the Mau Mau. They could track and think like the enemy; they could move fast and bear the cold and hunger and damp. Some members of the Regiment even maintain that the Kikuyu could 'see in the dark'. At first they were armed only with *simis* (native swords) and bows and arrows, but later were trained in the use of firearms and automatics.

Each post also had a supply of grenades, Tilly lamps and alarm flares, and was linked by wireless to other posts in the vicinity. The forts were built near or in a village, and the headman lived inside. Many of the Guards (and at some posts there were fifty or more) had their families with them. Patrols operated by day and night, but during the day normal work also continued; crops were cultivated, herds grazed.

Undercover terrorists made unpredictable enemies; there could be no well-defined battlefront, no waiting in lines of trenches. Action was sporadic and dissipated by periods of comparative quiet, so that by no means all memories of the Mau Mau Emergency are warlike or depressing. Captain Peter Browne, for instance, recalls several incidents when the wildlife, in which the area abounded, caused more of a stir than the terrorists:

One night at the Outspan Hotel, Nyeri, a rumour was spread by a Kenya Regiment sergeant that a gang was moving up the valley towards the hotel, carrying torches. Major Sherbrooke Walker, the owner and staff immediately took up a defensive position to protect the residents. I and three of the Air Wing pilots continued drinking, although we too had seen the lights. The stand-down was ordered when the torches were found to be fire-flies!

Once Sergeant Mike Pelly returned from a patrol wounded. He had failed to see a rhino until it was nearly upon him. In his dash for safety he had slipped and the rhino trod on his wrist.

On another day, a patrol was accompanied by an American journalist. When he came upon a steaming elephant turd he wanted to take it back with him to America! He was dissuaded, but later picked up a dried specimen which he carefully wrapped up in his knapsack.

But perhaps the leeches of Lake Naivasha caused more problems for the military than fireflies, rhinos or elephants. Soldiers wading into the lake found that the tenderer portions of their anatomy were extremely vulnerable to the leeches which infested the water. The medical officer had ordered that sheaths be issued to each man for protective purposes. A large number from Nairobi's stock were duly bought, but one company was commanded by an ardent Roman Catholic, who refused to submit to such heresy. Presumably his unfortunate men were forced to perfect the rhythm method of avoidance!

Throughout the early months of the Emergency visitors were permitted to spend the night at Tree Tops near Mweiga, originally constructed by Major Sherbrooke Walker, who started the Outspan Hotel. A visitor's book was kept for

11. Captain Wally Schuster inspecting men at a Home Guard Post in the Kikuyu Reserve, 1954.

12. "Stand-to" at a Home Guard Post near Ragati.

13.   B Company patrol leaving camp, Ragati, 1954.

14.   Mixed European and African patrol setting out, Ragati, 1954.

15. Davo Davidson on patrol in the forest, a
    ·36 grenade in his left hand.

16. Operation Anvil, 1954. *Left to right*: General Sir George Erskine,
    Brigadier George Taylor, the author.

17.   O Group. Major Nightingale giving orders to Sergeant Denis Hunter;
Mount Kenya in the background.

visitors to sign, and to record the various types of game they had seen. Among the game listed one wag included: '. . . and one Ray Mayers'.

A Mau Mau gang, reckoned to be led by Dedan Kimathi, burned down Tree Tops during 1953. Another Tree Tops was constructed, a much larger and more comfortable buidling, but the charm of the old one was somehow lacking and the original visitor's book was destroyed. In it were many famous names, such as Lord and Lady Baden-Powell and their Royal Highnesses Princess Elizabeth and Prince Philip.

The full history of the Kikuyu Guard could form a book in itself. By the end of 1955, they had accounted for 202 terrorists out of the District's total of 662 for all branches of the security services. Fifty-six members of the Regiment served in the Guard.

I Force
I (or Intelligence) Force was a mixed company of the Regiment, formed at Squair's Farm near Mweiga, under the command of Captain Neville Cooper MC (later Major MBE) and GM who was a Platoon Commander in B Company, assisted by Lieutenant Tony Vetch of the Kenya Police Reserve. Their original purpose was as an intelligence unit, who would penetrate the forest in search of gangs. To augment their number, ex-KAR Askaris and trackers were recruited into the Regiment, most, like the ones in Ray Force, armed at first only with spears, *simis* and bows and arrows, but firearms were soon obtained for them. Captured and de-oathed Mau Mau were also taken on and added greatly to operational efficiency. The members of I Force added a red flash to their shoulder straps and this was accepted by Regimental HQ, in spite of its irregularity.

Each patrol consisted of ten to twelve men, a mixture of Europeans and Africans, and later tracker dogs with their RAVC handlers. Here Brian Hawkins tells of some incidents involving tracker dogs where success was more elusive!

In one particular incident a rhino came on us suddenly and at the time I had two British Army dog-handlers attached to me. One of them had a labrador tracker dog and, as was common at the time, the poor old handler was only armed with a rather ineffectual .38 pistol for his own self-defence. So of course he took to the nearest tree and the funniest thing I can remember is him trying to climb a rather small tree with a 50 or 60lb pack on his back and his poor old labrador trying to climb up after him. I could appreciate the joke because I was safely up another tree nearby!

Another incident was caused by lack of firearms issued to tracker dogs' personnel: we were bivvying in a Mau Mau camp from which we had routed the inhabitants earlier that day. It was as comfortable a place as any to pass the night, but in that area we had to have fairly strong sentries. During the night someone did try to approach the camp and a sentry opened fire. I was sharing a bivvy with one of the dog handlers and for the next five minutes I was engaged in a bitter fight with this dog handler for my rifle which he had seized and wasn't going to give up for anyone!

On that same patrol, as we were going along in patrol formation, we were fired on and, in returning fire, got a rough idea where the micks* were and immediately charged up in that direction. The tracker dog was brought into play and got onto the scent which was so fresh being only a matter of minutes since they were there, that the dog of course got excited and went like the wind. There was the poor old handler hanging on at the end and his personal KR escort trying to keep up with him, but everyone got separated and when I eventually caught up with them there was the rather dejected handler minus his dog. Apparently the dog followed the trail round a tree, leaving the handler wrapped around it, and the dog got away. After about an hour the dog rejoined us, looking as pleased as punch and we are convinced to this day that he actually caught up with the quarry and then probably tracked back for his reward which would have been a titbit of some sort. He was purely a tracker dog – not trained to attack but from the look on his face I'm sure he did catch up with that quarry!

The companies invented their own methods of hunting terrorists and took the battle into the enemy's own country, the high-altitude bamboo forests and moorlands of the Aberdares and Mount Kenya. The news of their successes was most encouraging at a time when the situation was becoming depressing, with frequent reports of further atrocities and the growing confidence of the Mau Mau.

Every man going into the forest had to be able to kill silently, by knife, rope or hands, and all carried a length of blind cord for securing prisoners. It was important that each man should know exactly where all his equipment was; for instance that his torch was on his left, handkerchief in his right trouser pocket etc, because any movement had to be swift and silent. The sound of a voice, or a sneeze, could carry far in the forest. Hand signals were used for communication and sometimes, when moving in the dark, a patch of luminous paint on the back helped one man to follow the next along the track. Frequently the patrol would halt and move off the track since there was always a danger of being followed and surprised from the rear. Constant vigilance was needed, however weary one felt, in order to be able to cope with a burst of rifle fire from an unseen source, or a sudden charge by startled game. Patrols were often obliged to follow game tracks through the dense bush, which was the home of buffalo, elephant and rhino, to name but a few animals which could also be a serious hazard.

Breath becomes short at heights of 8–10,000 feet and each man had to carry a sleeping bag, water, ammunition and rations. Sometimes torrential rain could drench both load and clothes, so adding to the weight. At the same time the severe heat combined with the altitude was very inducive to sleep during the day,

* Mickey Mice – Kenreg name for Mau Mau terrorists.

56

while nights were often tense and sleepless, but to have given in to the temptation to doze on patrol could have meant not only that the chances of contacing a gang would be lost, but the patrol itself would be rendered vulnerable.

Patrols could last from three to fourteen days at a stretch: hot days of climbing up and down deep gulleys, and freezing cold nights. The entire operation was mentally and physically tense, to such a degree that some men suffered hallucinations and most became jumpy and short-tempered. Because it was vital for teams to act in harmony, friends were posted to the same patrols whenever possible. Certain men would be detailed off for safeguarding prisoners or assisting the wounded. Leaders had to develop understanding and the power to command instant obedience in moments of crisis.

Edwin Bristow recalls that patrols were:

tough – we weren't allowed to wash, weren't allowed to clean our teeth, we had to grow beards, and smelt terrible at the end of three weeks but it was the only way to combat the chaps we were trying to catch, who smelt even worse.

This was an important point: smoking, washing, shaving, talking – all the daily habits one takes for granted in normal life had to be abandoned in the forest. Iain Morrison, who was attached to Special Branch in Nyeri, quotes the following Mau Mau reply he received to his standard question 'Which of the Security Forces did you fear most?':

The *Wa Johnny* [British Troops] washed in perfume, their tin cans rattled, they could be heard and smelled two or three miles away, but the *Kenya Gombis* [Kenya Regiment] never washed. They left all their equipment in one place and patrolled quietly and were good trackers. They walked through the forest like us; that wasn't fair.

However, the British Army Sergeants and warrant officers never understood the Kenya Regiment type of discipline, according to Brian Hawkins, who tells the following story:

After a forest patrol, we got back into the base camp looking pretty dishevelled, and there was a shout from across the parade ground to the two dog-handlers. I think it was a Scots Guards warrant officer attached to 3rd KR. He asked the handlers what was the meaning of this, coming into camp in such a state? They answered that Hawkins, who commanded the tracker team, had ruled that they were not allowed to shave. Sergeant Major's reply was: 'I don't care what Hawkins might say – he is Kenya Regiment – they are a law unto themselves. You are British Army and will do it the British Army way!' So after that we had to shave on the last morning of patrol before we actually headed back for camp.

57

The Kenya Regiment was at an advantage in that our personnel were native-born and accustomed from childhood to move anywhere, with some knowledge of big game and experience in the use of arms. Africans were even more at home in the terrain; trackers were found to increase efficiency by 50 per cent. By 1954 there were around 400 trackers in the Regiment, and in all over 1000 Africans were recruited, several of them being later decorated for gallantry.

Forest patrols worked virtually blind, as map coordination in the Aberdares was at best mere guesswork. If there was information from a prisoner, or if a gang were suspected of being in the vicinity, small patrols would scour the area, starting from a firm base. The Mau Mau gangs used false hideouts and laid imitation tracks, walking backwards, breaking off branches or foliage and leaving scraps of food, clothing and even blood to suggest that they were moving in a particular direction. At the same time they camouflaged their real trails brilliantly, and could hide underwater, breathing through reed pipes for hours on end without any betrayal of their presence. Such methods are said to have been used by the American Indians with equal skill, and by the Royal American Regiment (later to become the 60th Rifles), in the days of Braddock and Amherst.

In order to take a gang by surprise, the patrols needed a combination of patience, skill and luck. Chance contact was occasionally made near a stream where a member of a gang, more often than not a woman, would have been sent for water. From that moment it was possible to make a plan and locate and attack the hide.

But luck was not something the patrols relied on: initiative produced techniques and equipment developed to fit the situation. It was recommended, for instance, that at least one man in each patrol should have a silencer fitted on his rifle, and the Regiment accordingly produced a pattern for .220s. 'Kiko' King of the Regiment invented a 'ray' which could detect gangsters passing through it up to the length of half a cricket pitch away. Although the War Office expressed no interest in the invention, it did work in the forest.

So fruitful were the activities of I Force that I decided to form as much of the Regiment as possible into similar patrol companies of twenty–thirty men augmented by trackers, ex-KAR and Mau Mau deserters. This achieved the hoped-for results and the seven companies based at Mweiga in March, 1953, were, in a very short time, inflicting heavy casualties on the many terrorist gangs in the forest.

The Regiment ran a jungle range at Mweiga on which British battalions were trained, run by RSM Pendry, 60th Rifles. The first to use it, besides Kenreg personnel were 1st Battalion the Buffs and 1st Battalion the Devonshire Regiment. (Other visitors to Kenreg were senior officers from the Imperial Defence College and the Provincial Commissioner, Mr Edward Windley, Generals Sir Cameron Nicholson, Matthews and Sir Richard Hull, and Field-Marshal Sir John Harding. Field-Marshal Harding fired on our range. As a result we were the first unit to receive the Patchett automatic. Later on, in 1955, we were the first unit to test and receive the FN rifle.)

Probably the most important development of all this was that the Regiment evolved what was later to be called the 'pseudo gang'. 'Pseudo gangs' were originally known in Kenya as 'impersonators'. Early in 1953 Captain Francis Erskine wrote a paper requesting official permission to carry out an operation with loyal Kikuyu disguised as Mau Mau. This did not receive the attention it merited, but was supported by the Kenya Regiment and Erskine went on to develop the method. He was subsequently awarded a well-deserved Military Cross. From this early start the regiment developed its own methods of defeating Mau Mau terrorists. The first regimental pseudo gang consisted of Bill Woodley, Steve Bothma and Gibson Wanbugu from Squairs Farm, where I Force was stationed under Major Neville Cooper. Gibson was decorated for gallantry.

By the end of 1953 all companies of the Kenya Regiment were successfully operating pseudo gangs and the Government recognized this type of unit and indeed gave the police the task of forming 'Special Force Teams' which used similar methods, though their aims differed from those of the Regiment. The Police Special Force Teams, working under the direction of the Special Branch and Intelligence Officers, attacked any target, and were detailed to eliminate a specific terrorist leader and his gang.* (The work of such a team is strikingly related in Senior Superintendent Ian Henderson's book *The Hunt for Kimathi* and in Frank Kitson's *Gangs and Countergangs*.)

The Kenya Regiment pseudo gangs worked with another aim: to eliminate, by killing if necessary, all the terrorists in their company areas, which could mean one small company being responsible for an area the size of Northern Ireland. Cooperation and liaison with the uniformed police and the Special Branch was close and continuous, though their operations were of such a different nature. Kenya Regiment projects would rarely last more than one night (although preparatory contacts might be made every night for several weeks). The pseudo gang would visit known sympathizers of the Mau Mau and would attempt to arrange a meeting or pass a message to them. They would dress in a variety of ragged garments in imitation of the genuine terrorists, and most sported greatcoats or mackintoshes. The Europeans darkened their faces and hands with various substances; cocoa powder mixed with soot, black boot polish, black greasepaint, all applied with great care, as no white skin must be left visible.

---

* Many of the Gang Leaders chose pseudonyms, partly because they did not wish to disclose their identity which would of course have compromised their relatives, or more likely it revealed a desire to remain a subject of mystery. To give only a few examples, Generals 'China' and 'Tanganyika' were typical. Another who was much sought after by the Police Special Forces was General 'Jojo Sabuni'. Although his progress was followed closely on the operations maps in Force HQ he remained at large. His true identity was never revealed, which is not surprising as he was a mythical character. 'Jojo Sabuni' is Swahili for 'Joe Soap'!

(One member of Erskine's team left a hut while talking with a gang, to urinate. He was lucky not to have been detected as he had not 'blacked up' this unexpectedly exposed part of his anatomy. Erskine fined him three days' pay for his negligence.)

The difference between the woolly, kinky, plaited locks of the Mau Mau and the often straight blond hair of the pseudo gang leader could be vast. Filthy cloth caps or hats were favoured as a cover, pulled well down; these hid the hair and the blue eyes of a European quite effectively, whereas the wigs which were made from close-fitting woollen caps and black wool 'hair' still left the eyes exposed. A coating of dirt and grease completed the disguise. It seems that occasionally the result was all too effective. Fergus McCartney, for instance, recalls:

'pseudo-ganging' was a very exciting pastime, especially when things went wrong and one found oneself pursued by the Home Guard with arrows and spears flying around, punctuated with the odd blast of buckshot. It was a case of getting to the nearest stream to take cover, get the boot polish off your face and hands and establish very quickly that you were Security Forces and not Mau Mau!

Weapons varied and included knives, *simis*, spears, grenades and Sterling sub-machine carbines which could be folded and concealed under the coat, with extra mazagine pouches stitched into the clothing.

Major Ray Nightingale describes here a pseudo gang encounter in which terrorists were expected to collect supplies from the labour lines of a farmer:

After considering all the information available I decided to send a pseudo gang into the labour lines to contact the terrorists and, if possible, capture them. A ring of ambushes were placed round all likely escape routes. The pseudo gang detailed for the task consisted of a subaltern [Nigel Bulley], two other ranks and four ex-terrorists. They were armed with three Sterlings, hidden under their greatcoats, and two homemade guns.

The appointed evening was moonless but the stars were very bright. The team set off, on foot, for the labour lines and when they arrived they lay down outside the perimeter fence to watch for any unexpected movement. When they saw that all was quiet one of the African members of the team slipped through the wire and tapped lightly on the door of the hut which he had been told belonged to the person the terrorists were to contact. He whispered that he and his companions wanted to meet the terrorists who would be arriving that night. He said that they had been harassed by the security forces of late and that he and his friends wished to join up with someone who could help them lead a less impossible life. He asked for news of government moves and, to conclude, asked for food as he and his friends were starving.

This approach appeared to satisfy the sympathizer as he opened his door.

He suggested that the team come inside the perimeter and rest in some nearby bushes while he and his wife prepared a meal. He said that when the terrorists with whom they wished to consult arrived he would arrange for them to meet. He then place a large bowl of black, unsweetened tea before them and returned to his hut.

After a wait of about half an hour, they saw their host approaching them, accompanied by one of the terrorists. Introductions were made and a bowl of maize-meal porridge was placed before them. The African members of the team began to talk to the terrorist and everyone began to feed, imitating starving men.

The terrorist was seated with his back to the wire and while he was eating he continually played with a large revolver which was tied to his wrist with a long piece of cord. The team leader sat opposite him and covered him with his Sterling MG which was hidden under his coat; he was considering the advantages of shooting the man where he sat or the possibly greater advantages of capturing him alive. When the terrorist mentioned that he was alone, the subaltern decided on the latter course.

The terrorist continued to eat and playfully point his loaded revolver at everyone in turn. The subaltern stood up, intending to walk round the group as though to squat beside the terrorist, but before he could do this, or even open his coat to clear his weapon to fire, the terrorist threw himself backwards, wriggled under the fence and disappeared into the darkness. Two hurried shots missed and frightened screams and wails broke out all over the labour camp. In the confusion the Mau Mau sympathizer, who had supplied the tea and porridge, quietly decamped and made for the forest but he was later caught by one of the ambushes around the farm. When all had settled down the pseudo team sneaked out and reported their failure to capture the terrorist.

Although this was a fairly typical operation, failure was not at all usual. And in fact the use of pseudo gangs contributed greatly to the defeat of the Mau Mau.

The following is the report of another operation written by the young officer who planned and commanded it. For obvious reasons some names have been changed.

On 15 December, 1954, following a report from a surrendered terrorist, Daudi Rubia, a member of Karii Mubenge's bodyguard, Lieutenant Bleazard decided to do some investigations in the area of the Kanunga Railway *landhies* (labour lines) on Kijabe Hill. With three of our ex-terrorists as impersonators, and two armed trackers in disguise, he made his way from the tarmac road up to the *landhies* shortly after nightfall. Arriving there at 2015 hours they made their way round the back of the building where there were some illegal mud and thatch huts. Here a young terrorist sentry was discovered sitting in the grass outside the hut. After the necessary exchange of passwords and greetings most of Mr Bleazard's party found another patch of long grass to lie in, while the impersonators, Karumbi and Mwangi Muchanga, made their way to the hut in which the sentry had indicated his fellow terrorists were.

A young girl was sent out to take food and water to our party outside, while Karumbi and Mwangi engaged the attention of the sentry and the occupants of the hut. There was only one other terrorist inside the hut; the other occupants, as we found out later, were Wakiri (Warimu d/o* Gichui), the female witch doctor with whom the Kiambu gangs consort regularly, Mwaura s/o† Gachaya, and employee at the *landhies* who is responsible for the feeding and welfare of the gangs, a Maragoli or Jaluo called Mukhambi s/o Kekhera, a committee member in charge of supplies and purchases for the gangs and two girls who were regular food carriers.

It transpired that these two terrorists were members of Kabati's gang, which they now said was twenty-eight strong, and was encamped in a hideout in a dry valley about two miles southwest of the tarmac road on the lower eastern slopes of Mount Longonot. The gang was armed with two DB shotguns, two .303 rifles and a revolver of sorts stolen from Colonel Orchard in Tigoni. Kabati was making his way up to Elburgen with his gang and wanted to move on to Munyu.

When this was reported back to Mr Bleazard, he told Karumbi to tell the terrorists that we had just come from the Munyu Station area. They were very pleased with this and asked if Commander Njuguna was still there and in good health and whether we could lead them to a good hideout. They said they could not go immediately as six of the gang had just gone up to the Lari area to steal four cows for food for the gang. So after further 'parl' it was agreed that we would meet up on Friday at 2000 hours to go with the whole gang. It was also learned from Wakiri that Karii Mubenge had been killed by O Coy Kenya Regiment, and that Mwana Mwende (or General Wairuingi) had been wounded in the stomach and left leg and was lying up on Kamonde Farm (Simpson's Tea Estate), Tigoni.

So on Friday 17th at nightfall we returned to the *landhies*. The Trojan party consisted of Captain Evans, Lieutenant Bleazard, Private Roberts, two armed trackers and five impersonators. We all had blankets slung across our shoulders and we approached from farther off this time. We were late in arriving in the area because on the way down the escarpment, just beyond Mayer's signpost at mile 28, Mr Bleazard with immaculate perception had detected movement in the grass on the side of the road. With tremendous speed he leapt from the Land Rover as it came to a halt and, seizing my Patchett, opened fire at a figure he had seen disappearing into the bushes. It was nearly 1900 hours and nearly dark but we searched the area and found the dead body of the man Mr Bleazard had just fired at, two shots having hit him, one in the neck and one in the bowels. This terrorist was none other than

* daughter of   † son of

62

Major Muhinju s/o Kinyanjui and known to my impersonators as the leader of the Kijabe and Escarpment Forest gangs. He had a packet of some fifty-six rounds of assorted ammunition in his pocket as well as documents, etc. His H/M gun must have been discarded as we did not find it. Also nearby we found that there had been a party drawing water from the spring who had left two *kikapus* (baskets) of empty bottles lying on the ground.

Thus it was not until 2100 hours that we approached the *landhies* where there appeared to be considerable coming and going. After being greeted by the sentry, Karumbi made the rest of our party sit down in the long grass above the huts. Presently they brought us a can of water and some food which was passed round. We recognized the sentry as Kiragenero the Dagoretti terrorist who had recently joined Kabati's gang after Arachuma's death. He had a blanket over his shoulders and a *simi* in his belt. After a bit I could just discern Mr Bleazard's figure standing among the terrorists outside Wakiri's hut. He was shaking hands with them all and joining in the general blackslapping that was going on. There were two girls and two men terrorists in the group. Eventually the two girls called us to follow them and we were led in single file down and across the railway. Just in the bushes we were halted and the girls went off a little way to call the gang leaders to meet us. Kiragenero and the other terrorist pushed off along the railway line to look for Kabati whom they were expecting to arrive at any moment.

After a few moments two of the gang's leaders arrived and started conversing with Mwangi Titi, Mwangi Kinanjui and Karumbi (our imperso-nators). We were expecting to be detected at any time so I ordered two of my men to prepare to throw their grenades and stood by. Then the conversation between my chaps and the terrorists seemed to become rather hostile and I heard them asking a lot of awkward questions. I got up and walked quickly round to the back of the terrorists and ordered them in Swahili to sit down and make no sound. They, however, preferred to make a dash for it; one was shot dead, and Mr Bleazard followed the other and shot him dead when he spotted him clambering down a nearby gorge. We also raked the bushes nearby with automatic fire and grenades. From the bodies of the terrorists some thirty rounds of assorted ammunition were recovered and documents showing that one of them was General Kibuta of Limuru Location, and the other was his 2i/c Major Nyama Ndito (Mwaura s/o Gathuyia) of Masai gang fame. We found food, clothing and blankets in the bushes not ten yards away where some ten other terrorists had been lying. (Later two other bodies were found in the bushes nearby. To conceal the operation a rumour was circulated to the effect that an inter-gang fight had taken place. Later evidence showed that the rumour had been accepted by the terrorists.)

The operations undertaken by the companies of the Regiment were many and varied:

A small patrol from B Company consisting of one officer, two sergeants, one corporal, one private and two unarmed trackers was sent off to follow the tracks of a large gang. The tracks were fresh and easy to follow.

The patrol was just crossing a low spur preparatory to entering a shallow valley, when a powerful voice shouted '*Simama!* ('Halt!'). As C Company were operating nearby, all members of the patrol thought, not unnaturally, that they had bumped into them and stopped instinctively.

As soon as the patrol halted, heavy fire, which fortunately was badly directed, was opened on it from short range by three Lanchesters and approximately a dozen rifles. This fire came from the front and right flank but the enemy were well concealed and remained unseen until they finally withdrew. The patrol took what cover it could and fired back immediately.

One of the sergeants, who had been leading scout, threw himself flat on his back on the path. He was kept there by a terrorist behind a log six feet away who fired at least ten shots at him. Each shot missed his head by only six inches; any move on his part would have been fatal and as he lay he wondered how long it would take the terrorist to hit him.

The enemy fire continued to be very heavy for five minutes and prevented the patrol who were firing back in the general direction of the enemy and searching for targets, from putting in an assault.

The gang leader then decided he had had enough and shouted 'Stop!' He then began to withdraw his men, one of whom had been killed and, as later patches of blood showed, several had been wounded. As soon as the fire slackened the patrol assaulted but the terrorists disappeared quickly.

The dead terrorist was searched and many documents and a No.4 rifle were recovered. Among his papers was found an invitation card from a prominent African politician to a farewell tea-party for an internationally known lawyer who had been the defence counsel at the trial of the former leader of the KAU. The area was well searched and it was proved that there must have been at least twenty weapons in the ambush party; much of the bamboo in the area of the patrol had been cut down by bullets, all at a height of three to four feet.

Immediate follow-up was impossible due to shortage of ammunition and approaching darkness and the patrol then returned to its base camp about a mile away.

Masai tracker Kuisa of B Company chased and speared a Mau Mau on Squairs' Farm:

On 16 May, 1953, a patrol of six and one tracker, with two Brens, from C Company, were returning to Mioro from a fruitless chase after a number of Mau Mau who had been seen watching their camp from the surrounding hills.

Moving down the ridge, the patrol came under heavy automatic and rifle fire from a copse about thirty yards away. Five huts stood near this copse and the area was surrounded by velvety Kikuyu grass, affording no cover for the patrol and no escape route for the terrorists.

The patrol took cover behind a road kerb a few inches high and engaged the gang. The Bren guns were placed on the flanks and, as the enemy were within range, '36' grenades were thrown into the copse.

After a short while ammunition began to run short, so a message was passed by 88 set to the camp at Mioro asking for further supplies and help. This relief was not expected for two hours, so the remaining few rounds were carefully conserved.

The gang must have realized that something was amiss and obviously some of them had had enough as a bunch made a dash for the huts beside the copse. A Bren-gunner killed two and another was accounted for by an accurate rifle shot and an arrow from the Elgeyo tracker.

The terrorists, now in two groups, fired intermittently at the patrol who were not only outnumbered but now very short of ammunition. One terrorist in a hut was more accurate than the others and becoming dangerous. A member of the patrol managed to crawl within twenty yards of him and threw the remaining '36' grenade. This, unfortunately, bounced back off the window sill. A very pistol was then tried and in a few moments all five huts were blazing fiercely. Four terrorists ran from the huts, one was killed by a Bren-gunner but the rest got away, taking with them a double-barrelled shotgun and a heavy calibre sporting rifle.

Reinforcements in the form of two Europeans and one tracker now arrived with fresh ammunition. The action was over in thirty minutes.

The patrol recovered thirteen bodies, one wounded man, five Lanchester SMGs, eight SMLE rifles, one shotgun and a large quantity of ammunition and many magazines. Later, when the huts cooled, two Lanchesters, three rifles and four bodies, all burned, were collected.

Another patrol in the same area the next morning contacted a gang, killed seven and recovered three precision weapons.

In January, 1953, an I Force Patrol of twenty men was given the task of trying to contact and destroy terrorist gangs in the forest areas west of Fort Hall. After entering the forest they established a base on the edge of a vast triangle of bamboo and small recces were sent out. Towards evening the Force Commander's party found a small hideout which had recently been occupied, with clear tracks of one man leading uphill into the bamboo 'badlands'. The following morning the Commander sent out two patrols north and south of the camp and he, with four Europeans and two trackers, followed the tracks of the lone man found the evening before. About 2 o'clock that afternoon the tracks came out into a broad, well-trodden path, obviously being used by gangs crossing the Aberdares. After a short recce forward it was decided to ambush the track that night.

By dawn next morning, after a very cold, miserable and unrewarding ambush, the patrol was well on its way to the moorlands on the crest of the Aberdares. At about 8 o'clock, while the patrol was eating a light meal on the edge of the moors, two men took a look half a mile forward. They reported a grass hut on the forest edge a mile further on, but no sign of life anywhere near it. A cautious stalk of the hut proved it to be old and dilapidated, but situated on a high vantage point with the approaches from most directions quite well screened. A rest was called here for the patrol to observe the ground and await the arrival of their next air contact plane. The map gave the patrol's position as on the headwaters of the Gura river.

Suddenly, a sharp-eyed member of the patrol reported movement on the crest of the next ridge. Everyone took cover and two pairs of binoculars trained on the ridge could make out a group of Africans moving parallel with the ridge and just over the crest. Twenty-two heads were counted.

At this moment the contact plane, Eagle Red, appeared over the forest edge. The Africans disappeared, thus proving they were Mau Mau. The patrol's wireless set was opened up and Eagle Red was told what had been seen and ordered to proceed as though she had seen nothing but to return in ten minutes' time.

This she proceeded to do. The gang immediately broke cover and started to move rapidly north east towards the forest edge, to reach which they had to skirt an isolated copse of bamboo and scrub on a low crest of some 900 yards from the grass hut. Again twenty-two persons were counted. Some could be seen to have spears and one carried what looked like a gun.

Eagle Red proved a little eager and came flying back to the area and, on sighting her, the gang immediately started running for the forest edge. The Commander made contact with Eagle Red and ordered her to dive on the gang immediately. This order was carried out very promptly, the pilot being only too anxious to use the two sten guns attached to his plane's wings.

At the first burst of fire the gang took cover in the tall, tussocky grass and lay still. The Commander then ordered the patrol to open long-range fire on them. The gang took fright and, like a covey of partridge, made for the copse with the patrol giving rapid fire and Eagle Red diving down firing her stens and dropping hand grenades timed to 'air' burst. Two gangsters were seen to fall during this engagement. Eagle Red continued to fly round the area of the copse and reported that it was completely isolated in the middle of a grass plain.

The Commander then detailed his four Europeans to vantage points round the copse and ordered them to shoot anyone trying to break out. He and the two trackers went to where the gang had been fired on. All positions were taken up within half an hour. Eagle Red meanwhile had been keeping the gang quiet with occasional dive-bombing attacks with grenades. Sniping started all round the copse and was to continue all day.

Eagle Red was then ordered to contact the rest of the patrol and get them to the copse by 5 pm that afternoon, a journey, as the crow flies, of about fourteen miles, probably twenty along the ground, and over some of the steepest and most impenetrable tangle of forest country on the Aberdares. Then Eagle Red was to fly back to Force base and organize continuous air cover over the engagement area until dark, and reserve ammunition, food and blankets were ordered for the evening drop.

All during the day shots rang out round the copse, quite a few coming from within it. One European had his water bottle shot through and the Commander had his hat blown from his head.

The two African trackers searched the area of the first engagement, which was in dead ground, and captured two unarmed and extremely frightened Mau Mau. They also found two very dead gangsters killed by rifle fire.

This was an encouraging start. The covering aircraft during the day dropped on the copse I Force's two secret weapons – 50lb home-made bombs called Gog and Magog. Gog went off with a shattering roar and wails of terror came from the copse. Magog, however, declined to explode and is there yet.*

By 5.30 pm the rest of the patrol had arrived and while they rested for a few minutes the Commander briefed them and gave orders for an attack on the copse. At 6 pm, covered by heavy grenade bombing from both Eagle Red and Eagle Black, the attack was launched.

The terrorists were not cowed and attacked I Force men with pangas and spears, but where shot down for their bravery. No I Force men were hurt or killed. After reorganizing, a thorough search was made of the copse and, as dark fell, the patrol was able to count eleven dead and eight prisoners, two of whom were badly wounded. The man with the gun was never found. The aircraft then flew off to base, promising to be over again at dawn.

Camp was made in a sheltered strip of bamboo on the forest edge but the rations which had been dropped that day could not be found. However, one of the prisoners volunteered that the gang had been carrying potatoes and a party under his guidance found several loads which were cooked by the prisoners for themselves and their captors.

Eagle Black arrived just after dawn, dropping very welcome reserve rations and some medical supplies for the wounded prisoners, and was asked to make arrangements for transport to meet the patrol at the forest edge that evening. The patrol was met at 3 o'clock some three miles inside the forest by porters to carry the wounded and at the forest edge by transport, food and refreshments for the weary patrolmen.

The copse where this engagement took place was afterwards called Battle Copse and it lies on what was later one of the main patrol routes of the security forces across the Aberdares.

* Magog was not in fact dropped on this occasion

Support Company was routed to Karatina via RHQ Nairobi, but at the last moment when all the trucks were packed and ready to move a 'phone message came through with an urgent request for mortar support in the Thomson's Falls area.

The Mortar Commander and three mortar detachments accordingly left the convoy and rushed to Thomson's Falls, where they had probably the most successful mortar shoot of the Emergency. It lasted about ten minutes and concentrated fire was brought to bear on a Rumuruti swamp in which a gang of thirty Mau Mau was reported to be in hiding.

After the shoot the detachment carried straight on to Karatina, via Nyeri, and was ready to welcome the main party when they arrived at the new company HQ the next day.

The results of the shoot were received about two weeks later – fourteen killed and their bodies collected and probably many more casualties but their bodies were not recoverable from the swamp.

At the beginning of 1954 the Regiment, still recognized as a formation of battalion size, was brought into Nairobi for Operation Anvil. In this operation the Regiment took an important part and by its thoroughness assisted the success of this decisive 'clean-up' of Nairobi.

After this the Regiment was once again required to change its role and show another aspect of its versatility. The Kikuyu Home Guard in the Reserves desperately needed European leaders to steady their flagging morale. The companies were spread over the Reserves and, under command of the Administration, were given immense parishes in which they were required to transform all the Kikuyu Guard Posts into reliable bastions. Only two men could be allotted to each post; thus these Kenya Regiment men found themselves overnight in isolated positions where great demands were made upon their initiative and sense of responsibility. They proved themselves equal to these tasks.

By the end of 1954, however, the manpower problem again became overwhelming and it was reluctantly decided to reduce the Regiment to one Operational Company of 120 men.

'Ops' Company became the only organized formation of the Regiment to continue the battle. But throughout the troubled areas and in almost every district there were Field Intelligence Officers with their pseudo-gangs and District Officers responsible for the morale, loyalty and security of several villages. There were many trackermasters serving with the British battalions: in fact, in every department of the Security Forces there were men of the Kenya Regiment. They were trained and prepared to tackle any job, however great a responsibility it entailed; they were essentially individualists but were welded together by their territorial esprit de corps.

It was at this time that the Regiment had its first two RAVC dog-handlers and tracker dogs posted to it. This number was later increased to four and several Kenya Regiment men were trained to handle the dogs. These dog-handlers joined platoons in Ops Company and immediately made their presence felt. In a very short time tracker teams were formed, trained and operating against the gangs. The handlers soon became used to forest operations and before long were the most experienced patrol men in the company. The close cooperation between the members of the tracker teams and the RAVC personnel was unique and this fruitful association continued until the company closed down.

Ops Company, under Major R. C. W. Nightingale, now inherited the regimental tradition of continually varying roles and ever-changing personnel. From its formation it was involved in numerous company moves, each entailing a different task in widely differing areas. Its reinforcements came from the Kenya Regiment Training Centre, the well-laid-out regimental training depot at Nakuru, where the recruits underwent their basic training. It was Ops Company's primary task to give these recruits operational training and experience prior to their secondment to the many jobs for which the Regiment provided men.

Lieutenant Alan Wisdom reports:

On 5 March, 1954, the District Officer of Fort Hall, Jimmy Candler, was driving near location 14 when a herd of cattle was driven in front of his Land Rover. While he was waiting for the cattle to pass, the terrorists opened fire from the roadsides. Jim dived under his Land Rover with his Kikuyu Guard escort but was wounded in both legs and, unable to fight his way out, he ordered his men to leave him. They managed to extricate themselves. When we found Jim he was shot and cut to pieces – hardly recognizable. While we were hunting the gang, a car arrived from Government House in Nairobi with an envoy who warned us that no bloodbath was to take place. We eventually found the gang submerged in a river, breathing through reeds. A few grenades made them pop out of the water like corks!

Jimmy was a great loss and was awarded the MBE in the New Year's Honours list. Operation Hammer started the day after he was killed and Payet and Taylor of Support Coy captured General Tanganyika. Complete cooperation existed between us and the Kikuyu Guard as every post had at least one member of the Regiment. Philip Morecombe's selection of DOs and police was inspired and the mixture of police administration and military was first-class.

THE KPR AIR WING

Another service which was indispensable during the Emergency was that given by the pilots who supported the ground patrols. The airfields at Mweiga and Squair's

Farm enabled us to initiate air-to-ground tactics which were to prove one of the deciding factors in the struggle. From members of the Aero Club and the Kenya Police Reserve Air Wing, a joint air/ground base was formed at Mweiga. 'Punch' Bearcroft, who in spite of having lost his right hand was a brilliant pilot and one of those best known at Mweiga, describes the role of the Air Wing:

The Police Air Wing started off in 1949 as a small facet of the Kenya Police Reserve and consisted of reserve police officers who were pilots and in most cases aircraft owners. Most of them were, as myself, farmers, and they were utilized mainly for community and recce work.

I was farming in the Elburgen area and had a Piper Cruiser which I used to use to fly around the country buying stock for other farmers and for aerial photography. I was one of the first to join the Kenya Police Reserve Air Wing but did very little police flying until the start of the Emergency. Everybody was called out at very short notice and none of us expected to be involved for more than a couple of weeks, but after about two months it became pretty obvious that the Emergency was going to last for a long time. I was then flying about a hundred hours a month, seven days a week and the farm was going to hell so I started the wheels in motion to sell it.

The majority of the work we did consisted of supply dropping, all of which was free fall with the supplies packed in approximately 30lb bags, and contact recce work which consisted in maintaining communication with forest patrols, helping them to move around.

These intrepid pilots added a new dimension to our operations, as ground troops could be kept alive by food drops, and kept in the forest longer. They could also signal the position of gangs by using smoke and flares.

In some of the earlier offensive operations in 1953 aerial bombing was forbidden by the War Council. It occurred despite the ban but disaster nearly overtook the Commanding Officer when, on a particular action in the forest, two excited pilots forgot to switch of their wireless sets and the air was alive with '1st stick of bombs gone now – 2nd stick. . . .'

Pacers and Tripacers were successful at strafing from the air, though when the Harvard Flight tried the same tactics, with their greater speed and lack of manoeuvrability, they tended to overshoot.

Much later the Lincoln bombers, while doing little actual harm to the gangs, made the elephant, rhino and buffalo more dangerous for those on the ground. They also started fires. Ten more Tripacers would have saved the Exchequer a large bill.

The Air Wing assisted the Government Survey Department, manned by men of the Regiment, in perfecting the ground maps as well as being on hand for the essential supply drops, reconnaissance, and for collecting casualties. For many isolated posts they were also a source of communications; newspapers might be dropped, as Jock Rutherfurd describes here:

70

[Loyal Kikuyu] Chief Njiri's homestead was near the forest edge by Kinyona. The Kenya Police Reserve spotter plane regularly dropped a copy of the *East African Standard*. At the first sound of the aircraft, the old Chief would order out all his wives and children to mark the fall, for should the paper miss the crest of the ridge, it might sail some distance away down the hillside. As the tiny white dot emerged from the plane, a mad scramble ensued. The paper was passed from hand to hand, until eventually Njiri would present it to the officer, requesting him to read out the following items of the previous day's news:

How many Mau Mau dead? How many bombs dropped?

How many guns for the Home Guard?

As the figures were usually, to Njiri's mind, unimpressive, he would then withdraw in silent bad humour.

Noel Simon had experience of KPR drops both on the ground, receiving supplies in the forest, and from the air, when he was involved in a less conventional drop:

We spent many days and night tramping the forest, scrambling up and down deep gulleys and ravines, ever on the move, constantly alert for fresh tracks and sudden ambush, and almost equally wary of unprovoked aggression by some of the larger wild animals. Keen naturalists that many of us were, we preferred our rhinos at a distance.

At night would come the welcome drone of the aircraft. If in open country, the plane would quickly spot us and down would come tumbling the day's rations as if from some giant cornucopia. The aim was usually alarmingly accurate and quick avoiding action was sometimes necessary to avert being laid out cold by one's own supper! In the dense bamboo it was necessary to light a fire as soon as the plane drew near. The thin wisp of smoke curling up through the bamboo acted as a marker easily visible from the air and the pilot aimed his wares at the smoke. This was a relatively safe procedure from the point of view of those at the receiving end as the bamboo broke the container's fall . . .

With the small number of personnel engaged, it looked as though the Emergency would be a long-drawn-out affair and we naturally tried to devise alternative and more effective methods of bringing the terrorists to task. It seemed fairly logical that, with the limited forces available, the most effective way of striking at them was from the air, and I was glad when an opportunity occurred of flying with an aircraft of the KPR Air Wing attached to I force. . . .

We approached someone in Nairobi who had some acquaintance with explosives and asked him to provide the necessary ingredients for a home-made bomb. In this manner were Gog and Magog conceived.

A great deal of preliminary organization was necessary before Gog could be launched on his one-way journey. It was decided that the most suitable

71

delivery would be at night as Mau Mau camp fires would provide a simple, worthwhile and unmistakable target.

The only place for assembling Gog was the verandah of the house in which we messed, and as work proceeded it was strange to see how many people found they had urgent business elsewhere. Being a complete novice so far as the intricates of explosives and detonators were concerned, I blessed the assembly instructions so thoughtfully provided by our tame boffin. Brief and to the point, they were interspersed with tactful comments such as: 'But do be careful. Gelignite will stand a lot of dropping but no sparks. Detonators will not stand either'.

All the ingredients haphazardly littered the verandah. It only remained to put them together in the correct order. Gog consisted of a 2½-foot length of 6-inch metal piping with four fins and a wooden nose cone. Thin metal strips, which would collapse on impact and set the bomb off, kept the nose cone separated from the business end. A wooden spacer inserted between the canister and the nose cone acted as an additional safety precaution to be removed prior to dropping. Fourteen sticks of gelignite had to be packed into the centre of the canister. These were kept firmly in place by a motley assortment of rivets, nuts, bolts and scrap metal, with a handful of .303 rounds thrown in for good measure.

Now came the really delicate part of the operation. The baseplate containing the cartridge holder was removed and the striker pushed down until its tip was flush with the base of the hole. Then the complete primer cartridge had to be inserted into the holder with the striker almost touching the percussion cap. The typewritten instructions explained that 'paper pasted over the percussion cap will prevent the striker resting with its own weight on the metal and accidents when charging will be avoided'.

Making up the primer cartridge proved an unnerving occupation. A 12-bore cartridge had to be partially dismantled, the shot and wads removed and a small hole drilled into the paper washer, behind which lay the charge. Then a hole had to be carefully drilled in the end of a stick of gelignite deep enough to take a detonator to its full length. This done, the detonator was inserted into the stick, rolled in the hand and the gelignite gently tamped around the deadly little phial to ensure perfect contact. So far so good, but I was appalled at the thought of the next step. The end of the stick of gelignite had to be pushed into the cartridge case, detonator first, to make contact with the charge. I read and re-read the instructions for fear I might have misconstrued the precise meaning of a particular phrase or sentence, but the wording allowed no alternative interpretation. 'Insert stick into cartridge case as far as it will go, without forcing, detonator first.' It was a tight squeeze but gradually the gelignite was pushed firmly home until it rested snug in the cavity.

With a feeling of intense relief I inverted the baseplate, to which was now attached the made-up primer cartridge, lowered it gently into place and screwed it firmly down. Gog was now ready for action and would detonate when dropped from three feet or less. Assembling and priming had occupied the entire afternoon. Meanwhile, Punch had been busy rigging up an extraordinary and distinctly inadequate looking contraption on his starboard wing strut. We coaxed Gog into position on this highly original bomb rack and strapped him firmly into place. When the time came, Mike Richmond in the rear of the aircraft would actuate the release mechanism by pulling on a string. It would be embarrassing if Gog declined to leave when called upon to do so.

After dinner the flare path was hastily laid. Punch and Mike clambered aboard and trundled down the strip into the air. The grass airfield was far from smooth and I was most anxious in case the bumps would jar the detonator into premature action, or that Gog would be jerked from his berth, and we all breathed a huge sigh of relief when the wheels finally left the ground. An hour later I batted the aircraft into a perfect touchdown, and from it emerged a jubilant and not entirely coherent Punch and Mike. Apparently everything had gone as planned. Shortly after take-off they had spotted a large Mau Mau camp fire in the depths of the forest. They carried out two or three dummy runs to gauge the height and the best method of attack. Then, approaching in a gentle glide, Gog was released right alongside the fire. In his determination to hit the target, Punch had approached rather lower than was wise and the force of the explosion threw the light plane violently into the air. It was impossible to say what damage had been inflicted on the gang but there could be little doubt that those squatting round the fire had their careers abruptly terminated, and if there were others close by they must have suffered a rude shock.

The following day strange rumours were circulating in Nyeri concerning a mysterious explosion heard during the night. Fortunately, nobody was able to throw any light on the matter and the incident was soon forgotten. Gog had shown the way, but it was decided that Magog should be saved for a special occasion.

In the meantime, normal routine went on. Constant contact was maintained with ground forces, and rations and supplies dropped to patrols operating in the depths of the forest. On one occasion John Bamber's section was camped at the very bottom of the narrow Gura Valley, which at this particular point must have been in the region of 1200 feet deep. The normal approach would have been downstream as the valley bottom fell away sharply. However, try as we might we could not approach from that direction owing to an overhanging pall of cloud enveloping the cliffs. If John was to receive his drop, there was no alternative but to fly upstream. We dived down, dropped the supplies and pulled away. Only then did we realize that the valley bed rose far more sharply than we had supposed. The ground came up to meet us and Punch had no alternative but to attempt to turn 180°. With throttle wide open and stick hard back, the cliff face loomed uncomfortably close but he managed to get us round with what seemed only feet to spare. For once I refrained from back-seat driving and we each kept our thoughts to ourselves.

Some time later, flying over the Aberdares, we spotted a freshly used track winding up through the forest to the high moorlands. By the side of this track could clearly be seen the remains of a recently used fire. Luckily Nev and John were not far away. We contacted them by radio and guided them to the position. Before long both patrols were in hot pursuit. The track twisted and turned, climbing ever upwards through the forest into the bamboo and out onto the moorland plateau at 10,000 feet. There in a small copse, only a few hundred yards from the point where the headwaters of the Gura plunged over a huge, spectacular precipice, the terrorists, either exhausted from their long trek or unaware they were being pursued, took their final stand. Nev Cooper, coming upon them after a strenuous hike of about sixteen miles in under four hours, soon had the copse surrounded and a brisk battle ensued. The terrorists had the advantage of thick cover while Nev was compelled to station his men in the open. It was then that we thought of Magog. Over the radio Nev explained that he would contain the gang in the copse until 4 pm but could not delay moving in to the assualt after that time or the terrorists might escape under cover of darkness. We roared back to the base, leaped out of the aircraft and rushed to assemble Magog. This time I was a trifle quicker but I cannot claim to have relished the performance any more than on the previous occasion.

Owing to the urgency of the situation, there was no possibility of installing a bomb rack. There was nothing for it but to carry the brute in my lap, hoping that my legs would cushion any shocks. While I was assembling Magog, Jimmy had ripped out the rear seat of the aircraft leaving a space sufficiently large for me to squat on the foor. With some misgiving I carried Magog to the plane, fearful that I would trip, and gently eased myself in. This was by no means as simple as it sounds as Magog weighed at least 50lbs, and the door of a Piper Pacer does not allow much room for manoeuvre. Jimmy had thoughtfully tied a stout rope to the outer door handle so that by pulling hard he could assist me to open the door when the moment came.

As we approached the target we saw Nev and his team firing at the copse and signalled to him to take cover while we went in. Jimmy pulled, I pushed, and the door opened a bare six inches. Our combined efforts could not succeed in opening it further against the pressure of the wind. One foot wedged in the door, I removed the spacer stick with unsteady hands and urged Magog's business end through the narrow gap, praying that the slipstream would not force the bomb into harsh contact with the fuselage. With throttle closed, Jimmy went into a gentle glide. Then suddenly 'Let her go'. I pushed Magog into space and as I did so Jimmy opened up to full throttle and went into a steep climbing turn.

Magog hurtled into the centre of the copse, a white glint of parachute trailing taut in its wake . . . But there was only silence. A silence broken at length by a flow of the most profane language I have ever heard or uttered. As we circled dejectedly over the copse, we saw the ground forces move in to the attack. By nightfall the entire gange of twenty terrorists were either dead or captured. It was the first major success of the Emergency and an outstanding achievement on Nev's part. But for Mike and me the cheers as the ground forces signalled their hard-earned victory served only to emphasize a profound anti-climax.

In early 1953 Wing Commander Robin Johnson, a famous wartime RAF pilot, took over control of Air Operations at Mweiga, under the overall command in Nairobi of Wing Commander Francombe, a distinguished pilot himself. Of all the Security Forces the Air Wing pilots deserved perhaps the highest awards for gallantry. Planes were always on standby on the numerous airstrips ready to collect casualties or carry out vital reconnaissance, as well as the more mundane supply drops. The ground patrols could never have achieved the same results without them. Every plane took off with a box of '36' grenades and sometimes home-made bombs and automatics precariously fixed to the wings. Fortunately fatal accidents were few but the loss of any pilot was a major disaster. The advantage of the light aircraft was that they could and often did land and take off on the main roads in the battle areas. Some of the pilots performed hair-raising feats such as taking off down-wind in mountainous terrain (or taking up a plane after an off-duty session at the bar!)

NOTE

JOINT GROUND/AIR STAFF
On 10 February, 1953, Tactical Headquarters formed on Marrian's Farm, Mweiga. The CO and Roly Guy were accompanied by operational staff consisting of:

The Air Wing
Wing Commanders Robin Johnson and David Hunt (both ex-RAF) Pilots: Punch Bearcroft, Jimmy Dodds, Mike Richmond, Peter Nicholas, Ken Holding, Tommy Thompson
RAF Harvards at Squair's, Marrian's and Nanyuki
(February – March, 1953, Tony Archer was with I Force)

I Staff in HQ Ops Room
Susie Marrian (Peter's wife)
Frank (KPR, ex-Scots Guards) and Tania Waldron
Mungo Park (KPR ex-Irish Guards)
Shaun Plunket (KPR ex-Irish Guards)
Sam Weller (Kenya Regiment)

Sam Weller wrote a monthly 'I' report on Mau Mau activities which was circulated to all HQs and police.

OFFICERS WHO COMMANDED COMPANIES DURING THE EMERGENCY

Major	Gillett	Captain	Schuster
	Josselyn		Nightingale
Captain	Mayers		Waring
	Brown		Klynsmith
	Cooper		Vetch
	Anderson		Riley
	Ragg		

CHAPTER 6

CLEANING-UP
OPERATIONS

THE TURNING-POINT of the war came on 26 March, 1953, when the loyalist location of Lari was attacked by Mau Mau. About a thousand terrorists under the command of Dedan Kimathi, the most notorious of the gang leaders, descended on the sleeping Kikuyu village. Each homestead was ringed and the whole location set on fire so that, as villagers tried to escape the flames, they were killed by the waiting Mau Mau. Over 200 houses were destroyed and at least as many people slaughtered. Sid Moscoff, whose platoon was the first army unit on the scene when 23rd KAR were rushed to Uplands Police Station that night, describes his experiences:

I shall never forget the incident when we rushed into Uplands police station and were confronted with lorry loads of chopped-up women and children who had been brought in from Lari Ridge where the loyalists were butchered earlier that night. The look of horror on the faces of our Wakamba askaris who suddenly realized what Mau Mau was about . . . when they saw the mutilated bodies of kids.

We shot off at dawn to engage the gang, long since disappeared. My platoon was guided by Dennis Kearney and the others by Kitch Morson, followed by hundreds of loyalists seeking revenge. Somehow we met some loyalists who had captured a dozen or so Mau Mau suspects whom we piled into a lorry to take back to Uplands Police Station. On the way there we were confronted by loyalists demanding our prisoners. Suddenly out of nowhere a car appeared driven by a Catholic missionary. He pleaded in the name of the Almighty that justice be done, whilst another platoon commander also wanted the prisoners handed over to the loyalists. Just then the 88 set crackled and Major Austin Maynard – God bless him! – asked me to report my position. I gave the facts, but did not mention that I was confronted with avenging loyalists or that missionary. What followed was a haze – I pointed my Patchett at the loyalists over the cab of the truck and ordered the driver to drive through them, while my prisoners lay flat shivering with fear. I shall never forget the look of disgust on the faces of the loyalists and later the loss of respect by my Wakamba askaris. I'm sure that hundreds of other Kenya Regiment men experienced similar instances which still haunt them.

The ruthlessness of the Lari Massacre eliminated much of the sympathy that Kikuyu and other Africans had held for the Mau Mau struggle. So too did the murder in October, 1954, of Arundel Gray Leakey (the cousin of L. S. B. Leakey and the father of Sergeant Gray Leakey who had been awarded a posthumous VC).

His body was found near Nyeri Hill, having apparently been buried alive. His wife was found strangled on the lawn. Their daughter, who hid in an attic above their bedroom (she was not strong enough to pull her mother to safety), was rescued later unharmed. These acts which were probably intended to terrify loyal Kikuyu once and for all into submission to Mau Mau only increased resistance against them and shocked the world into the realization that, whatever justification there may have been in Kenyatta's demands for African self-government, Mau Mau were terrorists and murderers who would have to be dealt with as such. It was ironic, but hardly surprising in view of Lari and other atrocities, that Africans, the very people whose freedom Mau Mau claimed to be struggling for, were fighting against them alongside the Europeans and white settlers.

On the night of the Lari Massacre, another Mau Mau forest gang raided the Naivasha Police Headquarters, including the armoury and a nearby detention camp. The result was that over 150 prisoners were released and Mau Mau departed with a large number of rifles, automatic weapons and a store of ammunition. The implications of this raid, and of the Lari Massacre itself, were frightening: Mau Mau was an increasingly well-organized force, becoming better armed and stronger, while police posts and civilians alike were comparitively ill-prepared to deal with them. Some, up till then, had not fully realized the urgency of the situation, as can be seen from this story told by John Toft:

One of the ——s from South Kinangop gave David Christie-Miller (DC, Naivasha) and me a hell of a lot of trouble, and refused to *boma* (enclose) his cattle (a prize dairy herd of 170) at night. A gang skipped in one night, drove the lot off and slaughtered them in the bamboo forest. We caught up with them later and killed the gang.

I was in the DC's office when —— came in to castigate us. David listened to him for a while, then walked across to his office window, beckoning —— to follow. David then said, 'You know Mr ——, you don't normally come to me with your problems, you normally see the Governor.' Pointing, he said: 'There is the road to Nairobi, I suggest you get on it!' We heard no more.

That year more rifles were issued to the Kikuyu Guard, which expanded to a strength of some 4500 men, and posts began to be more efficiently run, more effectively defended. New roads and bridges were built to connect the posts to one another. Alan Wisdom, who was stationed at Othaya, recalls that this work was hampered at first by terrorist intimidation of locals: 'the terrorists came at night and made the locals pull them up; next day we rebuilt, and so on.' But the defences were gradually improved and standardized; wide, deep trenches, filled with sharpened stakes or *panjis* were dug round the oblong perimeters of the posts. Narrow bridges spanned these trenches by day but were withdrawn when the gates were closed at dusk. The buildings within were roofed with corrugated iron to resist fire, while in the centre of each post loomed a tall tower with Tilly lamps manned by sentries round the clock. Men would sleep fully clothed, ready to run to standby positions at the first sound of an alarm, or to drive to another post in response to the bursting red stars of distress signals. This, at least, was the idea but, at times, the sudden nature of a night attack, combined with the inexperience of guards, could cause initial confusion in spite of preparations. Alan Wisdom describes the battle at Othayo garrison:

When the attack started at about 0030 hours they stumbled out of their quarters, lay on the ground and opened fire at us [the sentries on duty]. We had to silence them and, while engaging the terrorists, despatched Sergeant Spencer to show them which direction the terrorists were attacking from. About 300 terrorists were held off, but the battle was fierce. Their courage stimulated as usual with *bhang* [cannabis], a local drug, they came back and even under fire tried more than once to retrieve their dead. Davo Davidson crawled out with a bag of grenades and inflicted heavy casualties. This action saved the situation.

At first light, small patrols would leave the posts to make a quick search of the surrounding area for signs of gangster activity during the night. Occasionally a trail would be successfully followed; stolen food might be recovered, or the gangsters themselves confronted. On 23 June, 1953, a patrol of A Company KAR and Kikuyu Guard cornered a gang of fifty terrorists and food carriers in this way, near the forest edge on the Thika river track. The engagement lasted until dark and thirty-five Mau Mau were killed. It was the first success of its kind against terrorists in the district and was a source of encouragement to many.

Sweeps and stop lines were organized, in which bush, river banks, caves, treetops, huts, were all combed, while stop lines waited to intercept any fleeing terrorists. Considerable numbers of gangsters were killed or captured in this way during the large-scale Operation Buttercup. This was carried out in the area of

79

Ruathia Ridge by the 4th KAR,* the Kenya Regiment with Kikuyu Guard forming many of the stop lines. General 'Bobbie' Erskine had become Commander-in-Chief and with his support a new Mobile Patrol Company of Land Rovers was formed, mounting Bren guns and 3-inch mortars. Within a month of the start of Operation Buttercup the gangs in Ruathia were annihilated.

The smaller forest patrols were still probably the most successful of the offensive tactics; they were gradually catching up with the Mau Mau and beating them at their own game of hide and seek.

Those tense days and nights of eerie quiet shattered by sudden violence did, however, take their toll on the men. After a long period on operations, taut nerves would sometimes unwind without warning. A quiet-seeming man in the corner of a bar might draw his pistol and loose off at the bottles behind the bar. Without a word he would sign a chit for the damage and walk out into the night. As far as possible the men were encouraged to stick together in order to keep an eye on one another. Company commanders working out leave rosters would pass on a warning to 'look after so and so'. It was something the Regiment was proud of.

Nevertheless, regimental parties were often wild affairs, and rank was irrelevant since, unlike the British Army, all our men were entitled to use hotels and bars. Many were, in any case, members of the various clubs throughout the country, where social life continued in spite of the Emergency. I recall one party which developed in the Outspan Hotel at Nyeri after the Regiment returned from a lengthy joint operation with 4th KAR in the Fort Hall Reserve. Just as I was leaving camp to join the party, Sid Field, our Medical Orderly, reported that one of our chaps was ill. It was appendicitis, but the Medical Officer was already in Nyeri with the advance guard of party-goers. We loaded the patient into my battle-weary and ancient jeep and took him to Nyeri Hospital, where we discovered that the surgeon had also gone to the party. He was collected from the Outspan Hotel in a very cheerful mood and decided to operate immediately. Private Field and I had on green theatre smocks and masks and our hands were scrubbed. At the first incision there was a crash behind me – Field had fainted!

The operation was successful, the patient's only regret afterwards being that he had missed the party. In fact he had missed quite a lively party. When I arrived there from the hospital, it was to find the entrance doors of the Outspan missing – Sam Weller, our Intelligence Officer, had driven a jeep into the hotel. He explained this 'intelligently' by saying that he'd heard there was a fire and had rushed in to the rescue. He had tried to put out the 'fire' with the main garden hose. Luckily, the damp had not deterred the customers. Major Sherbrooke Walker, the owner, was delighted with the bar takings and honour was satisfied by the passing of a hat, which soon contained enough to pay for the damage.

* The 4th KAR (Uganda) was the one we knew best, as we operated for long periods with them in the Fort Hall area. Their CO, Donald Knott, was known as 'Warlord', a codename which may have puzzled Army Signals whose traditional names for the CO were different. My codename was 'Pasha', a rank I once held in the Sudan Defence Force.

Sport was also popular with the troops. Edwin Bristow, for instance, recalls getting 'requests every so often to rush up to the top of the Kedong Valley and play rugger against some other platoon in the evenings'. Another member of the Regiment 'was posted up to the Rift Valley at Kijabe, ostensibly to guard it and to patrol the railway line. Nothing much happened and we soon had a small pitch-and-putt golf course going.' Roly Guy remembers: 'playing golf at Muthaiga Club with a terrorist gang firing across the fairway. "Can't you shout 'Fore' before you shoot?" screamed one indignant golfer.'

Such diversions may sound incongruous in an account of a violent, bloody war, but in fact they helped to maintain morale and did not involve any neglect of duty or slackening of attention and discipline. Here Jock Rutherfurd describes how readily one member of the Regiment went into action in spite of being caught by Mau Mau literally with his trousers down:

George McKnight was suffering a go of the trots and had had to withdraw for much-needed relief. While hunkered down, there suddenly loomed up against the sky the unmistakable silhouette of a Mau Mau. Without more ado, George shot the man from the squatting position. The bullet went through the man's buttocks, knocking him down with his home-made gun. He later recovered and was taken to court but I regret that George's evidence was somewhat evasive as to the real facts of the action.

After continuous operations in the Nyeri and Fort Hall Reserves, the Regiment moved to Naivasha and was reduced from seven to four companies. The reason for this reduction was that the Regiment was being drained of manpower by the increasing demands for leadership throughout the Security Forces. Much work fell to the Kenya Regiment men as guides, liaison officers, interpreters and so on. The Regiment believed that, had this reduction not taken place, the active companies in the forest would have brought the Emergency to an earlier end. Our role was simple – to destroy the forest gangs. For a large operation we could have concentrated all our companies if necessary. With a tactical headquarters in control from one company base we could have dominated the gangs and forced them to move continually, which was not what they wanted as they would lose contact with sympathizers and food carriers. It would have taken some months, but the continual harry and pursuit tactics would have disorganized them completely.

The KAR battalions could also have played a fuller part in occupying vital posts in the Reserve and settled areas and, when combined with Kenreg units, they would have been invaluable.

British battalions could have played a full role in support by moving continually from farm to farm in the operational area which would have given a great boost to the morale in the more isolated places. The great advantage of this method of operation was that the Government forces would have had the initiative. We never believed that large sweeps were effective as the Mau Mau had a very fine warning system and they were quick to spot the arrival of troops in a particular location. It meant, as they well knew, that a search or operation was impending – and the gang in the area could be miles away by the time the Government started its own offensive. All movement of troops into an area should have had a cover plan which would have disguised the actual intention of our forces. As I recall it, large battalion or brigade operations were characterized by the arrival of a great convoy of vehicles. In the inevitable brew-up and noise no Mau Mau waited to shake hands; they disappeared and attacked an isolated farm thirty miles away.

Nevertheless, by the beginning of 1954 the Mau Mau threat, though far from defeated, was at least contained; the tide had turned. The Security Forces' next large operation was to be concentrated in Nairobi. A thorough search of the city was planned secretly, under the codename 'Operation Anvil'.

At dawn on 29 April, 1954, a ring encircled the area where wanted men were thought to be located. Four British battalions, one KAR battalion and the equivalent of two and a half companies of the Kenya Regiment, supplemented by clerks, artisans and HQ staff, and the Police were out in full strength, including twenty-four combat teams of Europeans, Asians and Africans. The scene was similar to an ant-heap stirred up by a stick. Barricaded doors were broken down, suspects hauled out from under beds or inside cupboards. Others broke through windows only to be caught by the searchers outside. Suspected Mau Mau sympathizers were collected into groups, searched, questioned and documented by special screening teams.

The police decided that suspects should be graded into 'hardcore', 'softcore' and 'followers', and that the 'hardcore' should be marked by distinguishing red chalk, 'softcore' by blue; but it was a day of drizzling rain and it was soon apparent that chalk applied to a man's shirt or coat was not going to last long. I therefore instructed all members of Kenreg patrols to use paint (procured from a conveniently adjacent decorator's shop) and not to put it on clothes which could be discarded.

Within an hour an agitated staff officer appeared and nervously ordered me to report to the Commander-in-Chief immediately. I found him waiting at a screening point with a large number of suspects lined up like ninepins. 'Take a look at these prisoners,' he ordered. 'What on earth have your fellows been up to?' With one accord the prisoners' heads turned towards me. Each one wore spectacles. Not ordinary spectacles: every pair had been roundly applied in thick red or blue paint!

That was not the only demonstration of over-enthusiasm by Kenreg men during Operation Anvil. At the offices of the Indian High Commission, doors had been shot off hinges, contents of drawers and filing cabinets were strewn around rooms and pictures were hanging askew on walls. Although it was true that four badly wanted men had been dragged out of hiding in the building, such an invasion of a High Commission is almost an act of war. My next meeting with the Commander-in-Chief was more turgid. He went through my report slowly as I watched. At last he looked up with a twinkle in his eye: 'You seem to have covered everything – as usual.' Next day we made our apologies to Mr Pandon, the High Commissioner, who luckily was very understanding.

Another incident that caused major concern was the very thorough search carried out by Second Lieutenant Moscoff of the Regiment of the Nairobi glassworks. Most of the staff were apprehended, so that some damage occurred to the process of glassmaking which took time to repair. Many of the staff were seen doubling with hands on head to the detainees' pen. What had been overlooked was that the machinery continued to function until, becoming choked, it ground to a halt.

Anvil continued until the end of May and 16,000 wanted Mau Mau sympathizers were taken in for questioning. Special Branch Police screening teams were gaining valuable data that led to the capture of more terrorists. Mau Mau activity in the Reserves was being neutralized. The pace had slackened. Women and children, who often acted as food carriers for the gangs, began at last to be seen in their true perspective. Instead of being ignored as harmless, they were now either watched and followed – used as leads to the whereabouts of gangs – or were detained and prevented from supplying the terrorists with food, thus forcing them to come out of hiding in order to get their own supplies. This was to prove more difficult for them than ever since a system of 'villagization' had been effectively employed so that cattle and grain were protected and kept inside stockades at night. Terrorists were forced to retreat into the forests and live on what they could snare for themselves, but they were weakening, becoming more isolated.

By this time, due again to the manpower problem, the Regiment was reduced to one operational company comprising both European and African soldiers. During the spell at Bexendales Farm above the Rift Valley they carried out offensive sorties on suspected gangsters operating below the Kinangop at Maguga.

During 1954 a War Council had been set up, its members including the Commander-in-Chief, the Governor and Deputy Governor and Michael Blundell, leader of the settlers in Kenya who had been dissastisfied with the Government's approach to Mau Mau and who wanted greater control of Kenya affairs independent of the Colonial Office. The wheels of political change were already turning. Oliver Lyttelton recommended a representative government through a multiracial Council of Ministers. It was a small step towards the independence which was originally part of Jomo Kenyatta's demands. Change, however, had been inevitable; in no sense was the Government yielding to the terrorists. The fight against them continued.

At our peak we had seven companies operating in the Forest and the Reserves. As demands increased for more extra-regimental appointments we were reduced to B, C, I and Support Company (the mobile patrol). Within months we were reduced to only one company which was known as 'Ops' or Operational Company, which was stationed at Narok in Masailand from March, 1955. A company of 6th KAR was stationed at Loliondo on the Tanganyika border. In the event of joint operations between Kenya and Tanganyika this company would come under my command. The object of the exercise was twofold – to prevent the Masai coming under the influence of the Mau Mau and to stop the gangs crossing the border between the two territories.

In fact this did occur in April, 1955, when Mike Higgins's platoon pursued a gang across the border. (There was, of course, no defined boundary.) Tanganyika reported alien bodies over their border and Kenya reacted promptly. The Deputy Governor, Sir Frederick Crawford and the Attorney-General, Sir Eric Griffith-Jones, myself and Ray Nightingale were despatched to Arusha for discussions with Sir Edward Twining, the Governor of Tanganyika.

The meeting was not without its moments of humour as, when the Attorney-General was introduced, Twining greeted him warmly and said: 'We have a Griffith-Jones in Tanganyika – a good fellow. I hope you are a good fellow too!' With that he asked me to accompany him to his office while the two teams of officials got down to business and I could tell him about the military situation. He proved to be a most amusing and generous host. When we returned to the conference, he went through the joint proposals very thoroughly and, when one of his senior staff queried the expense of hiring heavy lorries to transport troops to threatened areas, he said very pointedly: 'Provide the transport or buy a bowler hat.' In his youth he had been commissioned in the Worcestershire Regiment and had served in the 4th Uganda Battalion of the KAR. He was not in the least upset that Kenya forces had invaded his territory and he promised his wholehearted support.

Narok district stretched to the Tanganyikan border, a vast area of steppe and plain with patches of forest and thick bush. The Masai who lived there had once been the most feared fighters in Kenya, but in order to protect Kikuyu women from being carried off by them and to reduce cattle raiding, the Masai had been husbanded into allotted areas, where they lived with their herds in *manyattas* (villages) under their chiefs and headmen. They were unarmed except for long spears; shields were banned and they had little hope of defending themselves against Mau Mau armed with rifles. The morale of the Masai *Moran* (young warriors) was further undermined because, since they were no longer permitted to dip their spears with the blood of an enemy, their initiation to manhood was felt to be incomplete.

At a meeting held in Naivasha in May, 1955, Rift Valley officials, civil police and the military agreed with the Narok District Commissioner and the 'Ops' Commander that selected Masai ought to be armed with shotguns. 350 young *Moran* were eventually selected from volunteers in the Narok and Loita areas to assist the Security Forces. They were divided into groups of fifty and based strategically in especially built *manyattas*, most of them close to bases occupied by the Security Forces. They were paid by the Government and fed by the local headmen. However, it took some time for this process to be completed; but, armed or not, the contribution of the Masai warriors was considerable from the outset. The following comments I made in a secret memorandum at the time:

> The only drawback is that they can keep up a pace for days on end which far outstrips the fastest efforts of the Security troops. Their willingness to follow up gangs has had to be checked . . . In three months there have been eighty-five gang contacts. Eighty of these have occurred at *manyattas* which gangs have attacked and removed cattle. Most have succeeded as the Masai were unarmed, but nevertheless, so swift has been the pursuit that the cattle have been recovered on several occasions and Mau Mau have been killed and wounded by Masai spears.

The same memorandum stressed that, as more pressure was exerted against Mau Mau in the Aberdares, there was an added probability that the gangs would seek shelter in Masai land and that, unless the Masai were properly armed, a serious setback could result.

Eventually many of the Masai were issued with arms and, along with regimental patrols, they ranged into trouble spots and kept the terrorists at bay. By the end of 1955 Mau Mau activity was sporadic and the final race was on to capture the remaining gang leaders, notably Dedan Kimathi and Stanley Mathenge.

Those members of the Regiment not in operational companies were still active in a variety of roles – aerial survey, mapmaking or as custodians of internees, leaders of Kikuyu Guard posts and liaison officers with British Brigade HQ. Our men were also, as previously, attached to the British and KAR battalions. Others spent time back on their farms, some still participating in small pseudo-gang forays. The KPR Air Wing was always on hand but the early aerial sorties with home-made bombs and grenades had been displaced by more mundane tasks: reconnaissance flights, transport duties and so on.

Surrender leaflets had been dropped on known areas of Mau Mau influence and many came in and surrendered. There was the 'Green Branch' surrender scheme, in which the former gang leader General China, captured by Wally Young of Kenreg, agreed in return for his life to negotiate with the forest gangs, encouraging them to surrender. Some, possibly with large prices on their heads, remained in hiding, deep in the forests of the Aberdares and Mount Kenya. Action by Special Police Forces had only one object – to capture or destroy those gang leaders still in hiding. Although a few terrorists were still at large as late as 1960 – and it was not until 12 January of that year that the Governor, Sir Patrick Renison, signed a Proclamation bringing the Emergency to a close – Mau Mau was virtually defeated, and in 1956 the government forces and the loyalists were in the ascendancy and daily those who had taken oaths were wavering. Any association with a gang was fraught with danger, and the vast majority of the Kikuyu were thinking of their future.

I left Kenya in February, 1956, handing over command to Major C. S. Madden (KRRC) on 1 February. By the end of December all fulltime serving members of the Regiment had been released and on 1 January, 1957, the battalion reverted to its Territorial Force status.

There had been much criticism of the way the Emergency was handled. Even after the declaration, action was often slow to follow discussion and conference; critics of the War Cabinet suggested that there were too many senior officers. (By 1955 there were three General Officers – a Commander-in-Chief, a Chief of Operations and a Chief of Staff – besides other staff officers. There was a Deputy Chief of Staff, a colonel/brigadier, with attendant satellites. On the civil side were the Governor, the Legislative Council (LegCo) and the War Cabinet with staff, and Ministry of Defence. The police had a Commissioner and Heads of Departments and Districts, Special Branch, Kenya Police Reserve – in all a larger force than the army. The RAF Harvards and Lincoln Squadron and the KPR Air Wing with Tripacers were under command of the Commander-in-Chief.) Yet many Kenya settlers felt that Nairobi was out of touch and that results were minimal. Some members of the Kenya Regiment agreed and felt that they were not being fully exploited in the field. It is perhaps still permissible to question why no universal call-up of manpower was introduced. There were more able-bodied young men and women out of the forces than there were in them. Some could have been used in community roles, to staff hospitals or to act in pairs as guards on isolated homesteads. A short course in the use of firearms, first aid and wireless procedure would have been all that was necessary, yet this source of support was never tapped.

In spite of the difficulties, however, Mau Mau terrorists were eventually defeated. The commitment of Kenya Regiment members and loyal Kikuyu to this end was especially deep. It was their home country they were fighting for, Europeans and Africans alike. The cooperation which developed between the young Kenyan settlers in the Regiment and the loyal Kikuyu and trackers led to a better understanding between races when the Emergency ended. It showed the way to a peaceful handover to independence and the eventual development of modern Kenya under African leaders. It was an achievement almost unique on the African continent, something that most considered impossible; but, to those involved in the Emergency, this cooperation, which developed between races initially out of necessity, was soon to flourish in goodwill and respect. Thousands of lives had been lost, most of them Kikuyu, but within the eleven years 1952–63 the country was to achieve its independence, and the leader and planner of the revolt was to be the accepted leader and eventual first President of independent Kenya. Few, if any, citizens of the three races in Kenya in October, 1952, could have envisaged that such an event was possible.

18. An RAF Harvard on a sortie over the Aberdares.

19. Sergeant "Stooge" Stocker, later commissioned, on patrol.

20. 1 Company on patrol in the Northern Aberdares.

21. Mike Higgins looking over the Rift Valley.

22. The Adjutant, Captain Roly Guy, returning from a patrol in the Aberdares. Roly later became Adjutant-General.

23. A visit from the CIGS, 1954. *Left to right*: Brigadier John Orr, Field-Marshal Sir John Harding, General Sir George Erskine, the author.

24. The original Tree Tops, 1954. It was burnt down two days after this photograph was taken.

25. The last O Company patrol in the shadow of Mount Kenya.

On 18 May, 1954, the Archbishop of Canterbury laid the foundation stone of the Fort Hall Memorial Church to commemorate the several hundred loyalists who had died fighting against Mau Mau. The Church is close to the old cemetry where Lieutenant Hall is buried who gave his name to the Fort, now Muranga.

CHAPTER 7

PROBLEMS OF COMMANDING
THE REGIMENT

A commander's position is a lonely one and one of the greatest attributes of a successful commander is not to show to others the nightmare and worry that besiege you when weighty decisions have to be made. In an emergency of this sort, there were indeed some desperate decisions to make, some alarming risks to take, some unfortunate incidents to deal with and important principles to uphold – even to the point of resignation. The brandys and soda and gins and tonic in our office until the dawn hours on so many occasions lightened the burden.

It is never easy serving more than one master, but the CO of the Kenya Regiment had several masters – the army hierarchy, the politicians and the civil servants. Frequently the wishes of each differed and it was often extremely tricky trying to satisfy them all. More often than not it was necessary to play one against the other. It was in these sort of trying conditions that the Colonel of the Regiment, Colonel Dunstan-Adams, was such a tower of strength and a wonderful support to us all. A man of great integrity and stature and respected by everyone.

Guy also had to serve his men in a way which a normal Regular Commanding Officer would not be called upon to do. These chaps were not serving just for fun or, as we were, as professionals, but as citizens in uniform wanting to get back to their work on their farms and in their businesses as soon as possible to make some money, and they had to be kept fully occupied and convinced that their job was worth while. This was not always easy to do.

We were blessed in one respect: compared with similar terrorist-type operations today we did not have to contend with the media to the same extent. There were no TV interviews to give, no hounding by the press except on major issues. Thank God, is all I can say. I doubt we would have been as successful as we were had there been much press interest.

These words from my adjutant Roly Guy sum up the situation which faced us. My main concern was for the men of the Regiment, and the strains and pressures under which they had to operate. Many of the older members who had served in the 1939–45 war were continually being posted to vital appointments outside the Regiment, so that younger members with limited experience were holding their posts. Many, too, were not used to the ways of the British Army, and its, to them, top-heavy chain of command. They tended to act by rule of thumb and to cut through any red tape. This could and often did cause some raised eyebrows and the only way of allaying concern was for the CO or Adjutant to be where the Regiment was most active on operations. Our men and their methods were more easily understood by the units of the King's African Rifles and by the civil administration, the Recce Squadron and the Heavy Artillery Battery. The Kenya Regiment men were acutely motivated – it was their country and their livelihood that was at stake.

Our men were also working in pairs in Home Guard posts in the three districts of Kiambu, Fort Hall and Nyeri, besides being with the British and KAR battalions. Leave was given wherever possible but no guard post could be left with only one European and care had to be taken over who was posted to isolated spots as a clash of personalities could prove fatal.

It would have been impossible to exert any control from Nairobi, so, rightly or wrongly, I decided that I must remain in the centre of the operational area where I could keep in touch with political or military problems as they occurred. This ensured that I was in operational command and answerable to GHQ. Quick decisions had to be made which could be contrary to orders, but it was necessary. It also saved a sometimes quite junior officer from a difficult situation. Throughout the Emergency we had many masters, civil and military, and the distance from Nairobi often helped to achieve results which, otherwise, would have been impossible. Communications could break down, which provided good cover until an operation was completed! No commander in the field can ask for advice on what he should do in an unforeseen situation. It was a simple matter of 'Do it' and hope for the best. We had some near shaves but we achieved results and that was all that mattered.

I think it is surprising that there were so few occasions when it was necessary to replace individuals who failed for one reason or another. At times a man was moved; strain and exhaustion caused men to over-react. When reading of the activities of a patrol in search of a gang, with the advantage of air spotting, skilled trackers and a tracker dog, it may sound simple, but that was certainly not the case. Everyone has a limit of endurance and it varies in each man, but take into account also the fluctuations of the weather, the heat of the day, heavy rain storms and the freezing cold at the higher altitudes at night when men have climbed and descended numerous game tracks through thick bush that can tear clothes to ribbons, up and down gulleys, to be charged suddenly by a buffalo, elephant or rhino, or to meet a burst of rifle fire from an unseen foe. Breath becomes short over 10,000 feet and each man carried his rations, sleeping bag, water and ammunition – and damp clothes make the load even heavier. The heat of the African sun can be fierce and there is the added strain, known to all soldiers, of the need for vigilance by day and night, however weary one may be. All movement is in silence, as a voice travels far in the forest. None of the patrol have smoked or washed since before they started and they are on hard tack as only the bare necessities can be carried. All communication has to be by hand signals and each man must control the temptation to talk or stop to relieve himself or sneeze or cough. They are moving in a nightmare world where every bend in a track can produce an ambush or sudden charge of wild game.

The patrol is blind and depends on the skill of the tracker, or that of the dog and handler. One man dozing off – and the altitude can increase that desire – could cause the loss of a man's life and the chance of contacting and destroying the gang will be lost. Evacuation of a casualty is another hazard. It means waiting for the daily and nightly contact with their Pacer 'eyes', a change of plan, or in the worst event the termination of the task. This is the sole decision of the Patrol Commander unless Tactical HQ gives the order to abort. No plane could land in this type of territory and it would be a supreme task to convey a badly wounded man down several miles of track. The medical supplies carried were limited and a fractured limb, loss of blood and shock could prove fatal. Fatigue, both mental and physical, can affect the nerves and in extreme periods of tension can cause hallucinations or loss of sleep when rest is essential. Men can become jumpy and short-tempered and quarrels can start over trivial incidents.

The youth of our soldiers gave them strength and endurance but mentally some reacted in abnormal ways which taxed the forbearance of their companions. Wherever possible, friends were posted to the same patrols but this was not always feasible and any misfit had to be transferred. It was vital for all operational teams to act in harmony and patrol leaders had to develop powers of understanding which could achieve instant obedience in moments of crisis.

After these patrols, which were normal in the operational area, leave was given whenever possible, otherwise, with our manpower always subject to Government demands, rest was limited to routine occupations in the platoon or company HQ after debriefing. It is not surprising that the wilder element frequently caused alarm in the Outspan Hotel, the White Rhino in Nyeri, Philo's Bar in Fort Hall or the hotels, nightclubs and bars of Nairobi. A few eccentrics played Russian roulette, or parents reported that their son was having nightmares and firing at imaginary gangsters in the night. Extreme instances were rare but they caused a headache to Rear Regimental Headquarters on the Ngong Road in Nairobi.

Another contributory factor to the stress suffered by the young soldiers was that, although, when British regiments were posted to Kenya, officers' wives were permitted to live in Kenya, the wives of Kenya Regiment personnel were left alone on their farms. Accommodation was found for British and KAR officers' wives in various townships in whatever area their husbands were stationed. They faced little risk of death or mutilation and they had no land that could be devastated, cattle that might be hamstrung or wells poisoned, nor the loneliness and isolation of their farms. This obviously affected those members of the Regiment who were separated. Releases to rejoin their families were one of the major problems which faced Regimental HQ. Replacements for those released had to be made and it was not done by the Adjutant throwing a dart at the regimental roster, as many suspected! As guards could not be provided for the more remote homesteads, the owner was faced with the alternatives of trusting his staff or recruiting a labour force from another tribe.

This was not as easy as it may sound, as the livestock needed herdsmen and the farms needed those who had been trained as agriculturalists, drivers of tractors or skilled husbandmen. Many lost everything and left seeing a lifetime's work vanish beyond redemption. If anybody deserves commendation for courage and perseverance it is those aged farmers and the wives who carried on despite the danger which was always present. They stood to lose their crops on which their lives depended. Spending a night on an isolated farm in an affected area was an eerie experience: men and women carrying arms, windows barred and doors locked after dark. The house servant could only be let into the living-room at night by unlocking the door and covering him with a pistol. Tragedies did occur despite stringent precautions, as the cook and friend of years could herald a rush by armed terrorists when the door was opened.

Demands on our manpower were the biggest curse of our existence as men were needed for so many extra-regimental appointments. Our men, in the tradition of the Regiment, had to provide leaders, so a young soldier who had been a recruit a few months previously was posted as a sergeant to a British battalion with the task not only of acting as adviser to the Commanding Officer but also to lead a patrol in operations against the terrorists.

Some British battalions never fully understood the mentality of our young men who wore sergeants' chevrons after only six months' service and took responsibility for making decisions without reference to higher authority. Their approach was light-hearted and they did not always show the respect which was customary in a regular battalion. They were civilians in uniform and intended to enjoy life to the full, and needless 'bull' was anathema to them.

There was one occasion when a National Service acting lance-corporal was sent to the 1st Battalion The Black Watch at Naivasha with a sergeant's stripes sewn on his sleeves. The Colonel sent him back to OC Kenya Regiment with the complaint that he had asked for an officer and not an NCO. OC Kenreg gave the matter great thought and, opening the drawer of his desk, he took out a pair of scissors and cut off the three stripes. From the same drawer he produced the two pips of a Second-Lieutenant and fixed them onto the shoulder straps. Within one day, Private acting Lance-Corporal, temporary Sergeant Sydney Moscoff became a Second-Lieutenant in Her Majesty's Forces and he returned to Naivasha with the compliments of his Colonel. Sid was a great wit and, despite

91

his youth, of strong character, and he soon endeared himself to the Black Watch, as had his predecessor from the Kenya Regiment, James McKillop, a Highlander himself and a true eccentric: he always wore Harris tweed and drove a Rolls-Royce loaded with cases of beer with which he was most generous. He grew tea at Sotik and his view of authority was pithy and forthright.

Such men abounded in the Regiment. They were all older than their years due to their environment and the wide open spaces where they had been left to develop on their own. Fergus McCartney, like Sid Moscoff, rocketed to power:

In Field Intelligence one was usually stationed out in the bush with a District Officer and in my case I was initially at Egoji and then at Katheri in Meru. My DO went on leave and I was asked to hold the fort. The next thing I knew I was being pressed to become a DO (Meru Guard) for which post I was accepted. Before long I found myself as a DO (cadet) and started on a new career in the administration. The Emergency slowly faded away and the political war began. Many ex-Kenya Regiment men found themselves coping with far more complex and delicate issues than when they had started off innocently enough thinking it would be 'all over in two weeks'. I rose to the dizzy height of District Commissioner in the Northern Frontier District.

Another amusing story, told by Brian Hawkins shows the initiative of a Kenya Regiment Sergeant:

At one point in the Emergency when the 3rd Battalion KAR had come back off a major operation and it was understood that they would be on rest and not called in for operations. Most of the senior officers rushed off to various places: the company commander to watch the horse races in Nairobi, the adjutant to see his girlfriend in Nanyuki, etc. Unfortunately an urgent message came through from 70 Brigade, calling an 'O' group of all companies and battalions of the KAR for a major sweep being planned for the following week. Sergeant Danny MacCleary of the Kenya Regiment attached to the KAR suddenly found that he was the senior rank in camp. Danny got messages off in all directions to try and warn the officers what was happening but realized that it would be too late for them to get to the 'O' group, so he decided to attend himself. He put a camouflage jacket on over his uniform so that his rank would not show and went along to 70 Brigade HQ. He introduced himself as the representative from 3rd Battalion and of course by this time they were quite used to seeing Kenya Regiment officers in various positions in the KAR battalions, and he said he was deputizing for the battalion commander who was away. During the course of the proceedings, however, it got a little hot and, without thinking, Danny removed his camouflage smock, thus revealing the fact that he was only a sergeant. You can imagine that all the mud possible then hit the fan and there was a major blast to the battalion to explain the absence of any officers!

Not all such men were easy to handle, especially when it was a question of principle or they thought the well-being of their country was being mismanaged. Nearly all had political beliefs but they seldom agreed with each other on any one subject. It certainly added excitement to life but placing individuals together required much thought. This made the life of the adjutant a nightmare, as a misfit could cause trouble when it was essential to retain equanimity, but good humour generally prevailed and, when it did not, cross-postings had to be made. It says much for our young Adjutant, Captain Roly Guy, and the older Assistant Adjutant, Captain Angus MacDonald, who was Kenya-born and wise beyond his years, that between them they kept the peace and yet catered for all demands upon our manpower.

Sometimes men asked for compassionate leave for personal reasons and one I remember was certainly original: a pre-Emergency officer requested a month's special leave. When I asked why his case was exceptional, he stated that 'he had to make a son'. I did my best to keep a straight face and asked for further details. 'Well,' said the applicant, with great emotion, 'I just have to make a son, I need a son and heir.' When I told him that no one could ever have more than the special privilege of fourteen days, and that all I could suggest was that if he could not achieve the desired result in that time he had better try 'a change of bowling', the officer left the office with a heavy sense of doom. (I never heard if he was successful.)

Other cases that were difficult to handle were occasions when a man failed in command and lives were lost through loss of judgment. In one such, which was exceptional, the individual was sent on leave but was told on his return that he had to return to operations and it was up to him to prove himself. This may sound harsh but it was the only way we had in the Regiment – such was the demand for leaders. Most commanders have a belief that a man who lets you down once is always liable to do it again. This I found was not always the case, although in principle I shared that view. In the case I have in mind the NCO concerned proved later that he had outstanding qualities of leadership. At one time or another most soldiers have known a moment of total panic which stops thought and action, but this can be overcome. It is a case of knowing your men and trusting them. If they trust you, they will produce unknown strength just to prove your faith in them. Perhaps I can use the following joke as an analogy: a county captain asked the then captain of the Somerset cricket XI why he had played 'so and so'. 'Why, he can't bat, he can't bowl and he can't field.' 'Well,' replied the great 'Sammy' Woods, 'he's a helluva golfer.'

To the small coterie of men who ran the Regiment was added the Medical Officer and the Quartermaster. All our MOs did us proud. They quickly learned

93

our ways and knew when to turn a blind eye. Between us we shared many secrets when risks had to be taken or a smokescreen used. The greatest loss to the Regiment was our Regimental Padre. Jimmy Gillett's influence was immense. He and his wife Mary had taught many of the men and known them from childhood. Jimmy acted as a buffer; he would settle a problem and prevent any witch-hunt which might have occurred. We all felt a great sense of loss when he departed as there was nobody who could fill the gap. As elder statesman and friend he was a man among men, a Christian gentleman.

Overall I feel sure that what sustained everyone most was the spirit of adventure which motivated our men. There was always a sense of fun close to the surface and a 'damn you, Jack' attitude which was infectious. The only comparison I can think of is the 'Pals' or 'Chums' battalions of the First World War, young men who joined up together irrespective of class, station or education.

On the whole the Regiment had a good press but sometimes a few feathers were ruffled and some sniping was based on erroneous information or exaggerations of misdemeanours. High-spirited behaviour did occur when a few friends went on the tiles after a long spell in the forest. The Military Police were called sometimes but generally the hell-raisers succeeded in reaching safety and any damages were promptly settled the next day. In a few instances some were not so lucky and criminal charges were preferred.

Our sole aim was to 'locate and kill the terrorists', but we never kept score-cards as was the custom with certain KAR and British battalions, a practice which stemmed from Field-Marshal Templer's days in Malaya. Most kills took place high up in the Aberdares and on Mount Kenya where there was little possibility of recording them accurately after an engagement in deep forest and precipitous gulleys and spurs. Blood trails could be followed for a limited time only and were soon obliterated by rain. Badly wounded terrorists could not be brought back to lower altitudes, and the same applied elsewhere in the forest areas. Arms and identification, clothing, letters, etc, were brought back home and any recognized gang leader too if a support team could be sent to an RV.*

* As most of our operations were on a small scale, the number of Mau Mau casualties was also relatively small. the attack on the Othayo police post was an exception in which there were over seventy casualties inflicted on the gang, but, even so, many wounded men may have escaped unseen.

I have read accounts in a Regimental Journal where a bag of over 200 was claimed in the space of a few months, which is ridiculous. Casualties decreased after 1953–4 as the gangs were confined by the mile-strip policy to a hand-to-mouth existence in the forest, cut off from their food carriers. One man complained that he had not received a medal, although he had shot over sixty-nine people, but usually those who did the most damage kept quiet about it. Allowances must also be made for the tendency to exaggerate casualty figures of enemy fighters in order to boost the morale of the people the Security Forces were protecting.

Official figures stated in the Corfield Report up to the end of 1956 are to be found in Appendix III on p. 175.

The Regiment was often puzzled by the attitude of some of the professional politicians who appeared anxious to restrict and control all offensive actions of our ultimately small strike force still active in the field. I am glad to say that these efforts were strongly opposed and the Regiment remained active and under the command of its own CO. General Erskine, while C-in-C, was a tremendous supporter of the Regiment, as was General Hinde. Both understood our unique comradeship and fully committed attitude to destroying all that the Mau Mau stood for.

On the whole we were lucky in our relationship with the World Press and, if at times adverse comments were made, they were not blatantly adverse. Tony Lavers of the Regiment was our local representative with the *East African Standard*; Eric (Ed) Downton, a Canadian by birth, reported for the *Daily Telegraph* and we had an extremely friendly understanding with him when we formed our Tactical HQ at Mweiga. He also covered the activities of Ray Force and the newly formed I teams and I Force. We also had a close association with two well-known author/photographers – George Rodger of Magnum Photos and *Life* magazine and Hank Toluzzi, an American who had covered almost every revolution worldwide.

I had first met George in the Sudan in 1947 when I took him to visit the Kau, Fungur and Niaro bracelet fighters in the Nuba Mountains, about whom later a German lady author published a colour-illustrated book under the impression that she was the first European ever to have visited those hills. He and his wife Jinx were able to cover many of our operations round Karatina, Ragati and the Aberdares, besides interviewing government, military and colonial leaders in Nairobi and covering the Presentation of Colours to the 4th KAR by HM The Queen in 1954.

Hank was attached to Ray Nightingale's company and took many excellent photographs showing what it was like operating in the Forest and Reserves. He also studied the actions of Davo Davidson and his skill with every type of lethal weapon. He was quite oblivious of the risks he took to gain good action shots. Both he and George regarded this as quite a 'normal hazard'. During this period of early 1954 gang contacts were almost continuous and we had frequent visitors among whom were Field-Marshal Sir John Harding, Mr Oliver Lyttelton the Colonial Secretary, Hugh Fraser, General Sir George Erskine the C-in-C, Major-General Cecil Firbank, Victor Pike the Chaplain-General, and General Mike West, an old friend since 1938.

The British government often sent Ministers of State to see for themselves how the rebellion was being handled and to make suggestions for any further political and military action or equipment that might be necessary. Mr Oliver Lyttelton endeared himself to the Regiment by thanking the officers for giving him such an excellent meal at Ragati. The main course was rainbow trout. He asked David Gillett who was second-in-command what fly they had used to land such a beautiful fish. 'No.36,' replied David, without thinking. There was a momentary stunned silence and the great man looked up with a twinkle in his eye and said: 'I see – very good choice too'. Having served in the Grenadier Guards he knew immediately that the special fly was a 36 grenade! The company presented him with a long Kikuyu Chief's Stick, which he said would help him get round the Old Course at St Andrew's when his legs began to fail him. He admired General Erskine's approach to the Emergency, which was more forthright and tougher than Sir Evelyn Baring's.

Oliver Lyttelton insisted that the military should have greater control over the running of the Emergency, which pleased all sections of the administration, police, KPR, the soldiers, local settlers and executive officers like Pat Hughes and Roger Hurt.

Unlike the British or KAR battalions, the Kenya Regiment served under two masters, GHQ and the Kenya Government, and inevitably there were clashes both of authority and direction. Militarily we were under the Army Commander, but the Kenya government was responsible for our administration and for the financial backing for Army hardware. Another factor was that the Kenya settlers who made up the government were all friends, but had widely divergent views on how the country should be run. This came out very forcibly during the Emergency. They all tended to differ from the professional civil servants.

Several former members of the Regiment played a big part in the Government during the Emergency, particularly Michael Blundell, Humphrey Slade, Ray Cuthbert, Tony Swann, Wilfred Havelock, supported notably by Tom Neill, Geoffrey Ellerton and Hugo Dent. The Regiment was loyal to any decision taken, although individuals may have expressed their views forcibly if they met one of their politicians in the Muthaiga or the Nairobi Club where they could be challenged over a decision that seemed somewhat crazy to men who had just returned from a long spell in the Tribal Areas of the Reserves. Many of the politicians were their neighbours and were felt to be equals. Criticism was often unjust but to have satisfied everyone in a country where every citizen is a would-be politician would have been impossible. It is remarkable that animosities among the settlers were so rare.

All Kenyans are outspoken and forthright, and rank and position mean little when they are angry or aggrieved.

The press at times had offended many who, for instance, felt slighted when the Kenya Regiment was only allowed a small proportion of the number allotted to KAR battalions for the visit to England for the Queen's Coronation Parade. This hurt the Colonel of the Regiment, not so much as an affront to him but as an insult to the Regiment.

The Press generally talked about Kenya's regiment, which was a slight misnomer as the King's African Rifles with its Kenya battalions had more claim to be so called. To be more accurate, it was Kenya's European regiment, but that began to change when we first recruited African trackers and ex-KAR askaris. Although in the main the Press gave fair coverage to serving soldiers, some reports were exaggerated or distorted and caused pain to the parents of the individual held responsible for an act outside the law. Pressure often came from the older generation of settlers who said openly that Kenya's regiment was being treated badly and given little credit for the years it had spent trying to crush the insurrection in the swiftest possible manner.

However, the Regiment was much appreciated by many, including Sir Richard Catling, Arthur Young's successor as Commissioner of Police, who writes:

Looking back I have no doubt in my mind that the principal value of the Kenya Regiment to the then government of the country was as a reservoir of capable Europeans accustomed to military training, operations and discipline who knew the country intimately and were fluent in Swahili. Possibly a limited number could also get around in a tribal dialect or two as well but of this I am not certain. And it was from this reservoir that not only the police but other areas of the government service too were able to draw almost at will and straightaway get effective performance from the draftees. I felt pretty strongly in those days [1954/5] that as far as the intelligence side of the business was concerned, performance suffered as a result of the language gap (and to some extent the Regiment helped to fill that gap) . . .

I believe you chaps can say with every assurance that not only did you provide a sturdy contribution to the effectiveness of emergency formations like the Home Guard, police tracker teams, pseudo gangs, etc, but to the established government machine generally. It is in this manner that I judge your great contribution to have been made and I feel that it should most certainly be reflected in the Regiment's written history.

CHAPTER 8

'A RUM LOT'

PETER BROWNE, in one of the stories that follows in this chapter, remembers the remark of a British NCO when he saw how the Kenya Regiment men lived and behaved, which was quite unlike anything he had met before. He turned to another NCO of his regiment and said, 'What a rum lot they are!' This chapter attempts to explain what caused him to make that remark.

Sir Michael Blundell, formerly of the Kenya Regiment and one-time leader of the European community in Kenya and a member of LegCo, was able to take a wide view of the Emergency. He said that the Kenya Regiment had a tremendous name throughout the country and was a key factor in the fight against Mau Mau. He gives some insight into the character of the men who joined up, whom he classifies thus:

1. Those kept as a tough fighting force who could tackle the Mau Mau terrorists in the forests and in the reserves.
2. The specialist element which operated as liaison officers in the field with British battalions and Home Guard posts. In these roles they were excellent and formed the backbone of the administration.
3. Towards the end of the Emergency there were some whose parents thought they were brilliant but they were not so good. They tended to be bolshy and rude and were only too ready to criticize and show off.

The difference in character between the first two types he attributes to the different type of education they received in Kenya's two main secondary schools, the Prince of Wales' School and the Duke of York's School. The Prince of Wales' School, under Mr Fletcher, was a tough school with a stern military outlook and a strong Afrikaans element. This tended to make some individuals contemptuous of Africans, an attitude which amounted to racial arrogance. This criticism is in no way discriminatory against the splendid, healthy and well-disciplined sportsmen that made 'Old Cambrian' teams a match for any club in Kenya. Joining the OTC was obligatory and gave each boy the first groundings in military discipline which was patently apparent when they joined the Kenya Regiment Training Centre for their National Service courses. During the holidays many of the boys who lived 'up country' spent most of their time hunting, so they were brought up with firearms and many were expert trackers and game scouts.

The other boys' school, the Duke of York's, also in Nairobi, which started later than the Prince of Wales' School, was more polished and enlightened in its outlook and more emphasis was put on academic subjects and the humanities. The school did have sports teams and a cadet force but the type of boy who went there had a more mellow character. This in no way infers that its alumni were less sturdy, but their outlook was wider and the young men were better mixers. This was especially useful in a country of mixed races.

When it came to selection from within the Regiment with special reference to the appointments to KG posts, the selection board chose young men who could work well with the Africans, lead without resort to rough methods and generally build up a fine team spirit. It was essential too that they got on with the District Officers and the police with whom they were working. They needed something extra – cool brains and nerves of steel – and it was a real test of leadership to train and lead members of the Kikuyu Guard.

They were in no way inferior to those tough extroverts who were needed by the operational companies and Special Forces. These were outdoor types who were accustomed to act on their own initiative and who hit or shot first and argued afterwards.

Brigadier Donald Cornah, Commander of the 70th East African Brigade, writes:

The KR had a dual role, operating as company and detachment patrols, many used on special tasks and deep penetration work. By reason of their local knowledge and a spirit of cheerful 'have a go' they were able to dominate their operational areas to a degree not often found in regular units with their more formal operations. This is not to say that the Nelson blind eye had not to be used at the Brigade HQ from time to time!

Much of the less glamorous work fell to the KR: serving as guides, liaison officers, interpreters, etc, with British troops and KAR units. In my view these KR men were vital to the conduct of the whole operation. As an officer-producing unit, KR had a large number of men with leadership of a high order. A strong feeling for Kenya and its life led all ranks to feel deeply involved in the need to win the contest in the Colony.

Though details must naturally have faded, I remember the KR spirit as being on a par with that of the RAF pilots in Britain so that they gave one the feeling of hope and pride, something all too often not to be found in other organizations. A cheerful disregard of danger could result in a lack of military precautions at times. I remember once going to meet a KR patrol coming out of the forest. I found them just clear of the forest awaiting transport. The only sentry or lookout I could see was a Samburu tribesman leaning on his spear. He was picking his teeth with a twig and took no notice of me. I was moved to remind the patrol leader of the need to be alert even out of the forest and at the end of a patrol. The leader grinned cheerfully and said, 'Never mind, Brigadier, we are hellish alert at night!' I recall laughing to myself and often used this phrase afterwards!

Another picture in my mind is that of an inspection of a KR party drawn up with some formality in a forest clearing. The right marker was a splendid young man (a former Guardsman) [Peter Browne] in full jungle order standing to rigid attention. His rear rank file was the smallest and most wizened tracker I had ever seen, armed with an assortment of spears and a bow with variously assorted arrows. He held himself with a natural dignity notwithstanding. The contrast was so vivid it was impossible not to smile. While the Guardsman remained stern-faced as tradition demanded, the tracker smiled in return and his expression clearly said; 'Bloody silly, all this standing in line, but he (pointing to his huge companion) likes it, so I go along with him.'

After so many years, memory tends to fade but it was an exciting time – alarms, conferences, settlers, District Officers, inspections, raids, flights with KPR pilots (sometimes 'well-fortified'), fights with HQ, visits from MPs (some of whom thought the troops shot Africans just for fun), briefings, policemen, mountains and dust. One never stopped, it seemed. A good deal of laughter and much good company among a wide variety of folk caught up in the rebellion.

The men of the Regiment were high-spirited and often thoughtless of the feelings of others, but all were imbued with a close comradeship which activated their lives. Most of them were brought up in Kenya, the land their parents had helped to cultivate and civilize, and they had learned to live with the African, without whose help nothing could have been achieved. Not all were as considerate as they should have been but it was largely a difference of culture. When they enlisted in the Regiment it was akin to joining a club of which they were all members by birth and education.

Sid Moscoff writes:

Now I realize that the Regiment went through a lot of serious and tragic incidents especially through the Mau Mau days but . . . I also know that the majority of the hardcore, Kenya-born, Kenya-bred, strong-in-the-arm, weak-in-the-head chaps who served thoroughly enjoyed every minute of the

100

adventure, which it truly was – let's face it. I am sure . . . that the unique *esprit de corps* which us Kenyans enjoyed stemmed from our school days. Certainly between 1936 and 1950, when there was only a handful of primary and high schools in East Africa. For instance, most of the chaps I knew in the KR I had grown up with from kindergarten days and we became great *rafikis* [friends] when we 'graduated' from the Nairobi Primary to the Prince of Wales' School and eventually found salvation in the KR!

I can tell you that when the Rhodesian training scheme started, although it was classified under the Conscription Act, most of the chaps couldn't volunteer quickly enough to get away from the bull of civvy street. We all wanted to recapture our good old schooldays, and some of the chaps who became prematurely married (I know three who were married at the Prince of Wales' during the hols!) needed a break! I assure you that none of us ever regretted the decisions we made and left the Regiment feeling a lot more confident and mature! We regarded our experience in the Regiment as part of our education and not as a damn chore and I reckon that this accounts for the difference between KR chaps and other volunteers in TF regiments. However, I stand corrected as I met similar hardcore Pommies when I was with the Queen's Royal Rifles in the UK.

Also bear in mind that a lot of inspiration and encouragement was given to the chaps by our equally wild fathers who pioneered East Africa between 1900 and 1920. My dad, for instance (the first 'Vulgar Bulgar' to emigrate to Kenya in 1921), was delighted when I volunteered.

Rightly or wrongly I also think about our 'enemies', the Kenya-born Mau Mau *watu* (natives) who were also entitled to fight for their particular causes and beliefs. While I was seconded to the KAR I was very conscious of the deep inner feelings of the average black soldier/askari who was very confused with the entire situation. This was prevalent when I was briefly involved with the Home Guard in Meru and Fort Hall. I am sure that a lot of us KR chaps in similar situations had a lot of soul-searching to figure out when we considered the future of the beloved land of our birth. I also relate all this with the Rhodesians and Zimbabweans and the same psychological situations they must have endured during their war. It concerns me deeply how the South African situation will resolve itself.

The companionship which Sid Moscoff mentions was reinforced by the fact that men joined the company based on their own area and throughout the Emergency individuals served alongside their neighbours, either in the company or on secondment to other units. This gave an added feeling of strength and security which was not matched in other units. The same rule applied to platoons, which were based on towns within the company boundaries. Throughout the development of Kenya the settlers tended to remain on the farms where they had originally settled and the tradition of friendship among them was a living factor

101

within the Regiment. This had been maintained in peacetime during weekend camps and the annual camp in the Ngong Hills. The selection of leaders was made by the men themselves and was supported by Regimental HQ. Rank and promotion were given on a unique basis – 'an officer was only favoured amongst equals'.

Jock Rutherfurd 'was born and raised on a Kenya farm, which in those days had far more wild animals running round than domestic – anything from elephant to jackal! I don't think it would be easy to beat a boyhood spent with a rifle, a horse, a couple of hands and endless Africa.' He left school just after the end of the war and, as there was no OCTU in Kenya at the time, he 'decided to go on trying my luck in the UK and climbed on a troopship that was taking war-weary soldiers from the Far East back to England'. He spent eighteen months in the ranks, went to Eaton Hall and served in Europe for a while. On leaving the army he took on odd farming jobs 'to learn how they went about it', then bought, 'from an army salvage dump in Germany, a four-wheel drive, 15-hundred-weight Dodge truck' for £125 and, with a friend from Kenya, Ulrich Mittelberg, and a serving officer from the Gunners, Christopher Deverell, eventually drove back to Kenya. It took them three months, and was 'a great trip'.

He continues:

After having had recent service in the UK with the regular army there, the Kenya Regiment was a totally different kind of unit: it was very informal off the parade ground, but it worked. It was a regiment of professionals in their own backgrounds at home, whatever their rank, yet everybody got on perfectly. If you wanted the help of an architect or a veterinarian or a chief engineer you could be sure you'd find one standing around pretty near. I can well remember meeting, often working, with regular soldiers from Britain, who couldn't understand this at all, but we also got on very well with them. I can well remember taking a patrol up the Aberdares one day and we came across a party of British sappers who were building a track up the mountain. They were using a massive American bulldozer – a D6 type of thing – and it had run out of steering gear or something; it was going round in circles and they didn't know what the hell to do with it as they had no experience of the machine. One of the platoon commanders with me was a chap called Bill Fawcett whose background I knew to be an earthmover in a big way. He looked just like any other who'd spent three days on patrol in the wet and the mud like the rest of us. I called him and told him what the problem was and he took one look at this massive monster and asked for a screwdriver. This was duly produced and he flipped open a hatch on the side of the machine and turned something or made some adjustment inside, threw the hatch back and off the thing lumbered in a straight line! We left a bunch of astonished-looking sappers in the middle of the track.

While with 4th KAR at Fort Hall, I often took out shooting parties after

102

guineafowl or game on the Coles Plains across the Tana River. On one occasion I had agreed to take half a dozen British officers from 39 Brigade, who had brought out their own shotguns and were used to the precision attacks made on pheasant and partridge coverts in England. With twenty or so KAR Askaris as beaters – they always love doing this sort of thing – we found a pack of thirty-odd guineafowl. On the open plains, with no dogs, guineas run like hell and the only thing to do is to leg it after them as of course in the best of British traditions you should be half-starving before shooting the bird on the ground. After half a mile or so, the birds took off and landed in a patch of bush about half the size of a football field. I said, 'Right chaps, we've got 'em. All we have to do is to quietly surround this patch of bush. When everybody is in position I'll fire a shot, the birds will come out and the shooting starts.' I duly fired and in six different directions out shot six buffalo! As there wasn't one actually coming at me, I was able to stand back and enjoy the hilarious scene involving twenty-five fit men striving for Olympic records! So far as I know no one got to see a guineafowl, though in fact the birds had flown, and luckily no one had tried birdshot on a buffalo!

The character of the 'white hunter' formed the centre of the film *Mogambo* made in Kenya in 1953. Freddie Seed was billeted in Nanyuki at the Airfield Camp where Clark Gable and Ava Gardner and their camera crew teams were staying. They were allowed to use the Mawingo Hotel (now the Kenya Safari Club) on an honorary membership basis and were up there for dinner and drinks most evenings. He writes:

One evening I was at the bar with Bob Parke (who committed suicide later in Thomson's Falls), John Dugmore and one or two others. Also at the bar were several chaps just out from England, working as camera crew for the Gable/Gardner film. These fellows were really anti Kenya settlers, yet had only been in the country a week or two. One of them, particularly talkative and nasty, said to me: 'You chaps deserve all you are getting. The blacks should murder you all. I have no sympathy for you! You fellows have taken all they have and treated them like slaves . . .' etc. Quite an argument was going on when Guy walked by, probably deliberately. He stopped behind me, listened for a few seconds, and said: 'Throw him in the duckpond, Freddie, go on, throw him in the duckpond – he deserves it!' With that remark he walked on into the lounge to his party. I looked at Parke and the others and I could see we all agreed so I said; 'Come on chaps, grab the bastard.' We did this and lifted the Pommie up. He made a hell of a noise and cursed and swore, calling us bloody colonialists etc. I hit him to shut him up but he got my right thumb in his mouth and bit through it with his eye teeth. He would not let go and as the others carried him, I followed by 'the rule of thumb' so to speak, also yelling blue murder! At the pond, just outside the main bar of the hotel, I forced his mouth open with my left hand and, as we shouted; 'One, two, three', we tossed him into the water amongst the lilies and turtles and he landed with a splash and lost his glasses and was still shouting when we left him and went back to finish our drinks! Ava Gardner lodged a complaint with the management that her cameraman had been badly beaten up by those 'barbarian soldiers'. Gable, I heard, thought it a hell of a joke! Anyway, after that none of the movie crowd would dispute with us at the bar.

Freddie Seed himself was, like all of the others, able to converse on friendly terms, in Swahili with the Africans, as is witnessed by his other tale:

I was walking in the lines of the Airfield Camp at Nanyuki, when I heard the drone and wail of bagpipes. I decided to see the players so walked round a few of the wooden huts without coming across anything. At one hut I was challenged by one of the artillery battery askaris. The bagpipes were still playing and I listened and said to the askaris: *'Wapi Kinanda?'* ('Where's the music?'). He replied *'Sinji, Effendi, lakini hii nyama gania anapiga keleli mingi sana?'* ('I do not know, Sir, but what kind of animal is it that makes such a noise?') I replied: *'Hii, hapana nyama, hii ni ngoma ya* Black Scotch' ('It is not an animal, that is the music of the Scottish Regiments – called in Kenya Black Scotch'). The askari came up in his greatcoat and slouch hat and replied *'Mazuri, Effendi, lakini hawa* Black Scotch *analia sana. Allah!'* ('OK, Sir, but these Black Scotch are very noisy. By God!')

Edwin Bristow tells another story which shows that the Kenyan settlers were not generally arrogant and thoughtless towards the Africans:

The rules and regulations in those days, despite our protestations, prevented any bonus or anything for our trackers. So Ray and I mortgaged our pay for two months and with the connivance of all the chaps we managed to get this cash and had a little session outside the drill hall with the trackers and let them go two months before we actually packed up.

I had an old tracker from Marilal, a Morioni, and when we gave him his pay, he sat there with a face as long as your arm and said: 'No well, next time ... The first time, when the Queen asked me to come, I came. Next time she'll have to write to me because I'm not bloody well coming for nothing.'

Due to another hiccup in the rules, not one of their medals was available to give them. I was instrumental the following year in ensuring that everyone could be presented with his medal.

Michael R. Kemp (now the Reverend) was posted to the Intelligence Corps based at the Special Branch SIB Offices in Nairobi for work in gathering and collating Intelligence reports. He says:

I was involved in no deeds of bravery or daring such as Francis Erskine's lot were. One thing I felt pleased about was that some of the Mau Mau prisoners, whom I helped to interrogate while with the Intelligence Corps at the Special Branch HQ, later became my clients in the legal practice in Nairobi where several ex-Regiment people became partners (including J. D. M. Silvester, M. L. Somen, W. R. McA. Spence and myself). Among names that might be widely recognized who (through their companies) became clients of our firm, was Muraya Mucheru, the Number 3 to Dedan Kimathi, who was captured (if my memory serves me) in about January, 1956, and later came to Nairobi for interrogation. Both he and other ex-prisoners evidently trusted me personally and our firm both to understand them and to represent them effectively and honestly. Or perhaps they just got a 'kick' out of employing their ex-captors!

Another who shows sympathy with the predicament of the Africans is Michael Tetley, whose family came from South Africa. He himself was born in Nairobi. He joined the Regiment from the Training Centre in Southern Rhodesia when he was posted to A Company of 23rd KAR and promoted Second-Lieutenant in February, 1954. While serving with this battalion he and Bob Campbell of the Regiment engaged General Batu Batu's gang near Ragati. Batu Batu was killed but Mike was blinded in action. One of his askaris stood over him after he was wounded and saved his life. Since then his life-story has been a saga of courage.

After St Dunstan's, which taught him another way of living, he has been a practising physiotherapist, healing the infirmities of others when his own wound could not be healed. He is happily married and his wife has been a wonderful help and companion. To prove that blindness is not the end of life he went on a walking tour in the Himalayas and he and an Asian friend cycled the three hundred and twenty miles from Nairobi to Mombasa through the game parks. He attends our annual reunion every year in London, accompanied by his guide dog.

He believes that one of the causes of Mau Mau was that

if you bring African men from the reserve into Nairobi to work for whites, and they can only get home for three weeks in a year, this must break up the family unit. The men in Nairobi will look for prostitutes, the *bibi* [wife] on the reserve will be frustrated and the children will have no father to discipline them, a potential ground for trouble, and this was exploited. The British government should have known that the breaking-up of a family unit causes trouble. They haven't learnt yet, because the permissive society in the UK is breaking up the family unit and this will lead to trouble.

He remembers one occasion when two platoons of A Company were chasing Mau Mau down towards the Sagana power station:

105

I took over the wheel because I knew that the bridge across the river near the big waterfall was only made of two steel girders – one to take each wheel. When I came to the bridge we slowed down and went straight across. Boet de Bruin, the other platoon commander, also of Kenreg, looked at the askaris after we had crossed and said they all looked paler! After the action, when we returned to the bridge, all Boet's askaris jumped out.

For his gallantry and leadership in action, Mike was awarded the MBE. Every year, watching the old comrades march past the Cenotaph I pick out his tall, bare-headed figure in the ranks of the men and women of St Dunstan's.

A veteran of the Regiment whose courage was of a quite different kind was Davo Davidson, who was a PSI with Charlie Broomfield. He was born in Australia in about 1898. He went to sea as a fireman when a young man and his nose was flattened by another fireman with a shovel. Soon after this he jumped ship in San Francisco. He lived in the Wild West for some time, where he was befriended by a sheriff who taught him to shoot. At some time he drifted on to Chicago, where, so I was told,

he became a bodyguard to Al Capone, the notorious gangster. He once had a shoot-out with one Dapper Dan Durea. He said that D. D. Durea wore a large shiny belt buckle which gave him an excellent aiming mark. Davo himself never wore his belt buckle in the front, but over his hip. After killing Durea by using the buckle as target, Davo moved to the UK and joined the Cheshire Regiment as a Regular soldier. He was seconded to the 4th (Uganda) Battalion of the KAR and promoted to Regimental Sergeant-Major. He was a noted army boxer.

Charlie Broomfield first met him in Uganda in 1940 before Davo became CSM in the Kenya Regiment at Eldoret. Charlie was the RSM. After the war Davo joined the Labour Department of the Kenya government and gave many exhibitions of trick shooting. He was a showman and a brilliant shot with pistol, two pistols at once, rifle or sub-machine gun. He looked like a stunted oak tree with heavy beard and the cold pale eyes of a killer.

On the outbreak of the Emergency he soon made a name for himself as a 'free-lance' member of the Security Forces in pursuit of gangsters in the forest areas. His methods were far from orthodox, but they were successful – perhaps partly because he looked like a terrorist himself.

Nothing he did was conventional and he possessed an extraordinary instinct for danger. On one occasion I was driving in my Land Rover from a visit to one of our company forts on a spur of the Aberdares. The track was through dense bush with large trees on either side, where every bend was liable to be ambushed. Suddenly he whispered to me, 'Slow down and stop'. This I did. His automatic was across his knees, his pistol on his waist belt. 'Someone is watching us, don't move.' For what seemed a long time, although it was probably only half a minute, his eyes searched the ground ahead. The next moment, without appearing to move, he put a long burst into a fig tree about thirty yards ahead on his side of the road. A man crashed to earth from the branches some twenty feet above ground. A rifle fell with him and he was very obviously dead. He was no doubt a look-out posted by a gang in the vicinity. My wireless operator reported back to the company post we had just left but, beyond this and searching in the immediate vicinity, there was little we could do but continue our journey taking the body with us for possible identification. This is just an example of Davo's capability.

When General Erskine ordered Davo to seek out and destroy the gangs, Davo asked for members of the Regiment to join him. Shortly afterwards while on patrol searching for Dedan Kimathi, with Jock Rutherfurd of the Regiment commanding D Company of 4 KAR, Davo was not so lucky. He took three bullets, one of them being deflected into his groin as he was wearing an early model of a 'flak jacket'. He spent some time in hospital but recovered. He carried the normal hard-track rations issued to our men, such as biltong, but always added a bag of eggs. This ended in tragedy once, as a patrol of Ops Company he had accompanied came out of the forest and sat down for a meal. Davo placed his eggs, which he carried in his old knapsack, down and moved away to talk to me, the company commander. It had been a tiring night and the patrol sat down to eat. Micky Fernandez threw himself down on the first dry tussock he could find, in so doing flattening Davo's eggs. It was one of the few occasions when Davo was at a loss for words and it did not help matters much when Micky suggested that he could at least scramble them!

When he came out of hospital he was posted to the Battle School at Nanyuki as an instructor as his wound had shaken even his cast-iron frame. He taught unarmed combat and how to kill and he was an expert in both. It is said that he met his match once. It was his custom to call out a member from his class and use him as a guinea pig – this is a normal procedure in the Army. On one occasion he selected a very young officer, very thin and bespectacled, of the King's Own Yorkshire Light Infantry and told him to walk ahead of him. Davo winked at the squad and, following silently behind his victim, he suddenly threw a neck lock around him, only to be hurled several feet in the air on to the ground. The young officer said : 'I hope I didn't hurt you.' This was too much for Davo, who, noting the grinning faces of the others, said rather foolhardily, 'We'll try another approach – walk ahead of me.' Again Davo, more warily this time, stalked his prey, but again he was seized and rendered immovable on the ground. This story was told to me by John Humphreys of the Regiment who was another instructor at the School, under Major Keith Denniston of the Seaforth Highlanders, attached to the Black Watch. From then on, Davo had a very hearty respect for the second Lieutenant. I wish I knew his name and what happened to him!

Davo died some years back. He was a splendid chap to have with you in a tight spot and like most tough men he did not pick fights unless provoked, when he could be deadly.

It was the regimental consumption of eggs which occasioned the remark of the Royal Signallers (near link to the brigade) reported by Peter Browne:

'Rum lot, this mob.'
    'Yes, they get two eggs each for breakfast every day.' This was not surprising as not only were the local settlers very generous but Corporal Kruger (i/c rations) went shopping in Nairobi once a week. But even then the food only lasted three or four days – he shopped for the best at Erskine and Duncan, the Fortnum and Masons of Nairobi – so we had to live off the land for the rest of the time. I remember 'Lofty' Reynolds eating an enormous breakfast of eggs, bacon, chops, toast and five – or was it six – treacle puddings. Not far away was Dawson's Farm which had a dam full of unfished trout and a detail used to fish it most evenings. Once we fed an entire company: David Gillett, Peter Roller and 'Kiko' King brought home 114 trout after two hours' fishing.

It is possible that their fishing methods were similar to those used by men of the Regiment in other stories, such as the one of Oliver Lyttelton's trout, caught with a 'No.36' fly. Captain R. L. Plenderleith reports his initiation to this method:

My 2 I/C was Gerry Adams who asked me to go fishing with him and a fellow officer called Stan Bleazard. We jumped into the back of the Land Rover. 'Funny,' I thought, 'No tackle,' and imagined some hut on the river having it. We de-bused way up the mountain and made our way to the river. We arrived at this large pool and the next thing I knew these two bums had thrown grenades into the water and, yes, I was the one to get into the freezing pool to recover the trout. I've never been so cold in my life.

Another member who had a way with explosives was Captain Sam Weller, Kenya-born and posted to Mogadishu from the Regiment with Major 'Rouse' Barkas, who describes some of his adventures:

Sam Weller was an explosives expert to whom I once rather carelessly suggested that he boobytrap the company safe to discourage pilfering. One night a loud bang was heard and the sentry on the company lines, seeing smoke issuing from the commander's office, dashed inside where he found an askari and a wrecked safe. The unfortunate askari had lost a hand and most of the company pay was burning amongst other wreckage, including important files which were charred cinders. The thief had to be discharged after treatment as a one-handed soldier is of no military use and the ensuing Court of Inquiry decided that Captain Weller may have shown excessive zeal. This did not unduly chasten Sam. One evening afterwards he suggested to me that we should go fishing: he had hired a boat and we were to try gelignite as depth charges to bring up the fish. He had, he said, placed the explosives in a safe place ready for use the next morning.

So that was fine. We went to bed and never gave it a thought. At half past two in the morning there was the most awful explosion. I leapt out of bed and staggered outside and there was the whole sky absolutely red, things flying about in all directions and I stood there while Weller came out, also with not many clothes on and we looked at all these terrible things going on and eventually decided that we should go down and look a bit closer. We went down to my company lines – but they weren't there any more! The whole of the office block, the stores, the whole place had completely disappeared. I said to Weller: 'What on earth do you think's happened?' He coughed two or three times and eventually said; 'It must be something to do with that gelignite.'

The company storeman had evidently put the box under the head of his bedboards and struck a match on it and that was the end of him and of all the company arms, binoculars, compasses, papers and documents. Nobody seemed to mind about the Storeman – but they all said: 'Well he was a bloody awful chap, any way' – and after all the Courts of Inquiry and so on, 'Tricky Trev', the Commanding Officer, whom nobody liked either, got a severe reprimand for not having made adequate arrangements for the storage of explosives in his camp and Weller and I got off virtually scot-free!

There's another story about Weller, same time, same place. I had a little Topolina car, one of those little Fiats, and on this occasion Sam and I had been having a drink and decided it was time we went down to Paolo's for a good pasta. I switched the car on and started it, but nothing happened. So Weller got out, lifted the bonnet and – Good Lord – all the plug leads had been pulled off, the distributor nicked: so that was it! Weller, being a slightly hot-tempered fellow, grabbed the first bloke he saw and gave him the most awful belt in the jaw. The result was, the car didn't work and there was a bloke lying on the floor absolutely out for the count. We left them, and went down to Paolo's for a very good dinner. Much later, the car was still there, the bloke on the floor had gone, so we went to bed.

Next morning we went to find the whole battalion on parade. The Second-in-Command, Peter Chapman (60th Rifles), was officiating, so Sam and I went up and gave very smart salutes, and said: 'Sorry we're late, Peter, but we didn't know there was a battalion parade this morning.'

He said; 'Well, there shouldn't be really, but there was a terrible flurry in the town last night. The Luwali of Mogadishu had his jaw broken and he seems to think it's something to do with us chaps so we've got an identification parade to see if we can find the culprit. Funnily enough, it happened very near your house.'

109

I looked at Sam. Sam looked at me and said to Peter, 'I think, Sir, you can dismiss the parade because I'm the chap that did it.'

It ended up by Sam having to go to Mogadishu hospital, chat up the Luwali, say how very sorry he was, drink a lot of mint tea and everybody parted the best of friends. So once more, Weller and Barkas, having made the most monumental cock-up, succeeded in getting away scot-free!

Ray Mayers, commander of 'Ray Force', was a tea planter on the Southern Highlands before he joined the Regiment, but his extravagant behaviour lost him his plantation as well as his medical career for which he had begun to study at Cambridge. He and his wife Helen did various jobs, including running the Namanga River Camp, with George Adamson as the professional hunter, and helping to run a bakery for Joe Torr. It was then that he joined the regiment and was accepted, he thinks, 'on the strength of being able to cope with Dunstan-Adams's mount during a field day'. When war was declared, he was posted with his platoon to Nanyuki and having been kept waiting on the station until 23.30 hours by Colonel 'Sweetie' Barkas, the men were freezing cold.

Being Kenya settlers and the sons thereof, they had become quite outspoken to Major Hugo Tweedie of the Scots Guards which led to [them] being referred to at a later date as a bunch of 'rebellious reach-me-downs' by 'Blood on the Bayonet' Colonel Butt, at the first OCTU where [they] were sent to get some crash training in the principles of war.

The Regular Imperials were a bit dismayed at first by these 'bloody colonials' and it took a couple of months for them to realize that the old Regular Army (overseas) routine was in for some impromptu changes! One of these was when D Company of 5th KAR agreed to host a party to put the Wajir Yacht Club,* 'on ice' for the duration of the hostilities. I was detailed to organize the 'Q' side of the party. Some thirty cases of beer were laid in plus five cases each of whisky, gin and brandy, topped up with port, vermouth and sherry. Thirty-five members of the Squadron replied to the 'Storm Signal' and we expected some fifty guests on top of D Company personnel and other army ancillary units. We had Silver Jane, who flew a DH Moth on communications, and who agreed to transport any essential requirements that might arise. The party steering committee reckoned that we had underestimated the amount of whisky that would be consumed and it was decided to signal Flight Nairobi (Jane's official designation) and instruct her to supply two cases of whisky. Accordingly I despatched a signal over the army network: 'Flight Nairobi stop expedite urgently two cases whisky.' (At this time a member of the Shell Company, Kenya, had been installed as OC Cyphers.) After further discussion by the party steering committee it was decided that fifteen cases of hard liquor would suffice the hard-drinking Squadron members but it was thought that a

*The nearest sea is over two hundred miles away.

110

couple of FANYs would enliven the occasion. Accordingly I sent a further signal over the army network: 'Flight Nairobi stop reference previous signal stop need women.' This signal was not understood by the officer on duty at Flight Nairobi who passed it on to Cyphers thinking it was some pre-arranged code. Major Oak-Rind (ex-Shell and later awarded the OBE, I suspect for his massive decyphering of this intricate signal, and hereafter referred to as 'Oh, Christ') took three days trying to break down the hidden cypher before meeting Jane accidentally in Muthaiga Club, who cleared up the matter on the spot.

Unfortunately, the whole mystery had been sent to Army HQ as Cyphers thought it might have some bearing on important operational dispositions.

The Squadron party was a huge success, some eighty members and guests attending – including the GOC and his brother Dicker, the OC Intelligence! During the course of the evening some fisticuffs occurred between myself and Captain Ronnie Marsh which resulted in both parties acquiring a bloody gravel rash which could not be eradicated by morning when we were both summoned before the GOC. I had to explain how it came about that the army signals network was used for scurrilous code messages for women which had caused a three-day interruption of other pressing decyphering, and Captain Marsh had to answer for passing the signal for transmission. The GOC threatened me with relegation to sergeant and a return to the Kenya Regiment for further training, but on viewing the state of both our faces decided to close the incident with a severe reprimand.

Soon afterwards, during a crash course of instruction at Nakuru, Mayers, in a rugger match between the Colonials and Imperials, had all the muscles in his right leg torn, from his ankle to his thigh, and was in hospital for six months. Leaving hospital in late 1941 with his leg still in plaster he returned to the 5th. 'The CO was furious that I returned in such an immobilized condition and he immediately sent me off with Hector Munro, Stiffy Lees, 'Pud' Pudsey and Bertie Shields with the accompanying Kenya sergeants to form two new battalions at Bombo, Uganda (3/4th and 4/4th KAR).' Returning to the action, I was sent on recommendation by Humphrey Slade, to take over the military administration in Somalia 'where I . . . became notorious for building squash courts on all the stations to which I was posted, especially at Kismayu where I used the half-demolished Swedish Church under protest from Padre Cheeseman and Bishop Crabbe, who had me transferred to the Ogaden.'

In 1948 Mayers rejoined the Regiment as a private – 'after some undignified gambolling and jumping over chairs in the Mayor's parlour'. He was soon promoted Captain i/c of B Company while Neville Cooper who had joined up with him was made full lieutenant and platoon commander.

'After some time' Mayers was seconded to 49th Brigade where he served Brigadier George Taylor at Nakuru, which Brigade was then posted to Nanyuki.

111

Once when the Brigadier was giving out his orders for an operation, he placed his hand dramatically over the map which was on an easel, stating; 'The gang is here!' whereupon a member of his staff, Captain 'Pongo' Thornton, leapt to his feet, crying 'Hold it, Brigadier', and he outlined the Brigadier's large hand in blue chalk. The area denoted covered half the Aberdares and Mount Kenya and part of the Reserve!

Helen Mayers, Ray's wife, was a true Kenya settler. He recalls:

While I was liaison officer at Nakuru, in the early hours of one morning a signal came from a Brigade patrol saying: 'Mayers Farm raided. 19 Mau Mau killed.' I immediately went up to the farm and passed the farm truck on its way down with the dead bodies in the back. I found my wife and daughter very happy and proud of themselves, with a patrol of Kenya Police Reserve encamped there. My wife had got word of Mau Mau moving in the sawmill area and had been able to warn Mike Hughes of the KPR who had organized an ambush with great success. I was told that all necessary precautions had been taken and I could return to the Brigade.

When 'Ray Force' was formed 'The members . . . used their own vehicles which varied from a Rolls Royce (Captain James McKillop, Nyeri), a Bentley (another settler), to a common or garden farm vehicle. The architecture to the fortresses they had to defend was equally varied, some being built on the lines of Scottish castles and others palisaded crofts.' 'Ray Force HQ was based at Fort Hall together with HQ 4th KAR (Colonel Nott) and considered that hospitality given by other units of the army and administration should be returned.' They were also asked to accommodate visiting journalists and on one occasion they organized a tour of the Force's area of combat for one journalist, followed on his last night by a party at Ray Force HQ.

Everything was done that could give him cause to take back glowing reports of our hard living conditions etc. The wife of a certain administrative officer, whose husband happened to be away at the time, agreed to provide the banquet . . . She really put up a very fine feast. The mess dinner was a very formal affair and the loyal toast was drunk, cigars were lit and then an unrehearsed show was put on, entirely unbeknownst to the mess president. The lady concerned suddenly appeared in the nude and did a wonderful Salome dance on the table. Regrettably the journalist made more of this function in the widely read scandal sheet than any other report on our military prowess in the forest. I was asked to explain how this came about!

Of the members of Ray Force the outstanding pair of tearaways were Clutsom and Duffy who found a Nairobi lawyer in their prohibited area. When arrested he claimed that he was as good as any white man. They produced him in court the following morning in a jock strap with his body whitewashed. The magistrate took great exception to this. Luckily the Court House was in a distant part of Fort Hall district and Clutsom and Duffy were moved quickly to Nev Cooper's I Force, where Nev was told to keep them permanently in the forest.

Most of the outposts were very strictly commanded, however, and at one

the two Allen and Englebreght brothers were noted for their disciplinary measures. When they wanted information from their captives they said 'Here's a boxing ring: you must get into it and box each other. Five two-minute rounds and if we think that you are not fighting hard enough we will come in and fight.' They always decided to tell. Englebreght and Allen taught all the Kikuyu their boxing.

Mayers' old friend Douggie Collins, DO, was not one to miss an opportunity:

When stationed between Timau and Meru – 10,000 feet, bitterly cold, with the elephant raiding all the *shambas* in the forest that had been deserted by people running from the Mau Mau – Douggie picked up all the neglected potatoes and sold them and built his fort into a palace known as Potato Castle. He had a fireplace twelve feet deep which he would sit around with his guests each night drinking home-made potato gin.

When I (the author), accompanied by the C-in-C, inspected the Ray Force Company as Colonel of the Regiment, my convoy was greeted with a mock battle against some supposed *shifta* (bandits), with Bren guns, 2-inch mortars etc. We were taken aback completely and a few hard words were issued against Ray Force for not forewarning me!

After the Mau Mau were cleared out of the Kipipiri area of the Aberdares, 49 Brigade was moved to Nairobi to instigate Operation Anvil, really the last major operation of the Emergency. The story Peter Higginson tells concerns the mounted unit of the KPR who had some terrorists holed up on a kopje:

I had to be there by first light. I arrived with my troop in good time to find Digby Tatham-Water of Arnhem fame and some other redoubtables. I suggested to Digby that I lobbed a few 2-pdr HE, to which he responded, 'No way, we are going to charge in', and charge in they did, on their rather ponderous cobs, usual scene of trot, canter, gallop – horses slipping and stumbling, tails in the air. Reaching the kopje they perforce had to dismount (having expended much energy in various war cries and brandishing a variety of weaponry) due to the rocky terrain. A futile foot search ensued with odd horses galloping round the Rift Valley. To cut it short, my Turkhana tracker returned to say that the f-ing

Mau Mau had hopped it during the night. Shades of the last cavalry charge in the annals of the British Empire!

The Stag's Head Hotel at Nakuru was the scene of an exploit involving Private Richard Titman, of a platoon of B Coy camped in the Showground. They were making the most of a rest period, 'building up the Christmas spirit' there while some others were in the Rift Valley Sports Club.

The Kenya Women's League had their headquarters in the hotel and one of its members had made a large Christmas cake, beautifully iced: it was to be the showpiece of the Christmas Day party. Private Titman had fortified himself in a long session at the bar when he spotted the cake. By this time the manager felt the soldiery should leave – he was nervous that there might otherwise be a large charge for damages – and he asked our members to do so. After some argument, but all in good spirits, they left. Amongst the last to go was Titman. Spotting the cake, he grabbed it from its stand and flew out of the hotel. He was of course seen and several irate members of the Women's League, including the one who made the cake, took off in hot pursuit to the Showground camp. Our men went to ground and the ladies were barred entry but they made such a row that the police arrived. Shortly afterwards the platoon commander, Lieutenant Jack Barrah, returned from the Rift Valley Club and was informed what had happened by a raging mob of females yelling for blood. Jackie got his platoon together – they were in various stages of inebriation – and demanded an explanation as he feared an assault on his headquarters. There was not much to tell and no evidence of the theft as once inside their quarters the platoon had devoured the cake. Poor Titman did not get a bite as he had dived for cover inside the company armoury. In time the matter was reported to Kenreg HQ and action had to be taken as the President of the KW League had written to the Honoray Colonel of the Regiment and the Commanding Officer. Titman was found guilty and spent a short spell of detention in Gilgil. His one beef was that he had not managed to get a piece of the cake.

Peter Browne visited the Glasshouse (Military Detention Centre) at Gilgil to see 'one of our cherubs, Richard Titman' who had been incarcerated for fourteen days. As was customary I passed him a box of fifty Chipper cigarettes, but had forgotten matches. I was told this was no problem as the sailors and marines in Gilgil had taught our friend how to light up from a bulb socket!

There is no moral to this story except that an incident occurred the day after he returned from Gilgil – Titman that is. His Commanding Officer (the author) and Captain David Severn of the Black Watch had spent an evening at the Equator Club and driving home to the Ngong Road Headquarters they noticed that a lamp post beside Lord Delamere's statue was slightly askew, so they got out and tried to straighten it but only succeeded in getting it out of its pavement base. As they could not leave it lying in the road they began to hoist it into the back of the CO's Land Rover. As they were doing this, and it was very heavy, a voice said 'Do you want any help?' 'Yes,' we replied, 'Give us a hand; we will have to take it back to Headquarters.' 'OK,' the chap said, 'Can you take me too?' 'Yes,' the CO said, 'Hop in.'

Back at HQ we parked it on the parade ground, still with a large portion of its concrete base. It was then that I discovered that our helper was none other than Richard Titman, obviously very fit from his visit to Gilgil. We all promptly repaired to the canteen to celebrate the event.

The lamp post was returned next morning by our Quartermaster to the city authorities with an explanation that satisfied their pride and a contribution to a sports fund of their choosing was accepted with pleasure.

A similarly 'enlightened' attitude was taken by 'Rogue' Barkas on the 'morning after the night before' at a weekend camp on the Kongyta Range at Nanyuki, when he went into the mess and saw

propped up outside the entrance to his tent, an immaculate pair of elephant tusks. Being an old soldier, I recognized these tusks as having come from 3 KAR Officers' Mess and there was no doubt who was responsible for the deadly act. So I said to someone, 'Go and get Sergeant Parris. I want to have a word with him.' When he came I said, 'Congratulations. You've done a very good job. You took these things from 3 KAR Officers' Mess, didn't you?' He looked slightly sheepish and said, 'Yes, Sir.' So I told him: 'If you get 'em back by lunch time and nobody rings me up and says that damn Kenya Regiment have done it again – we'll call it quits.' Later that morning Wilfred came back wearing a very smart suit and said; 'Sir, mission accomplished!' and I never heard another word about it.

One club, the Travellers' Club, had the temerity to refuse entrance to Guy Catchpole (later the Reverend) of the Regiment and members of the Black Watch with whom he was serving. They were turned away

not because of our drunkenness or misbehaviour – in fact our behaviour at this stage was exemplary – but because we were 'improperly dressed'. This was manifestly untrue, becaue the Jocks were in their 'walking out' dress: kilt, Lovat hose, brogues etc, and I was in Kenya Regiment KD No.1 – tie, collar-dogs and all. Since there was no justice in our being barred, we picketed the place – no one else was allowed in. Panic ensued and all the revellers inside started streaming out down the steps. The police arrived in a '999' car and were summarily hustled down the stairs and back into their cars. They drove away, but returned in due course with the Redcaps. We realized that they would not be a pushover, and so, having spotted them at a distance, we decided

115

to disperse. By the time the MPs arrived at the Travellers' Club, we were halfway back to camp. Our Company Commander received a visit from an MP captain the following day and we were called in one by one, but of course no one had been anywhere near the Travellers' when the interrogation started! Whereupon Roddy Willett, our Company Commander, told the Redcaps to piss off and not waste his time. We were then called in and advised to take care – the worst thing we could do was to be stupid enough to get caught. Having got away once, we would have to keep it that way.

The smallest member of the Regiment was Cruickshank, the regimental goat. He arrived as a kid and was kennelled in the rear of our Regimental Headquarters. He was awarded his No.1 Dress uniform in our colours with buffalo badges on either side. He loved cigarettes and would advance rapidly when he recognized a smoker. He took a 'Clipper' very gently but tended to butt or paw for more as he was a tobacco addict. Some time later I heard that he had become bad-mannered and rather demanding but in his youth he and I were firm friends.

Jock Rutherfurd writes:

At the end of the active part of the Emergency in 1956, the Regiment was 'stood down' and we all went back to our civilian jobs and occupations. In 1957 the Regiment was re-formed with Charles Madden as CO. Many of us volunteered and, except for those who were going to organize companies, we all joined as we had always joined the Kenya Regiment, as private soldiers, regardless of the ranks we may have held previously . . .

After some time I went to Eldoret and took up my own farm there and, in doing so, Charles Madden asked me to take over the Eldoret Company which was a combination of Eldoret and Kitale and they were a good crowd. However, this meant in fact that I had now been commissioned three times from the ranks and so it was, until, sadly, but in the circumstances rightly, the Regiment was disbanded in 1963, just after the last annual camp.

I commanded the combined up-country company on the final parade in Nairobi and, at the cathedral ceremony afterwards as I watched Colonel Dunstan-Adams laying up the Colours, I thought there could not ever have been many men who had formed a Regiment of such high calibre and were still there at the end.

CHAPTER 9

THE REGIMENTAL
PERMANENT STAFF

SPECIAL MENTION must be made of the role of the Regular permanent staff with our Territorial Regiment. Their duties covered all aspects of military training, including a professional approach to discipline, organization, administration and military law. The Second-in-Command supports the decisions of the Commanding Officers, especially on the administrative side and sees that all departments work in harmony. For the first two years of the Emergency we had no Second-in-Command, so the Headquarters staff carried an extra load. After the CO and Adjutant left to form a Tactical Headquarters at Mweiga, the Regimental HQ in Nairobi was run by the Assistant Adjutant and the Quartermaster. Besides being involved in operational tasks, the Adjutant handled all the manpower demands, selecting members for a vast variety of requirements, and attending to leave and replacements.

The Quartermaster supervised all matters of clothing, equipment, food and transport and, in our case, the purchase of arms and ammunition, all of which had to be bought within the limits of the budget set by the Kenya Government each year. We also had our own system of pay and allowances as laid down by the Treasury and we were much later permitted to use the facilities of the NAAFI.

A Permanent Staff Instructor (PSI), a warrant officer or sergeant, lived up-country with B and C Companies, so he was always on hand for advice. They needed to be men of high calibre who were professionals and who knew when to curb a bolshy member. Headquarters staff paid frequent visits round the various platoon areas and gave lectures and demonstrations. They were also on the look-out for potential officer material.

The Medical Officer and Regimental Padre were responsible for the physical and spiritual welfare of the men.

117

Later additions to the permanent staff were Second-in-Command and Training Officer.

The first Adjutant in 1950 was Captain R. W. S. ('John') Moon (60th) who, with Colonel Cecil Valentine OBE ED and Major Edward de las Casas (Rifle Brigade) Second-in-Command, and Major Stan Blake (7th Hussars) Q M, reformed the Regiment.

John Moon was succeeded by Captain Teddy Phillips MC (60th), who had a good war record. He was a fine horseman and jockey, and a keen polo player and game shot. He was an excellent choice as Adjutant and was very popular with the Kenya boys. He left in July, 1952. His last job in the Army was as Military Attaché, Khartoum.

Captain Roly Guy (60th) took over from him and within days he was fully occupied with the Annual Camp in the Ngong Hills outside Nairobi. He had been Signal Officer of 1st Battalion 60th in the 33rd Armoured Brigade of the 11th Armoured Division. On the first day of the camp, Roly came across a huge private in C Company named 'Stooge' Stocker. Stooge was sitting on the ground banging an 88 set on a stone, swearing as he did do. This was too much for Roly. 'For God's sake, man, you can't do that to a wireless set!' Stooge looked up menacingly and replied: 'Give me three f—— good reasons why I shouldn't!' The new young Adjutant and the Commanding Officer moved on quickly.

Roly was Adjutant for three years and throughout his tour did a magnificent job. He was the ideal choice for service with the Regiment. He could see the humorous side of things, which was essential to gain the respect of our men and as the months of the Emergency lengthened he became the key link in our chain of command. He was asked to do many tasks which few Adjutants have ever had to contend with and, until we appointed an assistant, he, like the CO, was always on the move. Inside three months we had to form a Tactical Headquarters in the field at Mweiga under myself and the Adjutant. There were frequent trips back to Nairobi by car or plane, so one member of the staff relieved another, until returning to normal. Most of the decisions had to be made instantly, at times without offical consent.

He was the man who had to cope with the constant demands for leaders from the operational companies, Ray Force, every KAR and British battalion, Brigade HQ liaison, Field Intelligence Officers, the Mounted Section, the Recce Regiment, 156 HA Battery RA, field and aerial survey, interrogation centres, jungle warfare school, battle school, tracker combat teams, detainee camps and later Special Police Forces and the Kikuyu, Embu, Meru guard posts – and all the time a 'Release Board' was operating which depleted our strength. Such releases were given for farmers who, war or no war, had to get back to run their farms and protect the country's economy; or for members of civilian firms who

26.   Clive Symons (standing, left) at Eldoret. He was later killed in a grenade
accident in the forest.

The African Land and Freedom Army,
General Headquarters,
NAIROBI,
KENYA.
DATE:- K.I. 28/11/54.

These are the things which were given to Captain
Njoroge from Nairobi, and the Army Leader is investigating where
they are, they were money, ammunition, clothes and shoes. They were
as follows :-

35 Rounds of Rifle Ammunition
 6   "   " Sten Gun Ammunition
 1 Pair   of Shoes
350/- Three hundred and fifty shillings
 60/- Sixty shillings

I am very grateful to hear that you Captain Kariuki you
are alright. So I greet you very much, and I am very thankful for
things like ammunition, because we have got ways of getting them
now, and ways of getting everything is at hand. Another thing is
that now there is fierce battle of pangas, homemade guns, and petrol
fires. The Government are saying that they have never seen such
things before. A lot of damages, people cut into pieces, burning of
homes and those living in them, and at the same time firing of rifles
when houses are burning. So there is a fierce fighting here. The
leader of war is Mwangi 22, with 18 terrorists. I Kariuki I have
got more than 9 terrorists, or twelve. So wait patiently and hear
of our fierce battle. We were left with the gun which Njoroge had.
Mwangi 22 has got a big task of fighting. If Gods will you will hear
later and get the rifle, and other good things.

Writer (Mwandiki) 22.

I am Kariuki Ihai.

27. A typical Mau Mau letter.

28. Guard of Honour for HRH Princess Margaret, Nairobi, 1958. The
Guard Commander is Major R. C. W. Nightingale.

29. Kenya Regiment, 1962, with mixed European, African and Asian
members.

30.   The Regimental Colours being laid up in Nairobi Cathedral, 12 May, 1963; Colonel Dunstan-Adams and Major Paddy Deacon.

could not do without their principal executives. There was also the question of long overdue leave or replacing a misfit or casualty.

With all these demands to handle, his job would have tested the strength and experience of a much older man, but he never wavered, and retained his sanity and sense of fun. He was rightly awarded the MBE. He became General Sir Roland Guy KCB CBE DSO, Adjutant-General, after a distinguished career in several trouble spots. He was recently appointed ADC General to Her Majesty the Queen.

Here Roly writes about his time as Adjutant:

I certainly grew up in Kenya! For a rather immature 24-year-old who had barely cut his teeth in the comprehension of what living a full life was about, my posting as Adjutant to the Regiment in July, 1952, gave me such education, experience and satisfaction during the three years I spent in that beautiful country that I never ceased to be grateful for my luck in getting the job, and I continue to encourage young officers to grab at similar opportunities now – though regrettably there are only too few of them left.

I arrived shortly before the 1952 Camp. I found the Kenya Territorial a tough, gregarious, very friendly, hard-drinking, hard-working man and, in a sense, in need of the togetherness and comradeship which the Regiment provided for him. I think it was a sort of contrast to the quite lonely lives many of them led.

In one of my letters to my mother I wrote: 'There is no doubt that during the annual camp drinking is heavy, but for the rest of the year is quite reasonable and nothing for you to worry about!' I had only been in the country two months when I wrote that!

As a Regular Army Adjutant I was the senior captain. Many of those officers junior to me and indeed a large number of senior NCOs had served as officers in the War and were a darn sight more experienced than I was but they never made life difficult for me and, on parade, were always respectful and obedient. However, my authority over many of them was shortlived and it was not long before the likes of Captain Ray Mayers and Sergeant Walter Schuster were giving me orders after reverting to their wartime ranks during the course of the Emergency. The busy but more relaxed life of pre-emergency days was soon to change. The HQ became the nub of the Regiment to which Kenreg soldiers, white and black, always went when in Nairobi and many slept there.

He was succeeded as Adjutant by another young Rifleman, Captain Roy Eve in May, 1955. By this time the Government Forces contained what remained of the active Mau Mau terrorists and the Regiment was reduced to one company – known as the Operational Company – which was in Masailand clearing up that vast area extending to the Tanganyika border. He still had the knotty problem of release demands and keeping up the company and all our extra-regimental posts

119

which far exceeded our actual fighting strength. The KEM guard posts, pseudo-gang activities and officers and sergeants with the British and KAR battalions and all the other various posts were still required. The pressure was decreasing, but keeping pace with all the demands and, most important of all, the placing of the right man for the right job, was hard. Our new intake of recruits was not quite up to the high quality of the early volunteers, being younger, and some of the urgency had passed. Only a few of the hardcore gangsters were still at large, and Kenya was thinking of the future and of getting the country back to peaceful prosperity.

Captain Peter Welsh (60th) in due course took over the Adjutancy from Roy Eve, whose sterling work in the last serious year of the active battle then turned to the equally arduous business of building up the structure for peace. The new Adjutant was already one of the finest rifle shots in the Army and he assisted our rifle team in Kenya competitions. One of the highlights of his time there was when the Regiment's shooting teams swept the board at the EA Command meetings in 1959 and 1960, beating British Regular Army teams armed with the new SLR. Peter Welsh continued the work of reconstruction, which was by now fully back to peacetime conditions. Pater later served as the Divisional Brigadier, HQ of the Light Division, and is now a Major-General on the staff with an OBE and MC to his credit.

The last Adjutant before the Regiment was disbanded was Captain Christopher Adami (60th), round of frame and a leading light in the Amateur Dramatic Society. It was during his tour that the Regiment had become a multi-racial unit, which required tact and good humour of which he had plenty.

Miss Margaret Holden was another member of our Headquarters Staff who deserves a very special accolade. She originally came as the CO's and Adjutant's typist, but was soon occupying a position of trust as my personal private secretary. She shared all our secrets and we valued her advice and careful answers to any conundrums which came up.

She most ably officiated and added the necessary feminine touches to our Officers' Mess which was always open to visitors.

She is now living in Nairobi, happily married to Michael Horsley of the Regiment. They have five children and she is as attractive as ever.

ASSISTANT ADJUTANTS

Soon after we had set up a Tactical HQ, we found it essential to appoint an Assistant Adjutant who could swap over duties with the Adjutant, but whose main task was to be in charge of the Rear HQ with the Quartermaster. In fact, he was virtually Second-in-Command. Captain Angus Macdonald of the Regiment was chosen and for three years he handled all types of problems, acting directly with GHQ and the Secretariat. He never flapped, was calm, steady, humorous and very determined. (The very fact that he was either in the Field or in Nairobi allowed the Colonel to have one officer always with him.) He took over the responsibility of a Second-in-Command without any qualms and after a week or so you felt he had been there for years. He also possessed the rare attribute of tact and, being a Kenyan, he knew how to get the best out of them – they had all been to school together.

He never pushed his position or trod on tender toes but he had a strong will, and inexhaustible constitution and a tongue that could bite. He was one of the five members of the Regiment who received the Queen's Coronation Medal. The choice was made of one man of different rank in each company. British and KAR battalions received a much more generous allotment.

SECOND-IN-COMMAND

At the end of 1953 one of our own officers, Major David Gillett MC, was appointed Second-in-Command, which was a tremendous help, as the Regiment had been without one since April, 1952. Unfortunately this was only for a short time as he was released all too soon: his farm had suffered much by his absence. He lived at Ol Kalou under the Aberdares near Nakuru, the area known in the past as 'Happy Valley'. Almost the last job he did for us was to organize the superb lunch for the Colonial Secretary, Mr Oliver Lyttelton, and his party.

In place of David Gillett, my twin brother David, a major in The Black Watch, who had been in 4th KAR for a year, was appointed by General Erskine. During his tour of six months he did a fine job building up our garden at Headquarters. He also did much work in organizing our pseudo-gang activities and running Regimental Headquarters. When he left the Regiment he joined the staff of the Battle School at Nakuru.

On numerous occasions he was mistaken for me, a ploy which we both had used since childhood. It often got us into trouble and it could backfire, especially if it concerned a member of the opposite sex!

TRAINING OFFICERS

In 1954 we had a welcome addition to our staff – a training officer. The first was Captain Dick Cornell (60th), who came out as ADC to General Erskine. He planned many of our 'Ops', notably 'Anvil', and on other occasions when sudden demands were made to provide men for 'clean-ups', such as the one on the Athi Plain, and certain 'night activities' which were much used by the Regiment. He left us in mid-1955 and was posted to the Rifle Depot at Winchester, a post he was not happy about. He died tragically one morning under St Katherine's Hill which he knew well as a boy at Winchester. (His brother John is still serving with the Rifle Brigade as a brigadier on the staff.) I still remember him with great affection; he was one of a fine bunch of cheerful extrovert subalterns of 1/60th in BAOR with whom I had served before being posted to Kenya.

He was replaced by my cousin, Colin Campbell (60th), who did much to liven up any party. He was also for a time ADC to the Governor with his friend Charlie Douglas-Home, also ADC.

Following Colin Campbell came Gerald Carter (60th), to be succeeded by Captain Carol Gurney (60th). They were responsible for courses and all training weekends and the annual camp. On his departure Carol Gurney, with some friends, drove back to England, which was an adventure in itself. They went via the Kufra Oasis, where a Michigan University expedition in 1969 uncovered a Kenya Regiment badge and wrote to me asking for information.

The last training officer, Raymond Nelson (60th), led a mixed party of Africans, Asians and Europeans up Mount Kenya, reaching an altitude of over 16,000 feet.

QUARTERMASTERS

RSM Jimmy Cummins (Irish Guards), who had been first Regimental Sergeant-Major on the formation of the Regiment was also its first Quartermaster. Finally he became a lieutenant-colonel and Commandant of the Kenya Police Reserve. He was a man of commanding presence and outstanding character and no one who met him could fail to recognize his stature. The fire that he showed on the parade ground with an idle squad did not hide the true kindliness of his nature when recruits and instructor met off-duty. He was without doubt one of the most revered figures who ever served in the Regiment and his friends were legion. He died in May, 1984, but remained until then upright of figure and with the steady gaze and twinkling blue eyes that revealed the real Jimmy Cummins.

Major Frank Wakefield MBE of the Rifle Brigade took up his appointment from CQMS Slater, who had taken over after our previous QM had been relieved of his job. George Slater had done a splendid job and thoroughly deserved the award of the British Empire Medal. With the Emergency the 'Q' problems increased beyond anything a normal quartermaster would be expected to handle. He had to work within a budget the Treasury tried to impose which was insufficient to keep a battalion in the field. Frank and his staff were responsible for providing our increasing needs for combat uniform, jungle boots, tentage, weapons, ammunition, transport, barbed wire, explosives, Tilly lamps, latrine screens – to mention only a few items. He once bought 400 FN rifles from Belgium, and 600 berets from an Asian trader in Nairobi which were all paid for in cash. There was no time for argument: if we needed something we ordered it. Eventually, of course, it brought uproar from the Treasury or higher command, but it was too late then. We were fully committed and the risk of displeasure had to be taken. However, by the time the displeasure reached Nairobi our men were equipped and active on operations against the enemy. It was a matter of common sense – to fight you need weapons, clothing, transport and the whole mass of equipment and stores known in the Army as a G1098. We had no such backing.

Our budget began to leap by astronomical proportion from something like £50,000 in 1952 to around £800,000 by 1956. The CO was ultimately responsible for all of it! We may have jumped the gun but we were capable of taking on any task we were given.

Frank never appeared to be at a loss and, if he did not have an answer for a particularly pertinent Treasury enquiry, he produced one so convincing that no further questions were asked, at least for the time being. Thus he enabled us to operate efficiently with all the back-up supplies we needed. He and his staff did a magnificent job. He was always cheerful and it was a great relief to know that while he was on hand you would get what was required. What was even more endearing about him was that he appeared completely bland and innocent, yet when he confessed the sleight of hand he used to convince higher authorities it made one shudder.

The Regiment owes him a great debt of gratitude. His long days of work kept us in the field and enabled us to provide accommodation and entertainment for officers and other ranks of all the British and KAR battalions and brigades and a welcome for any visitor.

PERMANENT STAFF INSTRUCTORS

The Kenya Regiment owes much to its PSIs or Permanent Staff Instructors. From 1930 until the end of the Second World War they were provided by the Brigade of Guards, but from 1950 the Green Jackets (60th Rifles and Rifle Brigade) took over, as the Foot Guards could no longer spare the men. The connection was not altogether lost, though, as they sent many splendid Staff Instructors to the newly formed National Training Centre in Salisbury, Southern Rhodesia. The other instructors came from the Infantry of the Line. They were well chosen and I do not remember a single individual who was not excellent. Training recruits requires special qualities and they made a deep impression on the Kenya boys.

CSM (later Major) V. Bobbett of the Welsh Guards succeeded Jimmy Cummins as RSM and served with the Regiment during the period when they were training NCOs and men to become officers for the Forces of the East Africa Command.

Others of the original WO IIs were CSM Carter (Grenadier Guards), CSM Allen (Scots Guards) and CSM Broomfield (Grenadier Guards). Of these, Charlie Broomfield is the best remembered. He became RSM of the Regiment following V. Bobbett and also served with the King's African Rifles. Like Jimmy, Charlie earned a great name among all Kenyans. Many of his memories of those days are included in this history and they give a vivid account of how the recruits became leaders. He is still going strong and attends our UK reunions each year. He was in the mould of Jimmy Cummins, a strict disciplinarian but a sterling character of immense charm and wisdom. After many years of service including a long stint as Quartermaster to the Uganda Police, he retired as a Major.

The first official Regimental Medical Officer was Dr Billy Hargrave-Wilson who served with us until after the annual camp in 1952. He endeared himself to all ranks but was always quick to spot a 'skiver' who tried to pretend he had a diminished capacity for a full day's work, preceded by early PT, when in fact he was really suffering from a monumental hangover. We all regretted his departure when he emigrated to New Zealand, where he was needed as an orthopaedic surgeon. He died in 1983. He was replaced by Dr Donald Hicks, an outstanding character and a keen cricketer who formed the Wanderers Club. In his day he took many wickets with his spin bowling and was also a hard-hitting batsman. He was always good company and a great supporter of the Officers' Mess and any celebration in the Sergeants' Mess or the canteen. He accompanied many patrols and was with us when we formed our Tac HQ on Marrian's Farm at Mweiga. He left me with two scars, one on the ball of my left thumb, the other on the outside of my right knee, but that does not detract from his skill as a doctor! He was a good friend to all of us and to me especially. He was a heart specialist and died some years ago at an early age – from a heart attack! A man full of charm and most endearing.

He was succeeded by Dr Philip Crosskey, another man in the regimental mould, who soon learned our ways and when to turn a blind eye to some imagined illness. Like Donald he was always on the move, visiting outlying posts occupied by members of the Regiment. All our MOs knew how to deal with gunshot wounds, battle fatigue, mountain sickness and other ailments which occur on active service. We were lucky that all our MOs were blessed with a sense of humour, which is vital in maintaining high morale among the weary.

In due course he was replaced by Dr Dennis Alexander who lived up to the reputation of his predecessors. It may have been unethical but all our MOs carried weapons as they had to travel long distances through areas where armed gangs were active and our men were in posts high up in the Aberdares or on Mount Kenya. We never had enough men or vehicles to provide escorts. The loss of an MO would have been a disaster.

He was succeeded by Myles Dunstan-Adams, D.A.'s son, who also proved a great asset to the Regiment. Like other members, he has now made his home in Canada. I am grateful to him for lending me his father's files on the Regiment, which gave me access to all D.A.'s correspondence concerning the many battles fought to keep the Regiment in being.

REGIMENTAL PADRES

The man who held this post from the formation of the Regiment until he left Kenya in 1953 was the Reverend Jimmy Gillett, beloved by all ranks and one of the finest men who ever lived. He was also a schoolmaster, with a gift for imparting knowledge and humanity to all he met. Many of the Regiment's boys had known him at school. He was appointed Chaplain to the Prince of Wales' School in 1932 when it was opened as the new Secondary School for European Boys. He ran the scout troop there and led working parties to lay out the playing fields, hedges and gardens around the school.

Besides being Chaplain of the Regiment, he was also Chaplain to the RAF when they were stationed at Eastleigh, Nairobi, and to the Bishop of Mombasa. In 1941 he was appointed Headmaster of Nairobi Primary School and in 1949 was transferred to the Head Office of the Education Department in Nairobi and became Assistant Director of Education, a position he held until his retirement. He was a keen freemason and by the time he left Kenya he was Deputy Grand Master of East Africa. In 1953 he accepted a living in Warwickshire and became Rector of Stockton, moving in 1956 to the Isles of Scilly. On his retirement due to ill-health he moved to Falmouth, where he remained active until his death in 1976.

He was a warm and true friend to all, and wise in the ways of handling young boys and grown men alike. He was quick to note any form of trouble and all knew that they could take their worries to him and that his advice would be sound. He was one who inspired trust and confidence. He was much respected and a kind and generous man, but those who tried to fool him only did so once. He and his wife Mary were rare people who did much to instil the decencies of life in those they met.

Mary Gillett's brother was Ken Beaton whose parents were early settlers in Kenya. He was a former member of the Regiment and founded and ran the Nairobi Park and then the Uganda National Game Park, which was visited and opened by Queen Elizabeth, after whom it was called. He died of cancer on 22 October, 1954, having told no one of the pains he used to suffer, so that his sudden death was a great shock to his family and friends.

Mary herself won the Africa General Service Medal, Kenya, for her work with the Air Wing under Wing-Commander Francombe and later on at police HQ when Richard Catling was Commissioner and Howard Williams was in charge of her section.

The last Regimental Padre was the Reverend John De'Ath who remained with the Regiment until it was disbanded when Independence was declared. He started the regimental newsletters which are still sent out by our Association in Nairobi. Together with John, Jimmy Gillett and the Padre of the Green Jackets' Depot officiated when our Colours were laid up in the Garrison Church at Peninsula Barracks in Winchester. He also took the Remembrance service held there in memory of D.A. in 1978.

LIAISON OFFICERS

Another member of the Regiment who was invaluable in acting as a Liaison Officer or as a stand-in was Captain Bob Stanton, who was one of the older members. He was unflappable, cheerful and abounded in common sense.

Then there was Major Walter Schuster, who had shared a farm on the Kinangop with Eric Pardoe. He had some of the finest pigs in Kenya. His champion boar was a character; when Wally entered his pen he would lie on his side to have his tummy tickled and was rewarded with a carrot! Their farm had some of the best trout fishing in Kenya. He wrote a paper recommending a 'multi-racial' Regiment in 1955, which was excellent and far-reaching. Based on his plan it was introduced in 1961 and survived until Independence was declared in 1963. Personally, I regret that the new Kenya Army did not keep the Regiment as it was then. Since Independence, no European has been called up for service, which is a sad waste of valuable manpower and experience. Walter Schuster died in 1960 of a heart attack. He was a gentle, well-loved man, with a passion for Mozart, on whom he was a great authority. While he was PMC of our Officers' Mess we had the best food in Kenya and our parties were famous. Officers of all the British regiments, KAR battalions and other military forces were all honorary members (as were NCOs in our Sergeants' Mess and ORs in our canteen) and it was seldom that they failed to visit us in Nairobi.

Shortly after the Emergency started, a charming officer, Capitaine Ernest de Portère, was attached to us from the Belgian Congo, where he was a member of their Deuxième Bureau. He came out on a fact-finding mission and spent many months in our mess. He lived in the Adjutant's dressing-room. It was one of our boasts that we welcomed all service members and their wives or girlfriends. We could also provide beds for those who had no accommodation. Ernest proved to have a great sense of humour and was a very popular guest.

GENERAL ERSKINE

General Erskine was a 60th Rifleman who had had a distinguished career in the Western Desert as the commander of the 7th Armoured Division and, before being appointed GOC East Africa, he had been Commander of British Troops in Egypt. As a subaltern he had been renowned for his strength and sense of fun. He was always the leader in the wild and boisterous games played on guest nights in the Officers' Mess which seem to have dropped out of fashion in Army messes of today.

General Erskine was a man who had carried heavy responsibilities in his life but he never lost his youth. In Kenya his character was not always appreciated. He, like the Governor, was not the master at the helm. Kenya had a system of 'rule by many', if you include, as you must, the Colonial Office, the Secretariat and the administration, politicians and the high-ranking police officers. It was very different in Malaya where General Templer was 'supremo' and was able to assert his authority through a committee of civil, military and police without ever yielding to them his position and to many, especially the settlers, there seemed to be no sense of urgency at the high levels. He had one other handicap, for, when he drove round the troubled areas, his staff did not always organize his

126

programme to meet many of the settlers who had most to lose. Had he been better known his image would not have appeared to be so remote. At heart he was a very friendly man, who loved a good joke. I knew this better than most, for my father and uncles had served with him in his youth and when he needed to forget the daily trials and problems of his command, if we were in Nairobi, my brother and I were asked to come round and tell him the form and make him laugh. As his wife, Ruby, was in England, he was much alone with his MA and ADC and needed to be cheered up.

When General Sir George Erskine left after two years as C-in-C he was succeeded by Lieutenant General Sir Gerald Lathbury. For the Regiment this meant a change in direction. This is not unusual in the British Army and has to be accepted. Some of the close ties we had formed with General Erskine were lost and the atmosphere was to be more austere and remote, and tactics changed, which was inevitable as the war was now under control.

GENERAL HINDE

Another of Kenya's generals was Major-General Sir William ('Loony') Hinde, an international polo player and a 15th/19th King's Royal Hussar, whom I had known since 1933. He had commanded a brigade in the 7th Armoured Division with great élan. His appointment to Kenya in 1953 was opportune, and his brother Douglas was a settler near Nanyuki and he was immediately accepted. He believed in meeting everybody and, unlike some of the more senior officers, he drove about unescorted, with his driver, visiting isolated guard posts, police and soldiers, always with a cheering word and inquiries if there was anything they wanted. The very fact of seeing him made them feel good. He initiated the defensive structure which was to guard the Kikuyu Reserve and build up their morale and power of hitting back at the terrorists. He was always calm and inconspicuous; sometimes he wore no badges of rank and would drop in without warning. He possessed great charm and tact, not always a military attribute, and these fact-finding tours produced much-needed assistance and buffed up the morale of those who were bearing the brunt of the campaign against violence.

Evelyn, his wife, was a great character, who often got me into trouble when she decided that she and I should liven up a dull party. On one occasion I received two cracked ribs while we performed a daring exposition of a 'Come Dancing' routine. Their charming daughters were with them and had all inherited their mother's love of fun.

127

CHAPTER 10

THE LAST YEARS
OF THE REGIMENT

ON 9 DECEMBER, 1955, General Erskine wrote to me, telling me that the Colonel's Commandant had 'supported the application for the Kenya Regiment to be affiliated to the 60th and there were no conditions attached'. He had been consulted as to whether they ought to wear riflemen's black buttons and do rifle drill, but had pointed out the 'obvious difficulties'.

He then made this suggestion:

> It occurred to me that you might think it an appropriate moment to ask for the Regiment to be known as the Royal Kenya Regiment. It would be a mark of approval for the good work they have done and would I think be very popular with the chaps. I should think the Governor would be prepared to back it but I don't know if there are any hidden snags. It is of course nothing to do with me but just an idea which I thought you might like.

Unfortunately this remained only an idea as nothing more was ever heard of it.

The close association between the Kenya Regiment and the 60th Rifles was officially recognized in June, 1956, when Her Majesty the Queen gave official approval to an Alliance of the two Regiments. The following message was received by the Honorary Colonel from the Colonels Commandant, the King's Royal Rifle Corps:

> The Colonels Commandant, The King's Royal Rifle Corps, having just heard of the Sovereign's approval of the Alliance between our Regiments, send you and all ranks of your Regiment our greetings and best wishes for the future. This news has given to every 60th Rifleman a feeling of great pleasure and pride.

The following was sent in reply:

The Honorary Colonel, the Kenya Regiment, thanks the Colonels Commandant, The King's Royal Rifle Corps, for their stirring message. All members of the Regiment are proud that the close association that they have enjoyed with the 60th Rifles has now become a relationship recognized by Her Majesty the Queen. To become a partner of the 60th Rifles, whose allied membership and tradition has already spread beyond territorial boundaries, is indeed an honour which is fully appreciated by us here in Kenya. I reciprocate your good wishes and look forward to a happy and fruitful alliance.

To signify the Alliance the Regiment adopted the green beret and a green patrol uniform and now all 60th Permanent Staff Instructors serving with the Regiment wear the Regiment's lanyard.

The Regimental Music
The Regimental Quick March is composed of two marches, 'The Yorkshire Lass' and 'The Pipers of Dundee' which was suggested and arranged by Lady Stratheden.

The Regimental Call which is blown before all bugle calls except Reveille, Retreat, Fire and General Alarm, and First and Last Post, is composed of one and a half bars of the Regimental March and one and a half bars of the 2nd 60th Regimental Call.

The Regiment had no Slow March but after the Alliance with the 60th their Slow March the 'Duke of York' was adopted.

Lieutenant Colonel Charles Madden took over command of the Regiment on 28 January, 1956, having been Second-in-Command for five months. My brother David had been in the same PoW Camp as he after he was taken prisoner. He soon got into our ways and began to learn our methods of dealing with the various problems which we were now facing. Talk had already started about the future of the Regiment and volleys were fired at us which were alarming. When these were particularly heavy we always had the backing of our Honorary Colonel, Dunstan-Adams.

I left Kenya on 2 February, 1956. The worst of the Emergency was over and Charles was left with the task of reorganizing the Regiment. 'Ops' Company was still in the field but, other than sporadic sallies, no major events materialized. The Government was continuing to negotiate with those gang leaders still at large, but they were not entirely successful. The release boards continued to drain our manpower and many more applications to return to normal occupations were submitted.

Throughout his tour of command, Charles had to retain the Regiment in its active role, besides building up a sound basis for its return to normal life. The chief problem was to keep those serving in the field convinced that their task was still essential and to see that they were fully trained to take on any new Mau Mau offensive. An even harder task was to build a structure of officers and NCOs on which to form a peacetime regiment. Many had been away from their homes for years and they knew that they had to make good the losses caused to their farms or businesses when they were called up. A few unfortunates had to start afresh as they had lost nearly everything they possessed. Some, once out of uniform, felt lost, a few disillusioned, but the greater number knuckled down to the fresh challenge of rehabilitation.

Officers and all the junior ranks rallied round and gave Charles and his staff all the help he needed. The Regiment had to be ready at a moment's notice for active service, should the occasion arise.

By 1958 Flag Marches were carried out round the country and, as before, companies were based in the pre-Emergency areas. All who re-mustered, joined in the rank of private, despite the fact that they might have held higher rank at the date of their release. This was traditional and was taken for granted. Promotion was by selection and nobody ever questioned the decision of Regimental Headquarters. For the CO it meant continuous movement up and down the country, often to tempt a former officer to accept a vital position. This, of course, was a difficult decision for many to make. The task of starting a new life was not necessarily easy and even Territorial training makes demands on the time of those otherwise occupied. There were many who had suffered during their days on active service and who felt they had done enough.

Kenya was changing and a few may have considered trying their luck elsewhere. The future was uncertain and personal fortunes might be at stake. Throughout this period Charles Madden was a calming influence and it says much for his character and skill that it was all done smoothly. Sweeping up after a war is never easy and in peacetime conditions it is harder to take a strong line against any Government decision on a matter of principle. The Regiment always seemed to be faced with such problems. New ideas that seem ideal to politicians or GOCs can cause grave misgivings to Territorial soldiers who give up their spare time to help in the protection of their land and birthright. The future of Kenya depended upon the success of their civil occupations and they thought that they had the right to question any decision that might be wrong.

Weekend camps and training periods were carried out under the Regular PSIs, and annual camps were held for the whole regiment; the one in 1957 was held at Eburu in the middle of the Badlands and was attended by 400 all ranks. The training centre still operated at Nakuru and other courses took place at the Battle School. The lessons of forest operations were not forgotten.

By the time he left, Charles Madden handed over a keen and cheerful Regiment, fully trained, and the country was at peace. He has much to be proud of, as it is not easy to keep up interest in military life during peacetime. When the urgent and vital need to be properly trained is easy to recognize, the men know 'that their lives, when they go to join their fighting units, will depend on the standard of training which they and their comrades have reached'. However, Charles Madden comments:

When the fighting is over, compulsory service as was required by Kenreg can become a drudge ... It is for this reason that special mention should be made of the high standard maintained at KRTC after the Emergency. Major Bill Woodruff, Captain Lloyd Hailstone and other officers, CSM Cardy and all the other PSIs, by their enthusiasm, loyalty and hard work, kept the standard very high. Training included normal basic training and then more specialist leadership training for which the Regiment was so well-known.

Recruits then went to the TF company nearest their home or place of work and, if any did not have a job to go to, the Adjutant at RHQ, Captain Roy Eve and later Captain Peter Welsh, made a point of helping them into one. It should perhaps be mentioned here that the C-in-C, General Sir Gerald Lathbury, visited KRTC on a number of occasions to see the training of recruits and was quick to pick out any slipshod methods. He would also call me to his office from time to time to discuss progress of TF companies and assure himself that we were getting the administrative support from GHQ which we needed. The money, however, came from the Defence Ministry and on one occasion it took Colonel D.A.'s influence to get Kenreg a supplementary budget of £25,000.

Madden appreciated the help he always got from the Police Commissioner, Sir Richard Catling: 'He had a very realistic view of the future in Kenya and understood what the role and job of the army should be in the event of street riots and trouble before inevitable independence. Our main role could have been in support of the police and providing protection for convoys etc.' However, he declined 'to arm and train one platoon in each company with shields and pick helves for use on black crowds on the basis that the black head is harder than the white, and the panga more lethal than the pick helve'. He was given this order in 1958 by Major-General Tapp, following Kenya Police training seminars on the use of batons and shields for breaking up crowds, and on other internal security problems.

On 31 May, 1958, the Regiment officially celebrated its twenty-first birthday. In the morning 215 all ranks, led by Lieutenant-Colonel Madden, marched through Nairobi with bayonets fixed and colours flying, the salute being taken outside the City Hall by the Mayor, Alderman H. Travis. In the evening a ball was held in the City Hall which was attended by HE The Governor, Sir Evelyn Baring. On Sunday, 1 June, the Governor attended a church service at RHQ Nairobi, after which he opened the Old Comrades' Memorial Building.

The Annual Camp in 1958 was held at Nanyuki, near the Headquarters of 70th Infantry Brigade. The cooperation between the Regiment and the KAR at this camp was most valuable and did much to strengthen the ties between the two regiments. In November, 1958, the Regiment was reorganized onto a basis of four rifle companies and HQ Company. A and B Companies were merged into O Company with the Coast Platoon, formerly E Company, as an offshoot, and F Company because of its low strength became part of I Company. A 'Tea' platoon was formed in Kericho to tap the potential of the tea companies, many of whose members had already completed their National Service in the UK. A Recce platoon was also started in HQ Coy to provide the Regiment with a reconnaissance element.

Peter Welsh, who was Adjutant at the time, remembers the way the Regiment's Birthday Celebrations came about:

Acting Sergeant Baker of the Orderly Room mentioned to RSM Davey that the Regiment was going to be 21 that year. RSM Davey mentioned it to me as Adjutant and said that he would have a Sergeants' Mess party to celebrate. I went to Charles Madden and suggested we had an Officers' party too. He went to Colonel D.A. and it was agreed that we should make a regimental weekend of it! You can imagine the problems of organizing it all. All those on parade had kit inspections in their up-country HQ and then came down to Nairobi on the Friday for rehearsals and further kit cleaning and there we found that many of their shorts had been shortened Kenya-kiddy style!

All went well on the march through the city except that 60th officers, not knowing much about redcoat drill, had not heard of changing arms. So all 215 marched for half an hour or so with their rifles on their left shoulder and on arrival at the Charter Hall were almost unable to order arms, since their left arms were so stiff.

The only other smart parade we had to do was a Guard of Honour for HM the Queen Mother. It was drawn from I and C Companies – Nakuru, Kericho (the old F), Eldoret and Kitale and was commanded by Jock Rutherfurd, OC C Company.

Charles Madden was succeeded in February, 1959, by another 60th officer, Dick Vernon, and there were also changes among the other members of the regular permanent staff. The Regiment was now acting only as a Territorial Force, with no operational role.

The 4th (Uganda) Battalion of the KAR was back in Jinja and only Kenya battalions of the KAR still garrisoned Kenya. The aftermath of the Mau Mau rebellion was a rehabilitation period for former terrorists. Thousands of Kikuyu had died; the full total will never be known. Memories remained but they were becoming less bitter. It was a time of stock-taking.

Colonel Vernon's role was to keep the Regiment ready for any eventuality and to make the training interesting. His first Second-in-Command was Major Tony Vetch, a Kenya settler and member of the Kenya Police Reserve who had joined I Force at Squairs Farm in February, 1953. He was very popular and gave great service to the Regiment, but died quite suddenly. He was succeeded by Major

132

Paddy Deacon who had been serving with the Royal Irish Fusiliers. Captain Peter Welsh and Captain Christopher Adami, both Riflemen, served as Adjutants over his period of command, and it was at this time that the Regimental Rifle club was so successful, winning nine out of the eleven major rifle shooting cups, including Champion Major Unit, Champion Minor Unit (KRTC), Champion Individual Young Soldiers (Private Hopper), Champion Young Soldier Team, Champion Bren Pair in each class. In 1960 they won thirteen out of sixteen events. Captain Welsh was Champion Shot of East Africa Command, as well as running-up Queen's Medallist at Bisley. He and CSM Greenaway, one of the Greenjacket PSIs, trained the teams.

In 1959 the Regiment provided an ADC to the new Governor, Sir Patrick Renison. He was Second-Lieutenant John Yeldham, the son of Ronnie Yeldham, formerly of the King's African Rifles and a Kenya resident. The only other regimental officer to hold such an appointment was Colin Campbell who was ADC to Sir Evelyn Baring at the same time as Charlie Douglas-Home.

When Peter Welsh arrived in Colonel Madden's time

There were A and B Companies based in Nairobi, C in Kitale, D in Nyeri, E in Mombasa, F in Kericho and I in Nakuru where the KRTC also was. Later in 1958 A and B merged into one O Company, commanded by Paddy Deacon and then John Shaw. C was commanded by James McKillop before Jock Rutherfurd, D by Tony Vetch (later 2i/c) and then John Campbell and later Rogue Barkas; E Company in Mombasa was reduced to being a platoon of O Company (incidentally my first weekend with E Company was classifying on a suntrap of a range. My intake was four pints of beer, eight Pepsis and four Fanta and I did not pee the whole weekend!) and F, which had been under James McKillop, became a platoon of I Company commanded by Chris Tyler.

After a young white had completed his six months' training at the KRTC he had to do four years in the Kenya Regiment. His obligation was three weekends and a two-week annual camp each year. Each company had to hold a minimum of four weekends a year so that the Territorials had a choice and for the same reason there was an alternative annual camp. There was always a small nucleus of chaps who failed to complete their commitment and in 1960 I managed to have two of them brought up before the local magistrate. They were found guilty and fined! The weekend camps took place all over the colony but not too far from the company base. The annual camps while I was there were based in Nanyuki, mainly because of the help that 70th Brigade KAR was able to give. There were the usual stories of Kenya kiddies behaving wildly including that of Stocker strolling through camp whirling a puff adder around – the camp emptied pretty quickly! – or chaps waking up with a lion in their tent! I remember a cadet camp held at Langata in 1959 when a pride of lions used to walk through the camp every night!

133

The role of the Regiment was described in Sir Evelyn Baring's farewell speech as 'A role which prepares you, should the need arise, to play your part in defence of the Commonwealth in time of war and in the preservation of security in your own country.'

Field training was concentrated at a new site at Nanyuki which was ideal country for manoeuvres as it was close to the Northern Frontier District. Joint exercises took place with the British and KAR battalions.

As well as the regimental annual camp, camps were also held for the cadet forces of the Prince of Wales', Duke of York and St Mary's Schools. Companies held their own training weekends. On one occasion the Coast Platoon did an assault landing from a Royal East African naval craft against a general service unit.

Among visitors to the Regiment was the CIGS, General Sir Francis Festing in February, 1959. A previous CIGS, Field-Marshal Sir John Harding, had visited the Regiment on two occasions in 1953 and 1954.

It was now that a most important event took place. Colonel Vernon had settled into his post and knew that self-government for Kenya could not be long delayed. He visited 70th Brigade and was surprised to find that no real plans for leading the army to independence existed. So, after many late-night discussions with Tony Vetch, his 2i/c and the senior TA officer, they came to the conclusion that:

1. The Kenya Regiment was a fine regiment, worth preserving and worth leading into an independent black Kenya. Whatever happened, standards must not be lowered.
2. A purely European regiment, particularly one with the reputation for the great part it had played in defeating Mau Mau, had no chance of survival in an independent Kenya.
3. The only chance was to open the ranks to Africans and perhaps Asians. [Vernon did not know of the proposal to admit Africans into the Regiment which had been submitted to the government in 1955 by Major Walter Schuster.*]

*In this proposal he noted that

A fine spirit of comradeship and cooperation between the Europeans and the Africans has developed in many cases in the Companies. This is *something new*, for, although the KAR Askari give loyalty, trust and affection to his European Officer and NCO, he does not actually work side by side with them as the Kenya Regiment tracker does with the European personnel of the Regiment. This revolutionary new system of having black and white in equal ranks mixed within a platoon and getting down to any job of work together is something good and something *modern* and up to date. Its natural evolution during this Emergency proves in itself that it was necessary and desirable.

What better start could there be for sound and sensible multi-racialism than one guided by Army discipline, fairness and comradeship?

The proposal was rejected.

In retrospect it is incredible that this had not occurred in any of our colonial forces, whereas Sudanese officers had served in the Sudanese battalions of the old Egyptian Army and later the Sudan Defence Force from 1925.

134

4. If Europeans, Africans and Asians could be made to live together, be treated exactly the same and go 'through it' together, particularly at the KRTC and then at the Territorial annual camp, there might be created the first truly multi-racial society which could provide real hope for all races after Independence.

This was a most delicate matter as many of the Europeans in Kenya regarded the Regiment as the last bastion against a 'black deluge'. An elaborate plan was drawn up by the far-seeing Vetch, assisted by Colonel Vernon and Major Paddy Deacon, who had similar views and eventually succeeded Vetch as Second-in-Command. Vetch discussed the proposal in great secrecy with the Company Commanders and one or two others and obtained their support. Among these were John Williams, John Howard, Ham O'Hara, Fred Lee and John Shaw. Their contribution, in various ways, was considerable.

After much deliberation they went to the Honorary Colonel, who gave his appproval. The Kenya Regiment was everything to him.

The next step was to see the Minister of Defence (Tony Swan) and the Permanent Secretary (Geoffrey Ellerton). With their blessing Vernon visited the GOC. Next a working party was set up so that a detailed plan could be prepared before the Governor was approached. Many problems faced the planners, such as:

1. If European conscription continued, how to reconcile this with the selection of non-whites who were not subject to conscription.
2. If non-whites were to compete militarily, socially, mentally and physically with their young European comrades, they must be carefully selected.
3. How could non-whites be persuaded to volunteer?
4. How could young European recruits be persuaded to accept the young non-whites as comrades?

Vernon then visited the heads of the biggest firms in Kenya and took the line: 'You are trying to train Africans for top management and are having great difficulty. I can offer your best young men two things: first, six months' tough military training, doing leadership training if they are good enough. Second, they will live with young Europeans on an equal footing for six months. They will learn their outlook and how to behave in a senior position. They will also make invaluable contacts through the white European community.'

Both the Government and the senior European businessmen saw the sense in this and the first intake included seven Africans and six Asians, all very carefully selected, all with school certificates and therefore likely to be acceptable to their European comrades.

Dick Vernon writes:

The first public intimation I gave that changes were in the air was in the editorial of the Kenya Regiment *Newsletter* no. 10 of June, 1960 (I wrote all the editorials in my time) and this had a fairly wide circulation among the Europeans. Then when the great day arrived I enlisted the aid of the public relations chiefs of both the Kenya Government and East Africa Command. I held a large Press conference with reporters not only from the East African Press but also from nearly every UK national paper. I held a radio interview and a television interview. I took the line that this was a great day for Kenya – we were setting up at Lanet a truly multi-racial society – from little acorns big oak trees . . . etc, etc. My experience at handling the Press was minimal (unlike today when every officer in Northern Ireland had done a course on TV), but the Press was in favour of what we were doing and we were lucky and had a very good press.

In fairness to those who had doubts about the wisdom of setting up a multi-racial regiment, the recent Mau Mau troubles had left a scar of fear which was still very raw, and added to this there might be strong criticism from the Afrikaaner settlers. It was a bold step to take, but in my view it was the right one.

Colonel Vernon's views on the selection of recruits was far-sighted and present-day Kenya has proved that it was correct. As he writes, a number of Africans, as a result of experience in the Kenya Regiment, went on to be regular officers in the Kenya Army, an outstanding example being Brigadier Cromwell Mkungusi who recently became Chief of Staff to the Army Commander. Brigadier G. N. Mbau, Colonel F. A. Siddondo, Lieutenant-Colonels R. Khan and S. Mati and Major F. K. Musili are still serving.

Dick Vernon was replaced by Douglas Bright of the Oxfordshire and Buckinghamshire Light Infantry, who was to be the last CO of the Regiment. In 1961 Asians and Africans were recruited and for the first time the Regiment became fully multi-racial. As always outstanding recruits had the chance to become officers and many were commissioned. The influx of new blood was successful, leading the way to a smooth handover of power when Independence was declared in 1963.

Great credit must be given to Douglas Bright for his handling of regimental affairs over this transition of power. Few Kenyans of any of the races had ever quite thought that such an event could come so quickly, nor, for that matter, that it was even possible.

The man who helped as much as anyone to make it work was the Honorary Colonel of the Regiment, Colonel D.A. Many had misgivings, as it was for the government a complete 'about-turn', but the change came and it worked. 'Mzee' Jomo Kenyatta was elected the first Prime Minister of the new Kenya. Throughout his period of command, Douglas and his PSIs had shown great skill in binding together the new Regiment which trained and prepared the young

African and Asian officers to form the nucleus of leaders for the new Army of Kenya. They had been brought up in the traditions of the British Army, which are still evident if you meet or visit Officers and Askaris of the modern Kenya Rifles. It is heartening to see that they have retained the old numerals, insignia and traditions of the former Kenya battalions of the KAR. The British have left the same heritage in the Armies of India, Pakistan and Bangladesh.

I observed this myself when I spent several weeks in Kenya in 1981. On one occasion I spent a long session in 'God's Waiting Room' in the Rift Valley Sports Club with a very 'clued-up' young brigade major and Mike Hughes, formerly of the Kenya Police Reserve. He held his own with both of us and he used the same sort of language and told the same type of story as we did! (I should add that no ladies are ever permitted in this bar!) He must be an extremely gifted officer as he has attended two Staff College courses and is obviously highly qualified. He was a delightful and amusing companion. If all the Kenya Army officers are like him I feel confident that they will be a credit to Kenya. In modern Africa strange things can happen – none of our other former colonies has escaped turmoil and revolutions. They can break out suddenly and leaders fall, to be replaced by others who have a thirst of power. Kenya is a rich country which might tempt a hungry neighbour. Let us hope that Kenya's leaders and her armed forces are ready to defend their land against any aggressor.

Brigadier Douglas Bright recalls his time as CO of the Regiment:

When I took over the Regiment from Dick Vernon in 1961, it was still dependent on the conscription of Europeans. The six months' recruits' course at the Kenya Regiment Training Centre at Nakuru was based on the syllabus for an Officer Cadet School and, at the end of it, the standard of training was very high. Discipline was strict and administered by conventional Brigade of Guards methods. On joining the territorial companies, recruits had to adjust to the much more relaxed and unconventional leadership of the Greenjacket permanent staff and the settler officers and NCOs.

The limited number of carefully selected African and Asian volunteers had been absorbed satisfactorily up to that point, but they were all posted to the Nairobi companies and everyone was still on their best behaviour.

Obviously the outlook of the settlers reflected directly into the Regiment. The trouble was that the settlers were themselves confused and divided by the winds of change and the imminence of independence. Some saw no future in Kenya and were planning to leave. At the other extreme some announced that Kenya was their home, that they would take Kenya citizenship and would stay no matter what the future might bring. There were also all shades of opinion in between. In many families the parents decided to stay but to send their children back to England to make their careers there. This division of settlers' opinion and confusion of outlook was, of course, reflected in the ranks of the Regiment.

To complicate matters further, some of the older members of the Regiment believed that all those who served in the Regiment during the Emergency were on lists for liquidation immediately after Independence. Conversely others believed that the Regiment could serve as a form of Home Guard and an arsenal for the protection of up-country farms. Both these views were mistaken.

In the light of hindsight I do not think that many members of the Regiment really believed in a future for the Regiment in the long term as a multi-racial volunteer territorial force, although this was not said.

The GOC East Africa Command, General Sir Richard Goodwin, was a strong supporter of the Regiment and took a great personal interest. His staff were, on the whole, friendly and cooperative. They, however, quite naturally regarded the efficiency of the KAR after independence as their main preoccupation. The problem of the future of the Kenya Territorial could not have a very high priority on their agenda. There was a similar situation with the KAR Brigade. Its Commander, now the Duke of Norfolk, was friendliness itself and saw our recruitment of African and Asian volunteers as a promising source of supply of officers for the new Kenya Army, as indeed it was. Our role, however, had little relevance to the KAR and, once again, they had their own problems to worry about.

The Home Guard also had its problems. Ray Cuthbert reports that after the Emergency 'the Home Guard felt they were badly let down by Baring in 1957. Half felt they were made promises that were not kept, the other half felt they were heroes. The 1960 Lancaster House meeting did not satisfy the hopes of everybody. In 1963 on the Declaration of Independence, Baring's promises were nullified – but there was a good hand-over in 1963.'

Similarly the Europeans in the Government Secretariat who were leaving and the Africans who were taking over were not really very interested in the Kenya Regiment. They were, however, anxious to find a source of economies which was not sensitive with their political masters. This requirement the Kenya Regiment fitted perfectly. It was quite clear compulsory military training for Europeans could not continue and in June, 1962, the last intake passed out of the KRTC at Nakuru. HQ East Africa Command studied future roles for the Regiment and a summary of those agreed by the Kenya Government are given below:

1 An effective fighting unit to support the Kenya Army
2 The nucleus of a citizen army if expansion of the armed forces were needed
3 A framework for CCF or similar activities
4 A disciplined force to back up the Regular Army and Police if required.

These roles looked fine on paper but did not really carry very much conviction with anyone.

However, the significant economy found by the closing of the KRTC made it quite easy to get the money for a small increase in the permanent staff and for the building of a small barrack block at RHQ for our new system of recruit training. We decided on an initial fulltime course of three weeks, of which the final week should be spent in the NFD at a battle camp. Continuation training should be carried out during the first year of territorial service after recruit training. Intakes were carefully selected from the large number of applicants that we continued to receive. We only took about one in four. These intakes were, of course, predominantly African, but there was a significant proportion of Asians and we did manage to have a small number of European volunteers in every intake up to the end. In the climate of opinion in Kenya at that time this was quite an achievement, remembering that all races had to live a completely integrated life within barracks. As far as the existing European territorial element was concerned, we tried to encourage the maximum number to become volunteers. We had a fair degree of success in this, following our main effort at the 1963 annual camp. Indeed one whole company volunteered to a man.

Consequently we gave a fair start to a changed Regiment. Could we have succeeded in the long term? We might have done, but there were formidable obstacles in the way. The tide of colour would have risen rapidly. We already had an African corporal and we would have had to produce African officers very quickly. Future permanent staff would also have been Africanized very rapidly. It must be remembered that there were no seconded European officers within the structure of the KAR within a year of Independence. The effect of these factors would have made it difficult to retain a significant European element within the Regiment.

In any event we were not to be given the chance to continue rebuilding the Regiment on its new footing. The decision to suspend the Regiment was taken primarily because no one in the Government particularly wanted it to continue, and some latent hostility to it still existed. As I have said, the new roles did not carry conviction and any military unit without a convincing role is doomed. Many people believed in their hearts that it was time for the Regiment to finish. There were a very small number of Europeans who could have made an approach to the Government at a high level, perhaps to Kenyatta himself, to try and get a change in Government policy. They chose not to do so.

So it ended, and perhaps it was as well. We went out on a high note. We were able to make suitable arrangements for our Colours, property and funds and we formed the Kenya Regiment Association to keep our comradeship going until we are all too old. Perhaps this was better than the alternative, which might have been a territorial unit differing in too many important respects from its predecessor.

The Colours, according to a *Daily Telegraph* report, were laid up in Nairobi Cathedral when the Regiment was finally disbanded in 1963.

After Kenya became a republic the cathedral authorities felt that was no longer the appropriate place. So Winchester is to be the final resting place.

It announced:

Tomorrow the Colours of the Kenya Regiment will be laid up finally in the garrison church of the Green Jackets Depot at Winchester, thus closing another short African chapter.

CHAPTER 11

INDEPENDENCE
AND AFTER

WITH THE granting of 'Uhuru' in 1963, Kenya became independent. Its leader was Mzee Jomo Kenyatta who had been condemned as the originator of Mau Mau and served seven years as a convicted felon. He became Prime Minister and First President of Kenya. As President he not only surprised, but amazed the Europeans by his understanding, humanity and broad common sense in the rebuilding of the country after a virtual five years of war. He bore no grudges, nor did he penalize those of the administration who had judged him as a 'symbol of darkness'.

When he visited towns and addressed audiences of Africans and Europeans he received standing ovations. He proved himself to be wise, well-informed and broad-minded, and his policies were in the interests of all the races. Not all the measures were popular and many Europeans did sell up and leave, but the greater majority of Europeans accepted the change with some misgivings, though these proved to be unfounded and the country was able to settle down as a mixed society with potential for change and development.

The cry for land was nothing new and it was inevitable that more areas would be needed for the Kikuyu population. The first area to be chosen was the White Highlands, or the Kinangop area, of rich farming land in the Rift Valley Province. There will always be rancour over the sale of the land as the prices were low but the British Government offered what they considered to be a fair price. The Europeans who left were the losers as later on the land fetched astronomical prices. Land deals are always subject to fluctuation and no one is ever satisfied. Now this area is occupied by small African holdings and the value and amount of produce have dropped significantly – a phenomenon which applies to many other areas as well.

Gradually the country accepted the change. The end of hostilities allowed

141

people to think of the future and further development, though some adjustments were difficult for Africans, Asians and Europeans alike. Money from foreign countries built new roads which stretched to Lake Victoria and from the Uganda border to the Coast (it was said because the President disliked travelling by air!). Yugoslav, Israeli and other foreign companies were the contractors.

Nairobi was developed and all its old charm has vanished under towers of ugly concrete, dangerous roundabouts and erratic traffic lights. Mombasa and Eldoret are also expanding at great speed to cater for the population which has exploded at a faster rate than anywhere else in the world. The birth rate is said to have an annual increase of 50% so that the potential demand for land and jobs can barely be imagined.

All clubs, hotels and restaurants in Kenya are multi-racial. Driving through the country one notices that men, women and children are better dressed than in the past, especially the girls. Every village has a school and the children look smart in blue school uniforms with satchels. They are obviously in good health as they travel long distances to and from school, and when passed on the road they look cheerful and friendly greetings are exchanged.

The Kenya Regiment, after two years as a multi-racial regiment, was disbanded and the units of the army are now named after the old KAR battalions – 3rd, 5th, 7th, 11th etc. The Kenya Rifles use the old KAR badges and flashes. There are Asian officers alongside Africans.

Kenya was unique in that it was the only country in the British Empire, other than Southern Rhodesia, which permitted European settlement over a period of 50–60 years. After independence was granted to the new state no further grants of land were allowed. Those who have remained still hold the deeds to their land and they are part of the existing establishment. Any European who has remained has the choice of becoming a Kenya citizen with advantages that apply to all. Many have not taken out citizenship and there is as yet no sign that pressure may be brought to change their minds. The state does, however, prevent any influx of Europeans who may wish to work in Kenya and does not issue work permits. In time it is possible that non-Kenyan citizens of European extraction could be regarded as aliens. If such a law were passed, the choice would be plain. Every country is entitled to pride in its nationhood but one hopes that emergent countries can recognize the debt they owe to those Europeans who, against great odds, left their knowledge and the results of their labours in the country they loved. Many lost their lives in the endeavour.

In the recent droughts, wheat and other staple crops failed. Annexation of more land could seriously affect the preservation of the wild life and if this occurred it would be a tragedy. The destruction of game has become a major scandal. The depredation is carried out by well-armed poachers, mostly Somalis, backed by unscrupulous traders on the coast who sell the ivory, horns and skins to international exporters who make a fortune. Contacts have been traced to

Amsterdam, Singapore, Hong Kong and China, aided and supported by some high-ranking officials within Kenya.

The anti-poaching forces are fully stretched, even with well-trained trackers and light aircraft, in this battle for the survival of the elephant, rhinoceros and other wild life in the game reserves. The safari lodges run by European firms are still a big tourist attraction and their survival depends on financial aid from the United Kingdom, now suffering from a recession so that the grants previously available to retain the services of the European game wardens may soon cease. African game wardens are being trained but it is not an occupation that can be learned without years of devotion, skill and self-sacrifice.

The ivory poaching started [says Ian Parker of the National Archives, Nairobi] when the forest gangs came across elephant which had been killed by the Lincoln bombing raids. They cut out the tusks and hid them in caches, also rhino horn. Each gang probably had its own cache where they operated – often being moved by the Security patrols. After the Emergency the Mau Mau gang leaders returned to the forest and sold the ivory. Jomo Kenyatta permitted this as it was a method of rewarding the forest fighters. He himself did not deal in ivory to his own advantage.

This started some Press interest and there was an ivory rush similar to the discovery of gold or diamonds. Soon, fresh ivory, not the 'found' variety, came on the market and the dealers, middlemen and agents on the coast began to make huge profits. The more powerful the dealers became the more it helped Jomo Kenyatta: he used it as a political tool and again concessions were made to the Kamba to gain their support.

To combat this trade in ivory which was gaining wide publicity the Game Department realized they had to enlist teams to take on the poachers. Many former members of the Regiment were recruited and combined their duties as game wardens and rangers with anti-poaching combat teams of ex-Askaris, many being ex-Mau Mau who had served with the Regiment in the Emergency. Poaching, however, was by now a profitable business with an almost limitless source of game and vast profits to be made. Many of the most successful poachers were Somalis who had come down from the Ogaden, others from Uganda. These gangs were armed, good bushmen and highly dangerous and their activities covered a vast area of southern Kenya. . . .

One particular gang is still operating in the Tsavo area and has been pursued and strafed on many occasions. Light aircraft play a great part in the contacting and bombing of gangs but it is not a one-sided affair as poachers can travel great distances at high speed with no baggage. They are good shots and dangerous customers who can exist without water or rations for days.

To date the Kenya Army has not been used on anti-poaching duties as they would be unable to tackle the poachers on their own terrain.

143

However this could change if the poaching should escalate into a security threat from Somalia or Uganda who might wish to annexe more territory.

Long-term forecasts for Kenya's future vary between the pessimistic – like that of Michael Tetley: 'the population explosion seems unchecked, fuel sources in the form of wood are getting rapidly depleted: long-term prognosis – unfortunately, mass starvation' – to the optimistic and rosy like that of Hugh Hamilton:

Kenya now stands out as the most stable of the 'black' African states and it has already made an impressive impact on the Western world by its stability and democracy. This was very noticeable during and just after the death of Jomo Kenyatta. I would like to see Kenya become the 'bread basket' of Eastern Africa. It has the right climate and, provided the politicians have the will, I am sure the agricultural experts will give all the assistance required to improve the country's productivity, both cereal-wise and in livestock. This economy coupled with a thriving tourist industry – the two Bs (Beach and Big Game) – augur well for the future of the country.

As we have seen, the Kenya Regiment has been extinguished, but its members and their spirit had not. Some still continued to live active lives fighting ivory poachers, some were equally active in business, and some continued to be soldiers in other regiments, like the ones who joined the regiment to which the Kenya Regiment was affiliated – the 60th:

On 8 February, 1964, seven Kenreg members joined the Queen's Royal Rifles. They were Sid Moscoff, Richard Waldron, John Purvis, Raleigh Gilbert, Dave Howard, Len Weaver, and Iain Morrison [the writer of this letter]. Ted Lucas joined some months later and Guy Catchpole, who was at the time serving with the Honourable Artillery Company, transferred to the QRR. Iain Morrison remained with the QRR and, together with Guy Catchpole, transferred to the 4th (V) Battalion Royal Green Jackets when the QRR amalgamated with the London Rifle Brigade and Oxfordshire and Buckinghamshire Light Infantry. Guy left the 4th RGJ and returned to Kenya. Iain Morrison stayed on with the 4th RGJ and finished up as a medical sergeant in the HQ Coy at Davies Street.

Ray Nightingale was commissioned into the 60th Rifles and finished up as a colonel in the SAS.

A Kenya Regiment Newsletter of August, 1964, describes two weekend camps held by the Kenya Regiment Platoon of the QRR:

Seven men turned up and we underwent documentation, medicals and kit issue. We then did half an hour's training until the bar doors were flung open and we were able to settle down for the rest of the weekend elbow-lifting and

144

being paid for it! One QRR member was heard to say, 'I have heard that the Kenya Regiment lads are hard drinkers but never have I seen so much beer consumed by so few!'

The second weekend was more organized:

We camped under canvas on Farley Mount, near Winchester. The Kenya cars arrived slightly later than the main party but were well-equipped with beer, mattresses and extra blankets, in fact all the comforts necessary for a safari. During the afternoon we watched the QRRs doing section attacks and then, after taking ourselves off to Winchester for food and wine, we returned to camp to act as enemy on an exercise which started at 10pm. One of our number was to be dressed as a scientist and the rest were his bodyguards. After about an hour the scientist was captured and doubled away into the night, but then the Kenya Regiment rather spoiled the exercise by recapturing the scientist and avoiding all the patrols by sitting down for a quiet beer in the middle of a field. Alas, we were all eventually captured when the sing song began and we were taken back to camp where we had a nightcap or two round the camp fire before turning in for a couple of hours' kip until reveille.

On Sunday we were taken for a tour around the Green Jackets' Depot in Winchester, and after lunch we were introduced to our 'baby', a rather formidable weapon called the battalion anti-tank gun or BAT for short. At the same time we were issued with an officer, Lieutenant Brand, who was immediately nicknamed 'Willie'. We did a few gun drills, then paraded for our pay and set off on our various journeys home.

The third weekend was

a shooting weekend. We teamed up with the QRR A and C Coys and classified with the Bren (well some of us did!) on Saturday and with the rifle on Sunday. On the Saturday evening we found a very congenial pub and to cap the evening we were sent a bottle of whisky by Major Roy Eve, who was unable to attend the weekend, but wished to be with us in spirit if not in person.

This weekend was the first time that the new QRR/Kenya Regiment uniform was on show and we wore battledress but with the Kenreg colours surmounted with a silver buffalo on the left sleeve, a Kenreg lanyard and, of course, the Colorado beetle. We are hoping that bush hats will be allowed but this will probably not be until we have at least twenty active members, so come on, let's have a few more volunteers.

At the annual camp, 20 June–4 July, 1964, only five were able to attend and they were Corporal Moscoff, Lance-Coropral Waldron, Riflemen Morrison, Gilbert and Howard. The camp was held at Plasterdown, near Tavistock, Devon. This was the lap of luxury, by army standards anyway: stone barracks, proper beds, electric light, constant hot water and 100 WRACs next door.

The first week was spent training with the BAT and included two nights under canvas out on the moors on a battalion exercise. Two of our members passed their army driving test and so we then had two lorries and two BATs and therefore plenty of space to carry our necessary comforts. The fact that we loaded with crates of beer last – so they could come off first – before the exercise was viewed with horror. Colonel Keith Loudon-Shand got to hear about our supplies and seemed to visit us more than any of the other units!

We spent our spare time for the first couple of days reviewing the pub situation. The first night we drove down to Kingsbridge and visited the Ship and the Plough, which is run by Armour Hall (ex-Kenreg) and his wife, and has a very well-decorated African bar. We stayed until the early hours, drinking our ration and eating our fill of Cornish pasties.

The next night we found another pub called the Queen's Head in Tavistock which was ably run by Frank and Con Humphries from Road Hall Farm, Kitale. We took the place over as our RHQ and settled into camp life.

On Saturday 27 June there was a battalion parade in honour of the QRR's Honorary Colonel, Richard Wood MP. When we had been inspected, we marched past at 140 and, as if that was not enough, we then doubled past. Nevertheless, the parade went very well and impressed all who watched it, thanks to the expert training by RSM Rimmer, ex-Kenreg Training Centre. Major Roy Eve turned up after the big parade with some rather weak excuse and was then attached to Brigade HQ as head Pishi!

On Tuesday 30 June we went to the anti-tank range at Okehampton for the first time, to fire the BAT and compete against three other regiments for a bottle of whisky donated by the Brigadier. Much to everybody's amazement we (the Kenreg) won. There was some dispute, but we managed to convince the judges that the shots that they did not see hitting the target – a tank – actually went through the hole in the tank's turret. On our arrival back at camp we were presented with another bottle of whisky by our Colonel, Lieutenant Colonel Loudon-Shand, to mark an occasion that he thought he would never see.

On the evening of 30 June the battalion moved back to Okehampton in preparation for a divisional exercise. This was of course without Corporals Moscoff and Waldron, who were to umpire the London Scottish during the exercise; both slept soundly through the General's O Group. These two men spent their time jumping into and climbing out of marshes and rivers. The USAAF did some very impressive low-level bombing, during which everybody forgot the war and sat down to watch their display. Rifleman Howard for some unknown reason was with the I section (Intelligence) and had a pretty comfortable time. Riflemen Morrison and Gilbert were seconded to the mortars for the exercise.

146

Jock Rutherfurd continues the pioneer tradition, and tells the following remarkable story:

A year or so ago I was panning gold up in the Turkwell river which is on the border of Turkhana land – or rather I was organizing three or four hundred Turkhana, who were doing the panning. I was sitting under my dining tree one evening, reading. It was about 8 o'clock when a bullet went past my left ear. I didn't have any arms in the camp and the only thing I had with me right there and then was the camp chair I was sitting on and so I went for this guy who was only about ten yards away, and hit him over the head, which surprised him so much that his second bullet missed at point-blank range. But then I turned to get a panga which was lying not far away – if I had had it in the first place I would have clobbered him – and he nipped away a bit, fired a third shot and got me in the back. It went through my left shoulder and came out in my chest. He didn't realize he had hit me, and at that stage he either ran out of ammunition or he ran out of nerve – I don't know which – but he never came back. At the time one wasn't to know that, and I was bleeding pretty fast and thinking, 'Well, I've got about 15 or 20 minutes to go'. I hadn't been hit myself before, but I had seen plenty of others, and all my chaps by this time had bolted and there was nothing I could do. First, I thought, in this situation – like a drowning man – you're supposed to bring back all the memories of things you'd done in life – but I got nothing, absolutely zero, out of that. So I started stuffing cotton wool into the various holes; the one in my chest was pretty big. That probably, in a sense, saved me.

After about an hour or so some of my chaps started crawling back from out of the bush and, with what breath I had, I called them up – because they weren't to know whether I was dead or alive. The Turkhana were very good. The man who shot me was a Potok – people we were having trouble with and who had always been a cagey bunch to deal with any way. So the whole lot of Turkhana came in with their bows and arrows and sat around, which at least gave one a bit of confidence. One of my chaps, called – of all things – Christopher, was a real bushman and volunteered to go to the nearest mission station – which was seventeen miles across country on a pitch-black night and the whole area was littered with buffalo and lion – and I didn't think anything much more of it. I was trying to keep myself upright; I knew if I went down I would stay down. Meanwhile, all these chaps were around me snoring their heads off and quite happy.

About 3 o'clock in the morning, three rifle shots went off – not a great morale-booster at that time – but what I hadn't heard, because of the river running past just by the camp, was the Land Rover coming up on the other side. In the lamplight three tribal policemen appeared with their rifles. They had fired the shots since they hadn't known what was going on either. With the policemen was the most incredible vision in white. I was a bit down by now and

I thought, 'Cripes – I never expected to go up there. I thought I was going the other way!' But it turned out to be an Irish Catholic Sister from the mission station. Christopher had not only got there, but had given a fairly accurate description of what had happened and the Sister was carrying pain-killer, a bottle of drip-feed and an anti-bacterial. She took over the situation and I had to take orders from then on.

I did have a radio telephone, but they are no use at night; there is too much static, so we had to wait till the morning before trying to get hold of the Flying Doctors. By sheer coicidence I was due to leave the next day for two months and a relief man was being flown in so I knew there was an aircraft coming at some stage. But I didn't know how long I could hold out because I had lost a lot of blood.

In the morning the Sister refused to allow me to get up and handle the radio. I explained how to switch it on and she got on the air with no radio procedure whatever and, in the best of Irish, she shut up the whole network countrywide within a matter of minutes. All she was saying was 'Jock is shot' and that she wanted a doctor and an aircraft immediately, and the whole country was listening in. Having repeated this about fifty times, various people got on the air to say that they had got the message and they would see that it got there, and finally the Flying Doctors got on the air to say they would make it about midday.

I was not allowed to do anything, but managed to get a change of shirt and things. The doctor turned out to be a beautiful blonde and she took one sort of horrified look around this blood-spattered tent and said 'Let's go', and that's what we did. It was a pretty rough flight – two hours in the middle of the day over the Rift Valley – I can think of better things than that!

As everybody had got to hear about the business because it was all over the air, everybody turned up at the hospital to ask what was happening. Tom Pringle, who has run the laboratory there for years and is an old friend, took a pint of blood out of them and he was quite happy. After a few days in hospital I was OK.

As a sort of afterthing – Christopher never even bothered to come back that night, he was off on a party in Kapoeta or somewhere and didn't turn up again for two or three weeks, whereupon he got his right reward. Sister Cornissius, as she was called, would not take any kind of token or thanks in kind. Those are the sort of people who really keep us going in the bush these days.

KENYA REGIMENT RIFLE CLUB

The inaugural meeting of the Kenya Regiment Rifle Club was held on 16 June, 1952, under the presidency of Colonel Guy Campbell, Angus McDonald being elected chairman and Brian Hawkins secretary. Previous to this, club shooting had started in 1924 in numerous rifle and pistol clubs throughout Kenya which were all incorporated on 2 August, 1929 as the Kenya Rifle Association. Competitive shooting therefore has been well established for over sixty years. Teams have visited Kenya from the UK and elsewhere and our club members have competed annually at Bisley and in other countries outside Africa.

The driving interest of Brian Hawkins is the backbone of the club which celebrated its twenty-fifth anniversary in 1977. In conjunction with the Kenya Rifle Association, Kenya's shots have distinguished themselves all over the world. To name only a few: Charles Trotter, formerly of Kenya, who won the Queen's Prize at Bisley in 1975 when shooting for Guernsey, and Dave Drummond, several times Kenya Captain at Bisley. He served with great distinction during the troubled years of 1952–6 and now runs a successful safari business. Our Nairobi club room is full of trophies and photographs of visiting teams. The Kenya Team is now comprised of Asian, African and European members. Early names that figured prominently in our successes were Brian himself, RSM Jack Holland and CSMs Lew Jones and Ted Eves, and Captain Peter Welsh (now Major-General), a noted Army champion shot.

KENYA REGIMENT ASSOCIATION

When, before the shutters finally went up, all members of the Regiment, past and present, decided to form an Association, our museum was converted into premises which housed our Roll of Honour 1939–45 and 1952–7. Officers were appointed to run not only the clerical side but to provide meals, a bar and staff. Kamau, the head barman, is an old Askari and former member of the Regiment. It is a meeting place which welcomes all friends of the members and is now open to both Asians and Africans as associate members. The bar is well patronized and the staff provides meals. The committee meets monthly and sends out newsletters to all members in Kenya, the United Kingdom, South Africa, Canada, Australia and New Zealand, and wherever there are former members.

The Kenya Rifle Club, now combined with the original Kenya Regiment Rifle Club formed in 1952, shares the premises, using them as its headquarters. Wives, children and friends of members are eligible for election.

Our building takes up one small corner of the old Headquarters which now belongs to the Kenya Police. It is full of memories. The Regiment is very proud to have a signed photograph presented by Her Majesty the Queen. Also on display are plaques presented by numerous regiments and ships of the Royal Navy. Over the bar is the head of a female buffalo which killed one of our trackers during the Emergency. A photograph of Sergeant Gray Leakey and the citation of his Victoria Cross is a reminder of the Regiment's most famous son.

The UK Branch hold an annual reunion dinner in November in the Headquarters of the 4th Battalion the Royal Green Jackets in Davies Street, London. There is an active branch in Johannesburg and we hope members in Durban will follow their example.

Lieutenant-Colonel John Garvey is the perpetual chairman of the 'Old Comrades Branch' in South Africa, which flourishes with some forty members. He was one of the pre-1939–45 war officers of the Regiment, having enlisted at the start, been promoted sergeant in 1938 and commissioned in February 1939.

The Association does much good work in assisting members who need help or are ill. Annual gatherings are full of good company and nostalgia. None of us are getting any younger. Our ranks get thinner every year but we decided that we would keep going until we could no longer raise ten or more members.

Service with the Kenya Regiment was an experience for all members that none of us will ever forget and the friendships we made in Kenya were a reward for the hard work and long hours spent with a unique Regiment. How lucky we were to be given this opportunity! Though the Regiment is no longer in being, those of us who served with it retain the happiest of memories. The Association lives on and, judging by the letters and the occasional tape recording of a typical regimental reunion, they are still convivial. The language is as I remember it – full of expletives, but abundant with good humour and nostalgia. Many old friends have died, but, while the rest live, they will give a good account of themselves, whether it be in Kenya, South Africa, Australia, New Zealand, Canada or the UK – their lives are still full and success has come to many of them in a wide variety of occupations: the late Walter Schuster was a farmer, Ray Mayers has a vast cattle ranch at Voi in Kenya, so large that he has to pay £400,000 rates to the government: Billy Woodley (who is active against game poachers) still runs the Tsavo Game Park with Jackie Barrah in the Nairobi HQ of the Game Department; Sid Moscoff now lives in South Africa, with a printing business in Johannesburg where he is active in the Johannesburg Kenreg Association; Francis Erskine still lives in Kenya where his family is in the grocery business, and so on.

Here the story ends, and to all old comrades and loved friends I wish happiness and prosperity. Should there be difficult times ahead I am certain they will meet them with the same comradeship, humour and courage which were our watchwords.

I want to believe that when I leave this earth I will find in the hereafter a Branch of our Regimental Association who will welcome me into their midst and that from the open verandah I will have a view of the old Rift Valley road overlooking Lake Naivasha and in the distant haze the hills beyond Nakuru. We shall all be young again and laughter will fill the air.

APPENDICES

Author's Note

Every effort has been made to include all the major events in the life of the regiment. Any errors or omissions are regretted. Colonel Ray Nightingale and I exhausted our memories to avoid offending individuals by omitting their names from the text, but nevertheless not all the lists of personnel and appointments are complete, for which I apologize.

APPENDIX I

UP TO AND INCLUDING
THE SECOND WORLD WAR

A. Kenya Defence Force 1931

Among names in the Official List of the Kenya Defence Force, July, 1931 (Government Printer, Nairobi) are several which appear in the Kenya Regiment of later times, notably:

A. C. Lewin (Brigadier-General)
C. J. Valentine (Lieutenant)
A. H. W. Sheldrick (Captain)
H. C. Nightingale (Lieutenant)
A. C. Anstey (Captain)

Some of these names belong to Kenreg men and others to their fathers or other relations.

B. Roll of the Original Staff of the Kenya Regiment (TF) 1937

Brigadier-General A. C. Lewin CB CMG DSO ADC (Honorary Colonel)
Major A. Dunstan-Adams MC (later Colonel A. Dunstan-Adams OBE MC TD) Honorary Colonel of the Regiment, 1950
Captain O. Lennox-Browne
Captain C. J. Valentine (now Lieutenant-Colonel C. J. Valentine OBE ED) Commanding Officer March, 1950–April, 1952
Captain W. W. Mackinlay (now Lieutenant-Colonel) Commanded 1st EA Light Battery (53rd)

Captain C. H. Redhead ED (later Major)
Major The Lord Stratheden and Campbell (Coldstream Guards)
Captain J. Forrest (later OC Prince of Wales' CCF)
Lieutenant E. I. Gledhill (later Major)
Captain R. S. Boyd (later Lieutenant-Colonel)
Captain J. Oates (later Colonel, MC)
Surgeon-Captain J. Carman
Padre J. Gillett
RSM J. Cummins (Irish Guards) (later Lieutenant-Colonel and Commandant,
    Kenya Police Reserve)
CSM V. Bobbett (Welsh Guards) (later Major)
CSM C. Broomfield (Grenadier Guards) (later Major)
CSM Carter (Grenadier Guards)
CSM Allen (Scots Guards)

C. Kenya Regiment Establishment 1937–9
(list from Charlie Broomfield)

HQ: GYMKHANA ROAD, NAIROBI

Commanding Officer	Lieutenant-Colonel A. Dunstan-Adams OBE MC TD
Second-in-Command	Major J. Forrest
RQMS	N. Cole Curril
Clerk	Mr Enouff

NO. 1 COY – NAIROBI AREA COMPANY – NAIROBI

(HQ: at Regimental HQ)

Company Commander	Captain C. J. Valentine
Second-in-Command	Lieutenant G. H. Branston
Platoon Commanders	Lieutenants A. P. Manning, G. Luckham, A. M. Goldhawk, F. W. Bompas
CSM	CSM D. Powrie
Platoon Sergeants	Sergeants S. Ellis, J. Harvey, C. A. H. Swift

NO. 2 COY – NAKURU AREA COMPANY – NAKURU, THOMPSONS FALLS, RUMURUTI, NAIVASHA

(HQ: PSI's house in Nakuru)

Company Commander	Major Mackenzie

154

NO. 2 COY – *contd*

Platoon Commanders	Lieutenants C. W. F. Crawford, Ivor Lean
CSM	CSM Charles Corbett
Platoon Sergeant	Sergeant E. W. Temple-Boreham

NO. 3 COMPANY – ELDORET AREA COMPANY – ELDORET, KITALE, MOLO, KERICHO, LUMBWA, SOTIK, SONGHOR, FORT TERNAN, KISUMU, KAKAMEGA, MOIBEN

(HQ in drill hall next to Eldoret police station)

Company Commander	Major H. Buxton
CSM	CSM Sutton
CQMS	CQMS S. Churchill
Platoon Sergeants	Sergeants M. P. Byers (Kisumu), C. C. Gray (Kericho)

NO. 4 COMPANY

(HQ: Gymkhana Road, Nairobi with 1 Coy)

| CSM | CSM Allen |

UGANDA PLATOON

(HQ with No. 3 Coy, Eldoret, operated by PSI)
(The members of this platoon were mostly Government officials.)
Lieutenant F. H. Crittenden (later Major)

D. *Roll of Honour 1939–45*

Aggett H. B.	Harford S. R.	Nash R.
Aitken C. C.	Harvey L.	Nell L.
Alexander D.	Haslett F. S.	Newmark B. L.
Allen S. J.	Hasluck H. M.	Padkin G. C.
Ayre W. H.	Helberg F.	Park D. S.
Ball R. S.	Higgs R. B.	Paterson H. M.
Biddle N. R.	Hilton J. R.	Percival P. B.
Bingham K. R. DFC	Hinds D. P.	Phillips K.
Boon D. M.	Hirst R. F. W.	Pilling H. G. DFC
Booth H. P.	Horrocks D. W.	Pitkin R. L.
Brent T. M.	Hitchcock H. A.	Pollock S. R.
Brickwell W. A.	Hudson-Jones C. T.	Poppleton W.
Broughton D. H. MC	Hullneck C. R.	Pretorius M. M.
Brown S. J.	Human J. A.	Reynolds H. G.
Brown J. S.	Izzard J. L.	Reynolds-Ball R. C.

Chapman A. S. MC	Jackson F.	Rhys-Maizand K.
Charcal-Ambus A.	Jacobs L. A.	Robertson L.
Chinneck H. S.	Jacquemier P.	Robson D. V.
Clifford R. G.	Jarret S. L.	Roets J. N. J.
Confait A. E.	Jones J. B.	Ross A. P.
Cooke D. M.	Joubert L. S.	Shillitoe P. G.
Cootton P. T. DFC	Keel P. V. A.	Skelton R. S.
Copland C. M. R.	Kirk F. E.	Sladen E. C.
Copland J. H.	Lang J. D.	Smith A. W.
Corbet-Ward R.	Leach S. J.	Smith L. O.
Corynoon J.	Leakey N. G. VC	Smithyman W. R.
Coulson R. H.	Litchfield E. G.	Sossens P. V.
Cowen J. A.	Lloyd R. M. DFC	Spiers C. R.
Daly A. T.	Locke J.	Steenkamp R. C. M.
Dandy A. G. G.	Luck R. C. DFC	Stohr O. M.
Davie C.	Luckham E. H. C.	Suckling E. W.
Davis R. W.	Macdermott G.	Swift J. H. F.
De Haaff N. C. A.	Macintyre A. C.	Symons D. J.
Denchfield J. E.	Maclean J. A.	Tickwell M. L.
Docker F. A. M.	Maclean J. D.	Townsley G.
Evans G. A.	Magson R. W.	Van Plaster J. R.
Findlay G. R.	Marsh R.	West J. M. MM
Firth J. F.	Matthias M. N.	Wheeler G. Y.
Fittal L. A. W.	McClelland W. R. D.	White G. M.
Foster J. P.	McKenzie A.	White R. W. K.
Freeman M. H.	Measures H. T.	Widdows J.
Gardner D. M.	Meyer J. H.	Willbourn C.
Garland T. B.	Migeot A. E.	Williams L.
Genower J. A.	Millar W.	Williams W. H. W.
Gille L. A.	Miller A. W. D.	Williamson T. McD.
Girdlestone C. H. N.	Milward R. W. C.	Wilton R. N.
Gordon D. R.	Mole A. H.	Woods L. B.
Greensted D. P.	Montagu C. S. B.	Worthington R. B.
Griffin T. O.	Moodie B. S. CH	Wright L.
Hand J. R.	Naper M. O. L.	Young T. D.

E. Some Names of Members of the Kenya Regiment 1937–45
(from C. Broomfield)

A. Ball (No. 1 Coy)
A. Trafford (No. 1 Coy)
T. R. King (No. 3 Coy)

J. Hamilton (No. 1 Coy) to Major
John Percival
Ray Mayers MBE (No. 2 Coy)
Gregory Grant MC (No. 3 Coy Molo) to Captain
Peter Ragg (No. 3 Coy Sotik) to Captain
Robert Rintoul (No. 3 Coy Sotik)
Ken Beaton (No. 3 Coy Sotik) to Major
Peter Huth (No. 3 Coy Kitale)
John Gillett (No. 2 Coy)
No. 10 John Bamber (No. 1 Coy) to Captain
Brian Figgis (No. 1 Coy)
J. H. Jessop to Major
David Sheldrick MC to Major
John Poppleton (No. 1 Coy)
Rex Milford MBE (No. 1 Coy) to Adjutant 4 KAR – Major
D. H. Reid (to 4 KAR – Captain)
Colin Campbell MC (to 4 KAR – Major)
David Gillett MC (to 4 KAR – Captain)
Johnny Start (No. 3 Coy Molo – to 4 KAR Intelligence Officer – Lieutenant)
Peter Wilson MC (No. 3 Coy Kericho – to 4 KAR – Major)
'Beef' Barchard (No. 1 Coy to 4 KAR – Captain – wounded on Leik Hill,
    Burma)
Pat Gascoigne (to 4 KAR – Major)
D. Trent (to 4 KAR – Lieutenant)
D. Peddar (to 4 KAR – Lieutenant) ex-South America
D. Butcher (to 4 KAR – Lieutenant)
D. Cowan (to 4 KAR – Lieutenant)
Lon Wilkie (to 4 KAR – RQMS)
Captain C. J. Valentine to Lieutenant-Colonel
Lieutenant G. H. Branston to Lieutenant-Colonel
Lieutenant A. P. Manning to Captain
Lieutenant F. W. Bompas to Major
Sergeant J. Garvey MBE to Lieutenant-Colonel and Staff Officer 11th (EA)
    Division
Sergeant C. A. H. Swift to Major
CSM Charles Corbett to Lieutenant-Colonel
Sergeant E. W. Temple-Boreham MC (to 4 KAR – Major)
Sergeant M. P. Byers to Major
C. A. Richards (Uganda Pl) (became Resident, Buganda Province)
R. E. Dreschfield (Uganda Pl) (to 4 KAR – Captain – became Attorney-General,
    Uganda)
C. Powell Cotton (Uganda Pl) (became Provincial Commissioner, Northern
    Province, Uganda)

P. Thiel (Uganda Pl) (became Assistant Town Clerk, Jinja, Uganda)
J. Roe (Uganda Pl) (veterinary officer, Uganda)
J. W. Cooper (Uganda Pl) (veterinary officer, Uganda)
K. Pritchard (Uganda Pl) (became bank manager)
J. B. Hobson (Uganda Pl) (returned to legal profession)
John Keeble (Uganda Pl) (returned to legal profession)
P. R. B. Everett (Uganda Pl) (returned to legal profession)
J. Holcombe (Uganda Pl) (returned to legal profession)
Dicky Board MC Mombasa (to 4 KAR – Captain – Mortar Platoon Officer)
Peter Anderson MC (No. 1 Coy to 2 KAR – Lieutenant – Mortar Platoon Officer)
Jackie Black (No. 1 Coy) to Major
Gray Leakey to Sergeant (received the VC for action against Italian tanks – killed)
Ray Nightingale (to 4 KAR – Captain)
A. E. Sweatman to Lieutenant-Colonel
M. Berkeley to Major
G. Durrington to Major
N. Duirs to Major
J. Hart to Major
J. H. Simpson to Major
A. W. Hopcraft to Captain
D. Furse to Captain
O. Lennox-Browne to Major
W. B. Kerr to Major

APPENDIX II

THE RE-FORMING OF THE REGIMENT AND THE END

A. Kenya Regiment (TF) as at 20 October, 1952

Colonel A. Dunstan-Adams OBE MC TD	Honorary Colonel
Lieutenant-Colonel Guy Campbell MC	Commanding Officer
Lieutenant-Colonel Gerald Whyte	Second-in-Command (UK)
Captain Roly Guy	Adjutant
Captain Angus Macdonald	Assistant Adjutant
Captain Dick Cornell	Training Officer (joined 1953)
Dr Donald Hicks	Medical Officer
Rev. Jimmy Gillett	Chaplain
CQMS George Slater	Acting Quartermaster
RSM M. Pendry	RSM
CSM J. Holland DCM MM	CSM
ORQMS W. G. Hutchinson	ORQMS
Sergeant G. Nunn	PSI
Sergeant Hidden	PSI
CSM Croft	PSI

A COMPANY – NAIROBI

Captain 'Boxer' Brown	Officer Commanding
Lieutenant Bob Browning	Platoon Commanders
Shaun Franklin	
Mike Finnigan	
Pat Molloy	

159

Major David Gillett MC	Officer Commanding
Captain Ray Mayers MBE	Second-in-Command
Lieutenant Neville Cooper MC	Platoon Commanders
Peter Anderson MC	
Campbell-Clause	

C COMPANY — ELDORET/KITALE

Major Dick Josselyn	Officer Commanding
Captain Peter Ragg	Second-in-Command
Lieutenant John Klynsmith	Platoon Commanders
James McKillop	
Gerry Wigram	

B. *Decorations Awarded to Members of the Kenya Regiment (TF) Since 20 October, 1952*

OBE

Lieutenant-Colonel G. T. H. Campbell MC

MBE

Major N. M. C. Cooper MC	Colour Sergeant J. D. Campbell MC
Major R. C. W. Nightingale	Sergeant N. A. Powell
Captain R. K. Guy	Private P. H. Berry
Captain W. S. Gash	Private H. W. D. Kearney
Second Lieutenant M. R. M. Tetley	

MC

Major V. Fey	Captain R. J. Folliot
Captain F. D. M. Erskine	Lieutenant V. A. N. Swain
Captain F. W. de M. Woodley	

DCM

WO II J. A. Miller

GM

Major N. M. C. Cooper MBE MC	Sergeant I. L. Prichard
Lieutenant D. P. Brooks	Sergeant D. H. McCabe
Sergeant P. G. Nicholas	

MM

WO II E. E. Holyoak
Sergeant B. R. Hatfield
Sergeant D. R. Prophet

Sergeant V. J. Summers
Sergeant G. M. Plenderleith
Private P. J. S. Hewitt

BEM

Lieutenant J. A. McNab
WO II G. E. Slater
WO II N. G. Hales
WO II A. Mendel
Sergeant N. J. P. Hewett

Sergeant J. P. Tooley
Sergeant W. H. A. Botto
Sergeant E. T. Bruce-Low
Private J. M. Gore
Tracker/CSM L. Hoeden

QUEEN'S POLICE MEDAL FOR GALLANTRY (POSTHUMOUS)

Lieutenant J. A. McNab BEM

COLONIAL POLICE MEDAL

Tracker/Corporal Gibson Wambugu

Tracker Kitum arap Koech

MENTION IN DESPATCHES

Major R. C. W. Nightingale MBE
Major J. E. G. Vetch
Major D. J. S. Riley
Captain C. P. Beck
Captain J. D. Humphreys
Captain M. R. Higgins
Captain L. J. Gill
Lieutenant (QM) F. Wakefield
Lieutenant H. W. J. Willemse
Lieutenant J. H. H. Dugmore
Lieutenant J. D. Purves
Second Lieutenant J. F. L. Richardson
Colour Sergeant J. D. Campbell MBE MC
Sergeant W. M. J. Blanche
Sergeant J. A. Millar DCM

Sergeant B. D. McCleary
Sergeant D. S. Bush
Sergeant E. T. Bruce-Low BEM
Corporal J. A. Williams
Private J. M. Gore BEM
Private A. E. Brooks
Private F. C. Dansie
Private P. D. Owen-Thomas
Private C. S. Templer
Private N. M. Challoner
Private J. C. P. E. Kruger
Private B. U. Middleboe
Tracker/CSM Kagwa Layia
Tracker/CSM Githenge Gitui
Tracker/Sergeant Sarngarube Dadi

COMMANDER-IN-CHIEF'S COMMENDATIONS

Captain R. I. M. Campbell
Captain L. J. Gill

Private L. K. M. Pearse
Private J. T. Stephen

Lieutenant D. A. Veakins
Second Lieutenant W. Morton
Corporal F. Betts (RAVC attached)
Corporal S. Hayhurst (RAVC attached)
Corporal J. H. Sealey (RAVC attached)
Corporal W. C. H. H. Eastbrook

Private A. P. Pape
Private J. Russell-Pell
Private J. A. Blanche
Private P. D. Harvey-Kelly
Tracker/Corporal Yego arap Serikwa

C. Citation for Distinguished Conduct Medal for WO II John Austin Miller

By the beginning of February it had been discovered that a large Mau Mau organization existed on certain farms in the Thika Settled Area. It was decided to establish a mock gang in the area with a view to obtaining the enemy's secrets and breaking up his organization. The execution of this plan was left for the most part to Miller.

During the period 1 February–21 March Miller, disguised as a terrorist, attended, with his mock gang, a number of meetings of the top Mau Mau Committee. He also managed to eliminate some active terrorists, including one well-known leader. In addition, he was responsible for the recovery of two precision weapons.

On 21 March he again attended a meeting with all the senior Mau Mau office holders in the course of which he successfully directed a police patrol onto the scene so that all fifteen Mau Mau members were killed or arrested.

For the whole period Miller showed immense courage combined with careful planning and resource. One slip at any meeting would have resulted not only in the failure of the scheme but obviously in the death of Miller and his party which was always very weak in numbers. In addition the danger of directing a police party onto a meeting in which he was taking part should not be underestimated.

It was felt that Miller's conduct was of the highest order throughout, and rivals in cold courage anything achieved by the Security Forces during the Emergency. These incidents, moreover, crown a highly successful career as an FIO and are by no means the first occasions on which his courage has been noted.

D. Roll of Honour 1952–7

Baillon J. H.	Edwards D. R.	Pitt-Moore M. A.
Beckley V. R. S.	Fell H. S.	Purves N. H.
Bellingham D.	Gordon W. J.	Robinson A. A.
Bianchi J. V.	Luckes J. W.	Symons C. J.
Bingley R. R.	McNab J. A. BEM	Tomlinson G. A. E.

Boyce R. E.
Byfield A. M. D.
Cantounias M. C.
Chapman G. E.
Crowther A. F.
Dowey J. M.

Mouton C. J.
Norie D. A.
Parke R. C.
Paterson I. F. S.
Pearson J. M.

Webster J. M.
White D. A. J.
Wood-Whyte R. B.
Wortley F. A.
Wright J.

E. Officers Who Served in Operations Coy During the Emergency

Ray Nightingale MBE
Bill Woodley MC
Brian Williamson
Jerry Adam
Simon Reynolds
Mike Tremlett
Nigel Bulley
Stan Bleazard
Henry Willemse

Boet Ole Bruin
Eddy Bristow
Jack Harnett
David Durrant
Francis Erskine MC
Mickey Wright
Freddy Seed
George Newby
Mike Higgins

Scotty Meintjes
Denis Alexander (MO)
Tony Bannister
Bob Muir
Clive Catanio
Conway Plough
Dave Rooken-Smith
Dingo Plenderleith

F. Officers Who Served with Police Special Forces During the Emergency

'Kitch' Morson
Walter Gash
John Stanfield
Peter Hewett
Glen Cottar
Jim Stephen

Denis Kearney
Parry Verlaque
Derek Prophet
B. de Bruin
Jacky Millar
Bill Eastbrook

Eric Holyoak
George Hales
Don Bush
Peter Van Aardt
Laurie Pearse
Bob Folliot

G. Officers Who Served in the Kikuyu Guard

J. D. Campbell
G. H. Knaggs
E. C. Brooks
H. S. B. Thatcher
R. T. Polhill
A. C. Wisdom
H. Gallon-Fenzi
W. I. Pretty
W. R. Bosch
P. Owen-Smith
F. C. Dansie

H. A. Valentine
B. U. Middleton
H. W. D. Kearney
P. G. Nicholas
J. F. Weller
D. R. Petrie
T. T. Fjastard
G. R. Nightingale
F. Overdyck
J. N. Higginson
V. M. Drysdale

F. J. McCartney
C. P. Moore
R. J. G. Waldron
T. N. Martindale
F. Aagaard
P. W. W. Manger
J. Campbell-Gillies
A. H. M. Klynsmith
I. C. S. Parker
D. A. Alcorn
K. V. Payet

F. C. Dansie
R. B. Wood-White
I. F. S. Paterson
J. Lawrence
W. A. F. Young
J. A. Rutherfurd
M. J. Prettejohn
P. L. Upson
H. W. Storm

D. H. McCabe
F. V. Odendaal
N. R. Powell
J. P. L. Verlaque
J. O. J. Bamber
G. S. Catchpole
I. D. Campbell
R. C. Nightingale

P. M. R. D'Adhemar
C. S. Templar
C. E. Cade
A. T. Veakins
R. McConnell
D. W. Allen
B. D. Veakins

H. Kenya Regiment Training Centre Staff 1952–6

1952

COMPANY COMMANDER

Major A. D. Lewis DSO   Dorset Regiment

PLATOON COMMANDERS

Captain A. C. K. Barkas   Durham Light Infantry
        H. Bell   York and Lancaster Regiment
        K. C. Coutts   RAEC

COMPANY SERGEANT-MAJOR

CSM J. G. Cameron   Scots Guards

QMSI

CSM H. V. Ward   Army PT School
    T. Slack

INSTRUCTORS

Sergeant J. Bull   Royal Warwickshire Regiment
         J. Cameron   The Black Watch (RHR)
         R. Robertson
         E. Dargul   Gordon Highlanders
         J. E. Grindrod   Grenadier Guards
         A. Swinhoe   Coldstream Guards
         V. Glover   Grenadier Guards
         C. G. Prior   Royal Northumberland Fusiliers
         G. Unsworth   Loyal Regiment
         S. A. Turner   Royal Hampshire Regiment

164

1953

Sergeant W. H. Charmer	Worcestershire Regiment
N. A. Hawkes	King's Royal Rifle Corps
E. J. Sennett	Suffolk Regiment
J. Sharratt	West Yorkshire Regiment
A. Young	Royal Scots Fusiliers

CQMS

Colour Sergeant N. F. Eccles   Cameron Highlanders

1954

SECOND-IN-COMMAND

Major A. C. K. Barkas

PLATOON COMMANDER

Captain N. Clarke   Essex Regiment

INSTRUCTORS

Sergeant W. Millar	Seaforth Highlanders
S. Brayshaw	King's Shropshire Light Infantry
N. Lane	

1955

OFFICER COMMANDING

Major A. C. K. Barkas   Durham Light Infantry

SECOND-IN-COMMAND

Captain H. Bell   York and Lancaster Regiment

EDUCATION OFFICER

Captain W. Lynam   RAEC

PLATOON COMMANDERS

Captain W. Clarke	Essex Regiment
Lieutenant D. Hunter	Kenya Regiment

CSM R. W. Garner   King's Royal Rifle Corps

CQMS

Colour Sergeant W. Eccles   Cameron Highlanders

INSTRUCTORS

Sergeant W. Millar	Seaforth Highlanders
G. Adye	King's Royal Rifle Corps
S. Brayshaw	King's Shropshire Light Infantry
N. Hawkes	King's Royal Rifle Corps
S. Brisland	Gloucestershire Regiment
D. Humber	Coldstream Guards
K. Billington	King's Own Yorkshire Light Infantry

PHYSICAL TRAINING INSTRUCTOR

SSI J. Workman

COOK SERGEANT

Sergeant J. McDonough   Army Catering Corps

1955–6

OFFICER COMMANDING

Major W. T. Woodruffe MC

SECOND-IN-COMMAND

Major P. G. Grattan MBE

PLATOON OFFICERS

Major H. Bell	York and Lancaster Regiment
Major N. Clarke	Essex Regiment
Major J. Wetherall	Northamptonshire Regiment

COMPANY SERGEANT-MAJOR

CSM H. T. Stott   Irish Guards

Sergeant H. Brayshaw   King's Shropshire Light Infantry

INSTRUCTORS

Sergeant P. Scott-Davies   Scots Guards
          D. Humber   Coldstream Guards
          W. Hawkes   King's Royal Rifle Corps
          W. Millar   Seaforth Highlanders
          W. Charmer   Worcestershire Regiment
          D. Davies

APTC

Staff-Sergeant C. Workman   APTC
later – CSM R. S. Cardy   Irish Guards

I. Some Operations and Incidents

1952

| 20 August | Hoodlum | 25 October | Kiambu raid |
| 21 October | Jock Scott | 6 November | Tigoni raid |

1953

15 March	Dead Duck	1–3 July	Buttercup Leaf
21 March	Deep Valley	5–7 July	Final Chukker
27 March	Naivasha raid	20–23 July	Carnation I
18 April	Immediate	26–28 July	Carnation II
27 April	Thunder Box	27 August	Salt Cake
10 May	Immediate	10 November	Cartilage
6–12 June	Epsom I started	12 November	Light Armour
13–21 June	Epsom last phase	18 November	1st Lincoln raid
	started	11 December	Blowlamp
24–6 June	Buttercup		

1954

23 February	Barafu 25	24 April	Anvil started
3 March	First mention of Anvil		(ended 24 May)
6 March	Hammer	18 September	Search

1955

| January | First Flute |

After this date large-scale operations were not used.

J. A Regimental Song

(to the tune of Onward Christian Soldiers)

Onward plateau soldiers,
Marching round Ngong,
Doing f——— arms drill,
All day f——— long,
Get your lines in order,
Get those mess tins straight,
Get fell in you bastards,
Always bloody late.

Chorus   Onwards Plateau Soldiers,
            Marching round Ngong,
            Doing f——— arms drill,
            All day f——— long.

First day on manoeuvres,
Next day on a tewt,
Then down to the range Boys,
Cooley cup to shoot.
Alcoholic tremors,
Tongues all white with fur,
Try to spot a target on,
A bloody large green blur.

Chorus   Onwards Plateau Soldiers,

In C Company mess tent,
Asked 'any complaints?'
Some poor clot says 'Yes, sir',
Orderly Sergeant faints.
'What's your bloody grouse, lad?'
Ord'ly Officer yells.
'Taste these bloody spuds, sir,
And this bloody boiled egg smells.'

Chorus   Onwards Plateau Soldiers,

Our Platoon Commander,
Leads the bloody race,
We lump bloody Bren guns,
He a small map case.
Henry shouts out 'Double, lads,
Enemy in sight!'
Plateau voices answer him,
'F—— you, Jack we're all right.'

Chorus   Onwards Plateau Soldiers,
Marching as to war,
Get the bloody hell, boys,
Back to sixty four.

APPENDIX III

MISCELLANEOUS
PAPERS

A. Officers and PSIs Who Have Served in the Regiment

HONORARY COLONELS OF THE KENYA REGIMENT (TF)

Brigadier-General A. C. Lewin CB CMG DSO ADC
Colonel A. Dunstan-Adams OBE MC TD

COMMANDING OFFICERS OF THE KENYA REGIMENT (TF)

Lieutenant-Colonel A. Dunstan-Adams OBE MC TD	1 June, 1937–31 August, 1940
Lieutenant-Colonel T. L. Barkas OBE	1 September, 1940–1 March, 1941
Lieutenant-Colonel A. D. Stitt DSO MC	2 March–1 June, 1941
Lieutenant-Colonel C. J. Valentine OBE ED	28 March, 1950–1 April, 1952
Lieutenant-Colonel G. T. H. Campbell OBE MC	(9 December, 1951 2 i/c) 2 April, 1952–31 January, 1956
Lieutenant-Colonel C. S. Madden	1 February, 1956–17 February, 1959
Lieutenant-Colonel H. R. W. Vernon MBE	18 February, 1959–1961
Lieutenant-Colonel D. R. L. Bright OBE	1961–63

SECOND-IN-COMMAND

Cecil Valentine OBE ED
Edward de las Casas

David Campbell MC
Ray Nightingale MBE

Guy Campbell OBE MC
Gerald Whyte
David Gillett MC

Tony Vetch
Paddy Deacon MBE MC

PADRES

Jimmy Gillett
Jimmy Boxley

John De'Ath

ADJUTANTS

John Moon
Teddy Phillips
Roly Guy MBE

Roy Eve
Peter Welsh
Chris Adami

TRAINING OFFICERS

Dick Cornell
Colin Campbell
Gerald Carter

Carol Gurney
Raymond Nelson

QUARTERMASTERS

Major S. Blake (7th Hussars)
WO II George Slater BEM
      Frank Wakefield MBE

WO II George Blunden
      Jim Lane

MEDICAL OFFICERS

Billy Hargrave-Wilson
Donald Hicks
Philip Crosskey

Denis Alexander
Myles Dunstan-Adams

RSMS

RSM J. Cummins (Irish Guards)
RSM V. Bobbett (Welsh Guards)
RSM C. Broomfield (Grenadier
   Guards)
RSM M. Pendry (King's Royal Rifle
   Corps)

RSM J. Condon (King's Royal Rifle
   Corps)
RSM J. F. Holland DCM MM (King's
   Royal Rifle Corps)
RSM J. Davey (Rifle Brigade)

W. G. Hutchinson   Les Eveson
'Fluff' Sullivan

PSIS

WO II T. Eves   Sergeant G. Goodair
    Pat Garner   Hidden
    Fred Massingham   Stan Solomon
    P. Lawless   Selby
    Greenaway   Ward
Sergeant G. Nunn   McGrady

COMMANDERS OF THE KRTC

Major A. D. Lewis DSO   Major H. Gibson
Major A. C. K. ('Rogue') Barkas   Major P. Vaincourt-Strallen
Major W. T. Woodruffe   Major A. Athill

On the Long Roll of the Regiment are the names of all those who have served in our ranks. In all there are 7202. Between 1961 and 1963 our ranks were increased by 69 Africans and 50 Asians, including Arabs and Seychellois.

B. Organizations and Units in Kenya 1952–6

HEADQUARTERS EAST AFRICAN COMMAND

Lieutenant-General Sir Alexander   Lieutenant-General Sir Gerald
    Cameron   Lathbury
General Sir George Erskine (C in C)

BATTLE SCHOOL

Lieutenant-Colonel P. S. Douglas   Major E. F. D. Campbell

DIRECTOR OF OPERATIONS

Major-General Sir W. Hinde

TRACKER SCHOOL

Major Sandy Thomas

CHIEFS-OF-STAFF

Brigadier G. Rimbault
Major-General G. D. G. Heyman

Brigadier Michael Carver

COMMISSIONERS OF POLICE

Michael O'Rourke
Colonel A. Young

Dick Catling

POLICE OPERATIONS

David Cracknell

KENYAN FORCES

Kenya Regiment (TF)
Kenya Regiment Training Centre
Kenya Police
Kenya Police Reserve

Kenya Police Reserve Air Wing
Auxiliary Forces
Dobie Force (disbanded)
General Service Units

COMMANDERS 70TH EAST AFRICAN BRIGADE

Lieutenant-Colonel (Brigadier)
  G. Collins
Brigadier D. M. Cornah
    J. Orr
    John Macnab

Brigadier John Birkbeck
    George H. Goode
    Miles Fitzalan-Howard
    (now the Duke of Norfolk)

COMMANDERS 39TH AND 49TH BRIGADES

Brigadier J. Tweedie
    C. H. Harington

Brigadier The Lord Thurlow
    G. Taylor

HEAVY BATTERY

Major Pat Langford

Captain Christopher Deverell

KAR BATTALIONS

3rd Kenya Bn
4th Uganda Bn
5th Kenya Bn
6th Tanganyika Bn
7th Kenya Bn
23rd Kenya Bn

26th Tankanyika Bn
156 East African Heavy Anti-Aircraft
  Battery RA
East African Armoured Car Squadron
  (Recce)

173

1st Bn The Lancashire Fusiliers
1st Bn The Buffs
1st Bn The Devonshire Regiment
1st Bn The Black Watch (RHR)
1st Bn The Inniskilling Fusiliers
1st Bn The Royal Northumberland
Fusiliers
1st Bn The King's Own Yorkshire
Light Infantry
1st Bn The Rifle Brigade
1st Bn The Gloucestershire Regiment
1st Bn The King's Shropshire Light
Infantry

1st Bn The Royal Irish
Fusiliers
39th Corps Engineer
Regiment
73rd Independent Field Engineer
Squadron
Roadbuilding Section Royal
Engineers
RAVC Tracker Dogs
RAMC Unit Hospital, Nairobi, Nyeri,
Nanyuki
RAF Harvard and Lincoln
Squadrons

LOCAL UNITS

THE MOUNTED SECTION (KENYA REGIMENT/KENYA POLICE RESERVE)

Major Digby Tatham-Water DSO,
Commanding Officer (The Gallop-
ing Major – of Arnhem fame)
Major Hugh Massey (The Black
Major)
Mickey Buswell
John Dugmore
Robert Foster
Jon Wainwright

John Nye Chart
David Dunlop
Tony Nuttall
Bill Ryan
Francis Foster
Cyrus Morall
John Baker
Colin Campbell-Gillies
Derek Bentley

They operated around Nanyuki and the Rift Valley.

EAST AFRICAN ARMOURED CAR SQUADRON (CAVALRY AND ROYAL TANK REGIMENT)

Major Henry Huth (8th Hussars)
Captain Mark Fearfield (4th Hussars)
Captain Nick Carter (RTR)
Captain Tony Weston-Lewis (16th/
5th Lancers)
Captain Frank Poppleton (Kenya
Regiment)
Captain David Gibbs (3rd Hussars)

Captain John Mangles
Captain Colin Moody (RTR)
Captain Taggart-Langley (King's
Dragoon Guards)
Captain Jim Evans (Kenya Regiment
and 12th Lancers)
Captain Jack Hlwaty (Kenya
Regiment)

I FORCE

Captain Neville Cooper   Sergeant Francis Erskine
Lieutenant Tony Vetch (Kenya Police   Sergeant Bill Woodley
    Reserve)

MOBILE PATROL (SUPPORT COMPANY)

Captain (Major) Ray Mayers   RSM 'Dutchy' Holland
Lieutenant (Captain) Peter Browne

C. Statistics from the Corfield Report

Emergency Statistics up to end of 1956:

Terrorist casualties	Killed	Captured wounded	Captured in action	Arrested	Surrendered
	11,503	1035	1550	26,625	2714

Security Forces casualties	Killed	Wounded
European	63*	101
Asian	3	12
African	101	1469

(*Kenya Regiment)

Loyal civilians casualties		
European	32	26
Asian	26	36
African	819	916

Cost of the Emergency up to 30 June, 1954:

Grants from Her Majesty's Government	£24,250,000
Interest-free loans from HM Government	5,250,000
Borne by the Kenya Government	26,085,424
Total:	£55,585,424

175

BACKGROUND READING LIST

C. J. Wilson, *The East African Mounted Rifles*, Nairobi, East African Standard Ltd.
Christopher Wilson, *Before the Dawn*, Nairobi, English Press, 1952
                   Kenya's Warning, Nairobi, English Press, 1954
L. S. B. Leakey, *Mau Mau and the Kikuyu*, London, Methuen, 1952
                   Defeating Mau Mau, London, Methuen, 1954
'Bokkie', *Shambulia* (cartoons), Nairobi, English Press.
Ian Henderson, *The Hunt for Kimathi*, London, Hamish Hamilton, 1958
Frank Kitson, *Gang and Counter Gang*, London, Barrie & Rockliff, 1960
Leonard Mosley, *Duel for Kilimanjaro*, London, Weidenfeld & Nicolson, 1963
A. T. Chadwick, *Britannia Waives the Rules*, Cape Town, Nasionale Boekhandel, 1963
Iain Grahame, *Jambo Effendi*, London, J. A. Allen, 1966
Denis Holman, *The Elephant People*, London, John Murray, 1967
                   Elephants at Sundown, London, W. H. Allen, 1978
Charles Allen (ed.), *Tales from the Dark Continent*, London, André Deutsch, 1979
Elspeth Huxley, *Pioneers' Scrapbook*, London, Arnold Curtis Evans, 1980

INDEX

The index refers to references in the text. Lists of those serving in or with the Regiment will be found in the Appendices, pp. 153–175.

177

179